The Myth of Mondragón

SUNY Series in the Anthropology of Work

June C. Nash, Editor

The Myth of Mondragón;

Cooperatives, Politics, and Working-Class Life in a Basque Town,

SHARRYN KASMIR

State University of New York Press

Cover photo: "Mondragón's main gate (the *portalón*) with political posters" by Sharryn Kasmir

Published by
State University of New York Press, Albany

©1996 State University of New York

Printed in the United States of America

For information, address State University of New York Press, State University Plaza, Albany, N.Y. 12246

Production by M. R. Mulholland
Marketing by Bernadette LaManna

Library of Congress Cataloging-in-Publication Data

Kasmir, Sharryn.
    The myth of Mondragón : cooperatives, politics, and working-class
life in a Basque town / Sharryn Kasmir.
        p.   cm. — (SUNY series in the anthropology of work)
    Includes bibliographical references and index.
    ISBN 0–7914–3003–0 (HC : acid free). — ISBN 0–7914–3004–9 (PB:
acid free)
    1. Cooperative societies—Spain—Mondragón.   2. Working class—
Spain—Mondragón.   3. Arbitration, Industrial—Spain—Mondragón.
4. Mondragón (Spain)—Politics and government.   I. Title.
II. Series.
HD3528.M66K37   1996
334′.0946′61—dc20   96–40339
                                                                    CIP

10 9 8 7 6 5 4 3 2 1

Contents

Illustrations

Foreword

Sharryn Kasmir's book, *The Myth of Mondragón: Cooperatives, Politics, and Working-Class Life in a Basque Town,* is the first ethnographic analysis bringing together the interaction of cooperatives and communities in a holistic analysis of working-class perspectives on the form of industrial organization that has been hailed as an alternative to both capitalist and socialist organizations of work. From the perspective of workers, Mondragón differs little from managerial styles of private enterprises found throughout the Basque area. Workers do not take advantage of the democratic forms available to them and are, in fact, more passive in asserting their rights than are workers in private firms who engage in militant working-class action through trade unions. The very ideological stance of the cooperatives as harmoniously integrated worker–manager teams mitigates the expression of antagonism based on structural opposition that persists in these settings.

Another dimension of the myth is the portrayal of the cooperatives as apolitical entities. As Kasmir shows in her meticulous examination of historical archives of the community and her interviews with nationalist leaders and rank-and-file militants, the characterization of the cooperatives as lacking political commitments masks active and acrimonious debates carried from the workplace to the bars and neighborhoods. Workers and managers are, in fact, engaged in the Basque separatist issues, with the co-ops espousing conservative nationalist positions of the Basque Nationalist Party over those of the more radical and separatist Herri Batasuna.

Sharryn Kasmir's analysis enables us to penetrate the otherwise paradoxical situation in which cooperators in this putative postclass paradise are beginning to organize syndicates to protect their interests. The insights the reader gains from Sharryn Kasmir's book will enable us to go beyond the impasse currently faced by nihilist postindustrial critiques that deny the very existence of industrial production.

June C. Nash

Preface

I first learned about the Mondragón industrial cooperatives when I was an undergraduate anthropology student. I was taking a class on egalitarian societies and saw a film on Mondragón made by the British Broadcasting Company. Along with my classmates, I believed that cooperative workers derived satisfaction from their jobs and were actively involved in running their firms. I also imagined that the democracy practiced in the cooperatives was infectious and that the town outside the factories would mirror this egalitarianism. The existence of Mondragón and its long-term success inspired me to believe worker-ownership could generate equality within industrial society.

I know that such a vision of equality would mean a great deal to my own students, and to undergraduate students elsewhere. I understand the significance of Mondragón for a new generation of students, many of whom learn about Mondragón as the only viable counterexample to the seeming inevitability of inequality and hierarchy. I also understand how important the example of Mondragón is for community activists who, searching for models for economic development and solutions to deindustrialization, try to build cooperatives in their own cities and towns. It is with a genuine sense of responsibility that I wrote this book, which is the first in-depth criticism of the Mondragón system. I hope that dealing honestly with the problems of cooperative workplaces, the disaffection of co-op workers, and the ways in which cooperativism parallels other ideologies that are associated with new and often brutal forms of labor control is, in the end, a more fruitful endeavor than contributing to a prepackaged story of Mondragón, a story that I consider to be a myth. Furthermore, I hope that by unraveling the myth and showing the activism of Basque nationalist and working-class movements in the town of Mondragón, I will be able to offer alternative sources of inspiration to my students.

Acknowledgments

I am truly fortunate to have made lifelong friends and colleagues in Mondragón. Zapata, Mer, and Txomin were the first people in Mondragón to befriend me, and I do not think that I would have led such a happy life there or had such a successful fieldwork experience without their trust and companionship. From 1989 to 1990 and on subsequent visits, I lived with Maribel, Anuska, and Aitor. Their family life is exceptionally warm and open, and they graciously made a place for me in their home. Juan Ramón Garai's personal archives and love of history were indispensable resources for my work. Antxon Mendizabal, a native of Mondragón, an economist, and a political activist, was a wonderful informant and colleague. Throughout my fieldwork, I relied on the assistance of the people at the syndicate LAB, especially Basterra, and the members of Kooperatibisten Taldea, especially Joseba and Mila, who spent hours talking with me on many occasions. I thank the managers and workers at Fagor Clima for their help and cooperation, especially Montxe, Vitoria, Guerra, José Luis, and Jon, and the people at Mayc, S.A., particularly Ramón and the members of the Workers' Council. Pilar, Marián, and José María of Ikasbide were always generous with their time and resources. Not all of these people agreed with my interpretations of their experiences, yet they helped me anyway. For this I am extremely grateful.

More people extended themselves to me in Mondragón than I could hope to name. My day-to-day interactions with many intelligent, informed, and critical people in Mondragón are the impossible-to-cite sources that are the basis for many of the insights and analyses in this book. My friends at Bars Iluntz, Irati, Lagunilla, and Ekaitz, and especially the women at Bar Biona, taught me about Basque politics and music and took me to fiestas, demonstrations, marches, and funerals. I am especially indebted to Jaoine, Karmele, Sagra, and Pili for sharing their observations, analysis, and friendship. I am glad that so many people from Mondragón have visited me in New York City; I love my native city as much as they love their town, and we have enjoyed sharing our affection for these places.

During my graduate-student years at City University of New York (CUNY), I enjoyed the intellectual fellowship of the members of the CUNY Working Class Anthropology Project: John Antici, William Askins, Geoffrey Bate, Julia Butterfield, August Carbonella, Geraldine Casey, and Warren Perry. My work has been immeasurably enriched by our collective efforts. During my first two trips to Mondragón, I conducted collaborative fieldwork with Geoffrey Bate whose keen mind made an important impact on my work. August Carbonella and Geraldine Casey helped me think through much of the material in this book and were close intellectual companions throughout much of this project. For (repeatedly) editing several chapters of this work and for being collegial in the best sense of the word, I thank Ara Wilson and Karen Judd. Julia Butterfield saw me through the final edits of the manuscript, and her incisive mind was an inspiration to me. Dave Maynard, Ligia Simonian, and Ian Skoggard also edited and commented on manuscript drafts. Special thanks to Terri Vulcano, who always looked out for me.

I first learned about the Mondragón cooperatives from Arthur Keene; his interest in this project, from start to finish, has been an endless source of support. Jane Schneider pointed out insights and arguments that greatly improved this book, and she provided me with intellectual guidance over the years of research and writing. June Nash encouraged me to publish this book, and I would not have gotten this far without her example and assistance. For their invaluable comments and criticisms and for their good-hearted support, I thank Jacqueline Urla and Edward Hansen. Davydd Greenwood was a rigorous critic and generous mentor; I sincerely appreciate his help. William Foote Whyte, William Douglass, and two anonymous readers contributed helpful comments to drafts of the manuscript. I considered all of their criticisms carefully, but the responsibility for this book, and its shortcomings, is my own.

For giving me the time to write and for their kind tolerance, I thank Nancy Eberhardt and Jon Wagner, my colleagues at Knox College. Thanks also to Marty Eisenberg, Kathleen Seligmann and Sharon Clayton of Knox College. I am grateful to Arrasate Press for allowing me to use their photographs. Joy Nolan stuck by me during the arduous process of writing and rewriting; she is the best friend (and most accommodating editor) I could hope for. Benjamin Dulchin gave me tremendous support, energy, and love as I wrote.

Funding for my research and writing was provided by the following: the Council for European Studies; the Joint Committee on Western Europe of the American Council of Learned Societies, and the Social Science Research Council, with funds provided by the Ford and Mellon Foundations; a Fulbright Grant for Collaborative Research; the Mamie Phipps and Kenneth B. Clark Fellowship from the City University of New York Graduate School and University Center (CUNY); the American Association for University Women; CUNY; and Knox College.

My grandmother, Freda Yam, was the first to teach me that there is a fine line between history and myth. My mother, Eleanor Kasmir, gave me the courage and self-confidence it takes to be an ethnographer. My father, Stephen Kasmir, taught me by example to talk to strangers. I imagine that, throughout my life, I will discover many more ways in which they have contributed to my work, and I dedicate this book to their memories.

Notes on the Text

Throughout this book, I use Basque-language names and orthography for provinces, cities and towns. The Spanish-language names and spellings are likely more familiar to English-speaking audiences, but I have chosen Basque out of respect for Basques' political and cultural struggle to reclaim their language. In the text, the first usage of a place name is followed by its Spanish translation, and translations of place names are provided on the map on page xvi for reference.

An important exception is that I refer to Mondragón by its Spanish rather than Basque name, which is Arrasate. Since this book is concerned with the Mondragón cooperatives, known internationally by the Spanish name of the town, I use Spanish in this case. Likewise, I use Spanish rather than Basque names for cooperative institutions in order to facilitate communication with the body of literature on the cooperatives.

Throughout this book, I also adopt Basque spellings for personal names and, in accordance with orthographic rules, omit accent marks that would appear in Spanish spellings. In Basque, the suffix **a** indicates the definite article, and the suffix **ak** is a plural form.

MAP 1

The Basque Country and the Mondragón Environs

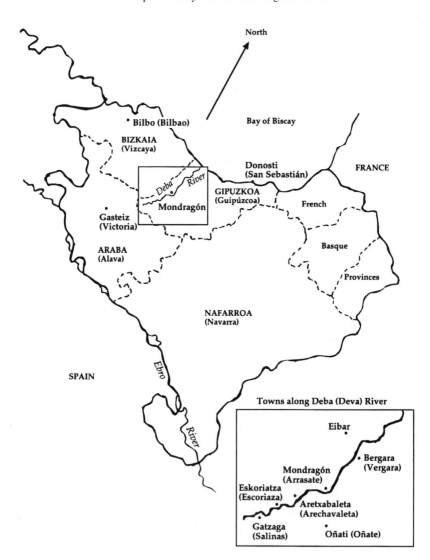

North

Bilbo (Bilbao)

BIZKAIA
(Vizcaya)

Bay of Biscay

Deba River

Donosti
(San Sebastián)

FRANCE

GIPUZKOA
(Guipúzcoa)

Mondragón

French

Gasteiz
(Victoria)

Basque

ARABA
(Alava)

Provinces

NAFARROA
(Navarra)

Ebro River

SPAIN

Towns along Deba (Deva) River

Eibar

Bergara
(Vergara)

Mondragón
(Arrasate)

Eskoriatza
(Escoriaza)

Aretxabaleta
(Arechavaleta)

Gatzaga
(Salinas)

Oñati (Oñate)

Introduction: The Mondragón Model and the Remaking of Industrial Working Classes

The fact is that a profound reshaping of the classes of contemporary British society is underway at the present time. It is perhaps as far-reaching as that re-making at the turn of the century.

—(Stuart Hall 1988, 5)

The reshaping of social class that Stuart Hall describes for Britain is presently underway throughout Western Europe and North America. This re-making comes in the wake of an economic downturn that dates to the mid-1970s; its full impact is yet to be felt and understood. Industrial workers who once held secure, full-time jobs in unionized shops face unemployment, irregular work, and a loss of the political power they once wielded through their unions. I mean this book as a contribution to anthropological research on this reshaping of working classes. I present the case study of the Spanish Basque town of Mondragón, which is internationally renowned for its worker-owned industrial cooperatives, and I examine the way in which the cooperative system has reshaped Mondragón's working class in the arenas of work, social life, politics, culture, and ideology.

Mondragón is an especially relevant case because the cooperative system is a leading model for transforming industrial working classes elsewhere. Scholars, business consultants, managers, and policy analysts from all over the world look to Mondragón for solutions to a range of economic problems. They see in Mondragón lessons for job creation, economic development, labor–management cooperation, and employee ownership. Worker participation and workplace democracy as practiced in the nonunionized Mondragón cooperatives are widely believed to be superior to the conflictual labor relations that characterize union shops, and Mondragón-inspired cooperation is seen as offering more satisfying work experiences and more justice on the job. Many of those who study the cooperatives have implemented aspects of the system in their home countries.

Cooperative legislation based on the Mondragón model was passed throughout the 1980s in Maine, Massachusetts, New York, and Vermont. The British Parliament approved similar bills to facilitate cooperative businesses. Moreover, the Mondragón cooperatives are discussed in universities, consulting firms, and unions. It is even reported that a video on Mondragón was shown in the White House while Ronald Reagan was president (Whyte 1982).[1] How have these transplanted experiences affected workers' lives elsewhere? What relationship do these changes have to the larger transformation of the working class described by Hall? By examining the lives of workers in the model system, I hope to offer some insight into the contemporary remaking of industrial working classes in North America and Western Europe.

Participation, Cooperation, and Economic Crisis

It is noteworthy that the Mondragón cooperatives were presented to an international audience in 1973,[2] the year that marked the onset of worldwide economic crisis. In the mid-1970s, all major industrial countries experienced a fall in production, a decrease in the rate of profit, and an increase in the cost of living. Structural transformations in the international economy began to change industrial organization, working-class social life, and cultural and political forms. What is the nature of this restructuring, and in what ways might the Mondragón model be linked to it?

David Harvey (1989) argues that a comprehensive shift in capital accumulation is at the heart of this transformation; the new regime of "flexible accumulation" is based on the casualization of labor contracts. The flexibility of the post-1973 period is replacing the Fordist regime that was consolidated in the United States and Europe after World War II. In Fordist factories, the assembly line, a rigid mental–manual division of labor, and strict managerial control over the production process propelled mass production. By offering workers a family wage and an eight-hour day, Ford linked this mass production to mass consumption. Workers (first in Ford's own plants and later in Fordist-modeled factories) could afford mass-produced goods and had a dependable schedule away from work, during which they elaborated family and social lives that drew on new patterns of consumption. For the first time in history, workers became mass consumers of the goods they produced, and this drove an expanding economy, especially in the United States, where Fordism was more highly developed than in other countries (see also Aglietta 1979).[3]

When profits began to fall in the mid-1970s, capitalists sought new markets, labor contracts, and forms of industrial organization. Capital investment was shifted to industrializing regions of the Third World, and U.S. and European workers were outcompeted on price by low-wage, nonunionized workers.

Workers in the United States and Europe, who had stable, unionized jobs during the Fordist epoch, are now employed in a variety of (insecure) ways. The number of unionized workers is decreasing and the number of temporary workers, part-timers, subcontractors, and worker-owners is on the rise. This plurality of labor contracts allows capitalists to limit investment in their labor force and to hire workers according to the demands of production.

Flexible accumulation and the loss of stable, unionized jobs have had staggering effects on working classes in the multiple arenas of daily life. Outside the factory, families are dislocated and communities dismantled (cf. Nash 1989). Mid-level managers are also affected by corporate downsizing; when they lose their jobs they too are dislodged from their communities and localities. Newman (1989) interviewed downwardly mobile Americans caught up in this transition who "spent hours reflecting upon what their old world meant and what the new one lacks" (x). Inside factories, the restructuring of work generates new divisions among workers. Temporary workers, hired on short-term contracts, do the same work as permanent employees but for lower wages and without job security; women and minorities, historically underrepresented by unions, make up a disproportionate part of the contingent work force (Judd and Morales 1994). In addition, entire factories are marginalized by large firms, which find it profitable to contract out portions of their operations to smaller subcontractors. In Japan, two-thirds of the work force is employed by these small firms that pay only 80 percent of the wages of companies such as Toyota and offer none of the benefits Toyota workers receive, such as housing, pensions, vacations, loans, and guaranteed employment (Shapiro and Cosenza 1987, 3–12).

Furthermore, new management techniques are changing the organization of industrial work. Many corporations (such as, Toyota, General Motors, and International Business Machines) are introducing labor–management cooperation schemes, including quality circles, the team concept, employee-ownership programs, and participatory management. Proponents of these schemes favor cooperative labor–management relations. Where there is respect for employees, they argue, unions are not necessary. Critics, however, see participation and cooperation as the cornerstone of a new mode of labor control that intensifies exploitation. Guillermo Grenier (1988) considers cooperation to be a form of "de-bureaucratized control" that replaces the bureaucratic management and the rigid division of labor associated with the assembly line. It undermines the shop-floor power of unions over seniority, job classifications, schedules, and wages and leaves workers without independent representation. Cooperation seems to be a key managerial strategy and a dominant corporate ideology of flexible accumulation. What are the effects of this new form of production on working-class communities and political forms? What is the impact of the ideologies of cooperation and participation

on the culture and consciousness of workers? In what ways might these ideologies comprise a new hegemonic discourse about industrial cooperation that
is international in scope?

Workplace Participation Programs

Labor–management cooperation is not a new idea. Examples of workers' councils and factory committees date back as far as the late 1800s, and
cooperative experiments are nearly as old as the factory system itself. Since
1973, however, there has been a systematic and international promotion of
cooperation—this is a new and notable phenomenon. Many scholars and policymakers believe that cooperation is an idea whose time has come, that qual-
ity-of-life issues that were central concerns of U.S. and Western European
social movements in the 1960s are finally being brought to the workplace.[4]
Ray Marshall, the U.S. Secretary of Labor from 1977 to 1981, believes that labor–management cooperation can go a long way toward increasing the competitiveness of the American economy, since workers who participate in the
design and implementation of technology are more likely to accept it and use
it to the best advantage (Marshall 1987). Other advocates argue that the kind
of democracy available in the political domain should be introduced into the
workplace; they believe that participation is a way to increase workers' self-
esteem and boost their productivity (Simmons and Mares 1985; Witte 1980).
The vast number of articles about employee participation that appear in major
business publications testifies to a growing belief that workers are more ful-
filled when they use their mental skills and have an emotional stake in their
firm and that this is good for managers, owners, and entire national
economies.

Quality circles, the team concept, and employee ownership are major
vehicles for implementing cooperation and participation. Western European
unions, especially in Germany, and some American unions, most notably the
United Auto Workers (UAW), have accepted participation programs. Recent
evidence suggests that productivity gains are higher when quality circles or
the team concept are implemented in union versus nonunion firms (Eaton and
Voos 1992; Wells 1987). Yet many unions remain skeptical. They see em-
ployee-involvement programs as management-driven organizations, akin to
company unions. Furthermore, the kind of flexibility employee involvement
requires conflicts with the union domain of monitoring job classifications and
seniority. Unions' rejection of these programs has often put them in the position of responding conservatively to what seems like a forward-looking managerial initiative. Despite the many failures of particular attempts at
labor–management cooperation, public sentiment remains supportive of these
experiments, while support for unions dwindles (Heckscher 1988). There is a

growing sense that cooperation is dynamic and that unions are outmoded and inefficient.

Nevertheless, there is reason to be skeptical about quality circles, the team concept, and employee ownership. Grenier (1988) details the way in which managers in a medical-products factory in New Mexico try to manipulate workers by appealing to their desire for more fulfilling work lives. In this firm, participation was purposefully planned to keep the union out of the newest plant of a unionized conglomerate, and an industrial psychologist was hired to control team meetings. This extreme example of manipulation described by Grenier is not unique. Union guides explaining the team concept and quality-of-work-life programs show how human-relations language is used to increase productivity, expand managerial control over the workplace, and weaken unions (Parker 1985; Parker and Slaughter 1988). Wells argues that quality-of-work-life programs do not offer genuine cooperation. Rather, they are a management strategy to discredit union conflict. "Power relations in the workplace are seen as *personal* conflicts—'adolescent,' or even socially deviant" (Wells 1987, 2). Quality-of-work-life seeks to overcome these conflicts without ceding real power to workers. "Management is no longer satisfied with making workers obey; it makes them *want* to obey" (Wells 1987, 5).

Quality circles were intended to replace the quality-control departments in Fordist plants. Quality control is typically the last phase of production, when finished products are checked for defects and then repaired. Instead, quality circles are groups of workers and managers who collaborate to evaluate the manufacturing process, checking for problems before they result in defects. In quality circles, workers and managers brainstorm to develop a list of problems in their section of the plant; they choose a problem to work on and develop a plan for tackling it. The team concept has many of the same goals. Whereas Fordist factories have assembly lines where the product passes by individual workers who perform single operations, teams are groups of workers who are multiskilled and who perform a variety of jobs. This team supervises itself and therefore is not under the control of a foreman. Since the team concept eliminates job classifications and seniority procedures and replaces them with job rotation, it strips unions of a primary source of their power and challenges the role of the union on the shop floor. Like quality circles, it also has a psychological impact on workers who evaluate and criticize each other's work (Grenier 1988). A central goal of quality circles and the team concept is to promote a common identity for labor and management.

Far from an everybody-wins proposition, these programs seem to be intended to displace unions. The firm Grenier studied was an extreme case. Job candidates were screened for the right psychological profile and nonunion background, team meetings were manipulated to create an anti-union sentiment, and colleague evaluations were used to isolate pro-union individuals. But in more typical cases, quality circles and the team concept are linked to just-in-time production (Whyte and Whyte 1991, 213–14), a system that offers little that is good for workers. Just-in-time production was first introduced at Toyota in 1973, after the oil crisis forced the company to cut costs. Toyota eliminated inventory and tailored production to incoming orders, thereby minimizing capital tied up in stock, a practice that also became common in the U.S. automobile industry. This flexible system of production was made possible by a new technology for changing presses, allowing for frequent model changes without much downtime. Thus, small batches became profitable, and style, targeted to smaller, more specialized markets, proliferated as a major means of competition (Shapiro and Cosenza 1987, 33–42).

For workers, just-in-time production means that schedules are subordinated to incoming orders. Workers are routinely sent home when there are no orders and forced to work weekends and overtime when demand is heavy. This threatens established patterns of socializing and family time as workers neither have reliable schedules nor can count on having free time when their friends or spouses are off work. Moreover, with production so tightly linked to orders, there is little room for rest or error. Frequently, just-in-time production is accompanied by a grueling pace of work; stress-related illnesses are common. A Japanese journalist wrote a firsthand account of his experiences as a line worker at Toyota, which is often assumed to be an ideal place to work. Quality meetings are held, workers are allowed to participate in managerial decisions, and interest-free loans are offered to employees, but workers also suffer from exhaustion and a host of stress-related illnesses (Kamata 1982; see also Parker and Slaughter 1988, 16).[5] Likewise, workplace democracy went hand-in-hand with important give-backs in the metal sector in Germany. The German metal workers' syndicate IG Metall won democratic rights for workers' councils, but it first had to agree to the introduction of numerical-control machine tools. IG Metall previously opposed numerical control, since this computerized system increased the pace of work, routinized operations, and de-skilled laborers (IG Metall 1984).

On a social level, the team or quality circle can supplant prior relationships and networks. The group throws parties and usually gives itself a name, which is sometimes embroidered on jackets or caps to be worn by group members (Parker 1985, 9–15). The choice of embroidered caps is significant. According to Hobsbawm, the flat cap became a symbol of proletarian identity for the English working class by 1914, when "British male workers had taken to wearing a badge which immediately stamped them as members of a class. And, moreover, they knew that it did" (1984, 200). In Britain and elsewhere, male workers have historically worn such markers of class identity. Similarly, they have shared their leisure time with members of their own class, especially in pubs, taverns, and bars and in participating in and watching sports. Female workers have sometimes participated in the sociability of the bars and have often created rituals of their own to celebrate life-cycle events (see Lamphere, Stepick, and Grenier 1994, 10–15). By interrupting these patterns of sociability, quality circles can challenge previously existing collectivities and attempt to replace them with social groups that are cross-class, comprised of workers and managers alike. These groups can further jeopardize links between factory and community life.

Another vehicle for participation is worker ownership. According to the National Center for Employee Ownership in Washington, DC, more than nine thousand U.S. corporations had employee stock option programs (ESOPs) in 1991; in some cases, workers see considerable financial benefits. Sometimes, voting rights are attached to the stocks, thereby involving employees in corporate decision making and supposedly democratizing management. More often, they are nonvoting shares. Regardless of the kind of stock issued, major corporations see employee ownership as a way to motivate workers to identify with the company and to embrace its gains and losses as their own. In some instances, corporations institute ESOPs in the hope of generating employee identification with the firm and staving off a union drive (see Rosen 1981). Ownership is seen as a powerful device for forging an alliance between workers and managers, an alliance that is not always beneficial for workers (see Kasmir 1991; Russell 1984, 1985; Schiller 1987). Russell (1984, 1985) situates the ideology of worker ownership within larger myths about nation, democracy, and equality, showing how ESOPs perpetuate the myth that the United States is a country of small-property owners. As Americans' standard of living declines (with the demise of Fordism) and the number of homeowners falls—the home is the most important American symbol of small property—the U.S. government promotes employee ownership, giving tax breaks to firms that offer stock to workers. Employee ownership is a stand-in for home ownership and represents the existence of a property-owning middle class in a country that is experiencing a concentration of wealth and the loss of its middle strata.

While there is ample evidence to suggest that workplace democracy and ESOPs are at least partially intended to control workers, the nature of cooperatives is less clear. Unlike ESOPs, cooperatives are fully owned by workers who also have the right to manage their firms. In the face of capital flight from historic industrial centers, workers' purchase of their firm is often the only alternative to unemployment. Academics, community activists, and some unionists argue that worker buyouts are a way to combat deindustrialization (Bluestone and Harrison 1982; Lindenfeld 1982; Lynch n.d.; Royal Arsenal Cooperative Society Ltd. n.d.; Schweikart 1984). Cooperatives are also seen as a way to spur regional economic development (Greenwood 1986), especially in underdeveloped areas (Nash, Dandler, and Hopkins 1976). Yet cooperativism is clearly more complex than it seems. One commentator (unknowingly) hints that the cooperative may be better understood not as a unique business form but as one of the multiplicity of flexible business and management arrangements:

> Here is a fantasy for managers. How would you like to spend 5% on industrial relations . . . ? The unlikely way to realize this dream. . . is to manage a well-organized workers' cooperative. (Searjeant 1978)

While I was in Mondragón, a management team from Polaroid arrived to tour the co-ops. Polaroid was considering offering an employee stock option plan to its employees. Their guide, a high-level manager in the Mondragón cooperative system, told me that the team's mission was to determine if they could transfer ownership without yielding power. The Polaroid managers hoped to find in Mondragón a formula for using ownership to manipulate workers.

It is noteworthy that within Mondragón, local factories display a continuum of participation. Several small owners initiated employee involvement and profit sharing. They claim that they, too, are implementing the goals of cooperativism, despite the fact that ownership of the firms remains in their hands. Significantly, their firms have a lower rate of syndicate (union) membership than other town factories. In order to genuinely understand cooperatives, we must consider these worker-owned business forms within the contexts of the reorganization of production and the reshaping of working classes.

Cooperation as Ideology

Participation schemes are often more ideological than real; they generate considerable public enthusiasm (Heckscher 1988); and when they fail, they tend to die a quiet death, without the public fanfare or press coverage associated with their inauguration (Grenier 1988, 9). Employee participation is also a language, a way of changing how shop floor and class relations are talked about (Grenier 1988; Lamphere et al. 1993, 12); perhaps they have their greatest impact at an ideological level. What is the effect of this ideology both inside and outside the workplace, on those with a variety of labor contracts, the unemployed and underemployed, and those who work in different factory regimes?

One example of the emerging discourse of cooperation is familiar to TV watchers and magazine readers in the United States. In 1990, General Motors (GM) unveiled Saturn, an American-made small car that was meant to compete with Japanese models. Inside the Saturn plant in Tennessee, work tables replace the Fordist assembly line, and job rotation within work teams makes Taylorism obsolete. Quality circles reportedly bring managers and workers together to meet a common goal called "Total Quality." Saturn employs three thousand workers it calls "team members" (General Motors 1990). GM presented Saturn as the symbol for a new age of production, when cooperation and participation would set the tone for labor–management relations. Using a Hollywood-style advertising campaign, GM told consumers that Saturn was not just another car but that it heralded an era of industrial production, characterized by cooperative and friendly relations with managers.

Television advertisements present personal narratives of employees who came to Tennessee in search of a better life, where they could participate in decision making and take pride in production. A recent television spot shows a couple in their thirties arriving in their new, large home, looking a little nervous. In the next scene, viewers follow the man to the Saturn plant where he is about to shut down the assembly line because he has detected a small quality flaw in one of the cars. After fixing the car, he reports that this is one of the most memorable days of his life; he was able to exercise control.

The ads are touching. They are meant to sell more than just a car: they sell a whole vision of industry. But that vision is purposefully selective. The ads do not discuss the use of just-in-time production. Nor do they show us that many Saturn workers moved to Tennessee and uprooted their families only after they experienced massive layoffs in Detroit, where the three major auto companies have been decapitalizing plants for years.[6] Nor do they detail how the United Auto Workers compromised its standard bases of shop-floor power—seniority and job classifications—in order to win a union shop in Tennessee rather than see GM move production out of the United States (Parker and Slaughter 1988, 4–5). Thus, the Saturn media campaign decontextualizes and idealizes participatory workplace programs, and contributes stylized notions of cooperation to a larger discourse on the transformation of work. "Cooperation" and "participation" have become decontextualized buzz words, even symbols, for new labor relations in the post-Fordist epoch.

The Myth of Mondragón

In this context a kind of cottage industry has emerged to promote the transfer of the Mondragón model to other countries. Several institutes have been founded to create Mondragón-style cooperatives. The Industrial Cooperatives Association in Massachusetts, for example, is instrumental in establishing Mondragón-style cooperatives throughout the northeastern United States; a division of the organization is named "Dragon Mountain," the English translation of Mondragón. Scholarly panels and conferences are held to discuss and disseminate the model. Tours are organized for groups of scholars and community activists. Moreover, a vast, interdisciplinary literature exists on the co-ops. Despite extensive research, however, no study situates the cooperatives in their social and political milieu. This decontextualization is parallel to the

process by which cooperation and participation have been stylized and produced as symbols.

As we shall see, this packaging of Mondragón, like the packaging of Saturn, consists of a selective process of representation; workers' experiences are
overlooked, critical perspectives are minimized, and the co-ops are taken out
of the context of the contemporary world economy. I consider this process of
representation to constitute myth making. Throughout this book, I analyze the
construction of this myth of Mondragón, and I attempt to portray another cooperative system, one that is successively contextualized within the broader
changes of global capitalism, within the historical development and class structure of the town itself, and within the Basque political milieu. And I try to give
voice to workers' perspectives.

I made four trips to Mondragón from 1987 to 1992. The bulk of my research was carried out over an eighteen-month period, from February 1989 to
August 1990. Some of my research was done collaboratively with Geoffrey
Bate, an anthropologist studying Basque politics; Juan Ramón Garai, a local
syndicalist and one of my key informants, became a kind of collaborator, as did
economist Antxon Mendizabal. During my time in Mondragón, I engaged in
the anthropological method of participant observation, taking part in daily social life with townspeople and attending political demonstrations and meetings.
My premise was that the best way to evaluate the cooperatives was from within
their cultural, social, and political contexts. In the town of Mondragón, these
contexts were shaped by a historically militant working class and a thriving radical Basque nationalist movement.

The absence of politics in the literature on the cooperatives is an important aspect of the myth of Mondragón. In chapter 1, I discuss a series of historical and contemporary arguments that suggest that economic democracy is
possible—indeed, preferable—without engaging in union or party politics. I
show how these arguments are essential to the packaging of the Mondragón cooperatives as a model for industrial change. Nonsyndicalized and reportedly un-
connected to Basque politics, the Mondragón cooperatives provide a paragon
for new labor relations. This curiously apolitical status is considered all the more
impressive in the Basque region, where Basque nationalism, most radically expressed by the armed organization Euskadi ta Askatasuna (ETA), has pro-
foundly marked public life. Furthermore, while the Basque region has a history
of working-class activism, the co-ops are thought to have created a classless society by inventing a person who is neither worker nor capitalist but cooperator
and who benefits from neither syndical nor party politics. Ironically, as writers
in other parts of the world conjure up the image that the cooperatives function
all the better without the intervention of politics, as we shall see in chapter 7, cooperators in Mondragón are turning to syndicates and political parties. (Syndicates are the Spanish equivalent of U.S. unions, yet laws regulating syndicates

and unions differ in key ways, as do syndical and union structures. Syndicates have less circumscribed membership than do unions; members are not restricted to sector or trade, and syndicates have more leeway to organize managers and the unemployed. Moreover, several syndicates can have delegates within a single shop, and workers in the same trade can affiliate with different syndicates. Most syndicates are tied to political parties.)

A Working-Class Perspective

My daily interaction and friendships with workers convinced me of the necessity to present their views on cooperativism. Workers' feelings and experiences are often at odds with those of managers, yet managers' points of view are those that are reported in the popular and scholarly literature. Moreover, workers express frustration about claims that cooperatives are classless institutions when, from their point of view, class differences are obvious (chapter 6). Despite the fact that workers and managers share the formal class position of co-owners of their firms, there is a tangible difference between them.

A related problem of categorizing the class position of California sharecroppers was tackled by Wells (1984). The sharecroppers Wells studied are autonomous in some aspects of their work and own some of their own tools, but their working conditions are worse and more precarious than those of many wage earners. Drawing on Wright's (1976) analysis of classes in contemporary capitalist societies, which are populated by many people who are neither fully workers nor fully capitalists, Wells shows that political and ideological dimensions are often more significant for actual class position than are strict property relations. In this book, I draw on this notion of class elaborated by Wells and Wright; cooperative workers have different experiences than do managers, and these experiences lead them to develop distinct perspectives.

This book is written from what I consider to be a working-class perspective. I adopt this perspective for several reasons. First, as I note throughout this work, the literature on the Mondragón cooperatives relies primarily on managers or public-relations personnel as informants; this is part of the myth making. By drawing on data collected through participant observation with workers, and by considering materials written by working-class organizations and political parties, I hope to provide a corrective to the existing literature. My own experiences figure in as well. While in graduate school, I helped to form the City University of New York (CUNY) Working Class Anthropology Project along with fellow students. At a time when the relevance of perspective was the topic of much that was new in academe, especially among postmodernist theorists, we experimented with viewing society and culture from the point of view of the working class. I hope my work does some justice to the richness of our exchanges.

Herein I apply this perspective to the town of Mondragón, where the cooperative complex has been thriving for more than thirty years. In the intensely associative environment of the Basque region, a working-class perspective necessarily turned my attention to a variety of organizations in which workers participate: friendship groups, voluntary associations, syndicates, and political groups and parties. Situating the cooperatives in their social and political contexts, I examine the relationship of the cooperatives to Basque syndicates and parties. Two parties are particularly important: Partido Nacionalista Vasco (PNV) and Herri Batasuna (HB), respectively, represent moderate and radical views of Basque nationalism, and compete in many spheres of daily life.

In chapter 2, I address these questions: Why did the cooperatives develop in Mondragón? Why was the cooperative form chosen over some other business form? Not only have these basic questions been absent from the literature, but answering them takes us to the heart of the national and class debates that have marked the Basque nationalist movement since its inception and that underlie the present-day competition between PNV and HB. In chapter 3, I consider the emergence of cooperativism in the historical and political context of post–Spanish Civil War Mondragón. I use Gramsci's concept of hegemony to explain the founding of the cooperatives and to analyze the way in which they imposed middle-class values on the town.

Throughout the book, I assess the implications of the cooperative project for working-class social life, politics, and consciousness in Mondragón. I ask if the cooperatives represent workers' interests better than the many social groups, syndicates, and political parties do; not only does this question test the claims made by literature, it also reflects a Basque working-class perspective that strong collectivities and independent organizations benefit workers. In chapter 4, I discuss the strike that took place in the Ulgor cooperative in 1974—one of the most divisive events in Mondragón's recent history. The Ulgor strike highlights the political tensions between competing visions of nationalism in the Basque region and the political dilemma over how to evaluate cooperativism. I also discuss how the cooperative experience has generated a division between cooperators and those who work in regular factories. I introduce the Basque concept of *ekintza* (taking action), which is a core cultural value in Mondragón (cf. Zulaika 1988), and consider the implications of cooperativism for ekintza among co-op workers.[7] The division between cooperators and other workers, and the inactivism of cooperators, was most recently acted out in 1990, when cooperators failed to join town workers in their annual ritual of protest, the strike for the metal-sector contract that establishes the base pay for the area. This event is discussed in chapter 7.

In chapters 5 and 6, I present the results of my comparison of the cooperative firm Fagor Clima with the privately owned firm Mayc, where syndical representation is strong. This is the first extensive effort to compare a local private firm with a Mondragón co-op. I discuss how workers in each firm evaluate their ability to exercise their rights, their level of participation, their feelings of solidarity with co-workers, and their level of job satisfaction. In chapter 7, I outline recent shop floor and organizational changes in the cooperative system, including automation and the centralization of decision making. These changes, along with a political shift in the Basque nationalist political alliances, have moved workers to organize against management. Syndicates are currently exploring options for organizing in the cooperatives. In the conclusions, I discuss the ways in which these developments transform the nature and meaning of the Mondragón model and suggest a future direction for workers' organizations elsewhere.

1

Making the Myth of Mondragón

On 15 November 1978, just before 6:00 P.M., six people were shot, three fatally, in Mondragón's Udala Plaza. A major car and pedestrian route, the plaza was filled with workers leaving the nearby cooperative factories of Fagor and with students heading home from the cooperative Polytechnical and Professional School. Workers, students, and other townspeople saw Civil Guardsmen approach a car and take aim at the three young men inside. Two were killed. In the shootout that followed, three passersby were hit, including one middle-aged woman who died instantaneously. The three youths had been followed by police after they fired shots at the Civil Guard station of a neighboring town. They were members of the autonomous faction of the Basque separatist organization Euskadi ta Askatasuna (ETA). Making their way to Mondragón, they were caught in rush-hour traffic in the plaza when the Civil Guardsmen opened fire on them. While the official police version of the incident reports that the three were likely responsible for the shootings of the townspeople, eyewitness accounts indicate that the bystanders, as well as the three young ETA militants, were shot by Civil Guardsmen.[1]

In November 1989, on the eleventh anniversary of the shootings, I was attending a birthday lunch with several Basque friends in a restaurant near the Polytechnical and Professional School. We celebrated over a long, elaborate meal, with plenty of wine and talk. My friends told me that one of the ETA members killed was the brother of a close friend of ours. I was struck, as I had often been during my time in Mondragón, by the proximity of politics to daily life.

Our conversation turned to the latest issue of the Spanish edition of *Geo* magazine. The magazine was being discussed around town because it featured a twelve-page article on the Mondragón cooperative system (Chrisleanschi 1989). I read the title aloud, "The Empire of Mondragón." Someone else picked up the magazine and read to the group. The article proclaimed that the co-ops are such egalitarian institutions that social classes no longer exist in the town of Mondragón. It also asserted that Basque nationalist politics do not intrude on business operations because the co-ops have the full support of even the most radical nationalists. The article sparked a passionate discussion about the way in which the town of Mondragón was portrayed in the growing popular and scholarly literature on the cooperatives.

The Mondragón cooperative system is a network of industrial, agricultural, and retail firms that produces a range of goods from bicycles and copper tubing to computerized machine tools and industrial robots. The system has its own bank for internal financing, a social security co-op that provides pensions and health care, a research and development center, and schools from the primary to the masters level. Its growth rate, measured in terms of sales, capital sources, and job creation, and its low rate of business failure are impressive for any medium-sized enterprise. The system is all the more impressive because the individual businesses are fully worker-owned; no one who is not an employee holds stock in any of the firms. The businesses are also democratically managed. Every member, from the assembly line to top management, is entitled to one vote in the General Assembly and a representative voice in the Governing and Social Councils.

Because it successfully combines business acumen and market viability with worker ownership and democratic management, the Mondragón system is seen as a model by all types of economic reformers who believe that Mondragón-style businesses have the potential to spur economic development, transform labor relations, and provide alternative property structures for state-run factories in formerly socialist countries. These reformers—academics and business consultants by profession—have found in Mondragón a new kind of economic system, neither fully capitalist nor socialist (e.g., Bradley and Gelb 1983; Campbell et al. 1977; Ellerman 1984; Morrison 1991; Oakeshott 1978b; Whyte and Whyte 1988).

However, in the process of distilling a business model from the reality of Mondragón, these reformers have made the co-ops into mythical institutions, where labor and management collaborate easily for the good of the firm. And they have made the town of Mondragón into an imaginary place where social class has disappeared. My friends were already aware that the cooperatives were internationally renowned, and found it amusing that their home attracted journalists, scholars, and social tourists from all over the world. (The issue of *Geo* sold out from town newsstands.) Yet they did not fully realize the extent to which the cooperatives and the town are idealized. This portrayal contrasted with their experiences; to them, the history of cooperativism was also the history of reformist ideologies and politics that competed actively with radical positions in the arenas of Basque nationalism and the labor movement. The cooperatives had also transformed the town's working-class life. While the *Geo* story was not unlike hundreds of other articles, books, and theses that popularize the cooperatives by idealizing town life and by ignoring political questions, the day itself was different. It marked a painful anniversary for Mondragón, when many townspeople recalled the demonstrations and general strikes in commemoration of those killed and the days of police reprisal and fear that followed. It was simply more difficult to accept the utopian imagery on that day.

I, too, came to Mondragón to study the cooperatives. My original goals were not different from those of other researchers. I largely believed what I had read about the cooperatives, and I expected to find that they were democratic institutions and that the town of Mondragón would reflect this egalitarian industrial structure. The first paper I wrote on the cooperatives in graduate school depicted them as working-class institutions within which internal conflict would generate more democracy. My early research proposals stated that the contribution of my research would be ethnographic. Mine was to be the first ethnographic study of the cooperatives, and in retrospect, I think it is this ethnographic vantage point that most distinguishes my work. The literature already included many studies of the institutional history of the system; Gorroño (1975) and Whyte and Whyte (1988) are the most complete. The economic success and profitability of the cooperatives were evaluated by Thomas and Logan (1982), who found that worker participation increased productivity. The democratic management structures developed in Mondragón were described and analyzed by Greenwood and González et al. (1989) and Whyte and Whyte (1988). Bradley and Gelb (1982) argued that the model is transferrable elsewhere, and Ellerman (1984) pinpointed the cooperative bank as the key ingredient for replicating success. For the most part, managers were the informants for these and many other studies of the cooperatives. Drawing on our discussions in the CUNY Working Class Anthropology Project, I undertook (like many ethnographers) to study the cooperatives from the "bottom up." This undertaking yielded surprising results. I found that the cooperatives looked quite different from this perspective than the literature had led me to believe: There was considerable discontent among co-op workers; they perceived class inequalities in a system that was supposed to have eradicated class; and they felt they had little control over their work lives yet were largely uninterested in exercising the rights to which they were formally entitled.

I also found that the town itself was quite another place than I had imagined. Mondragón is rife with activism and is marked by the political culture of radical Basque nationalism, which calls for both independence and socialism for the Basque nation, called Euskadi in the Basque language of Euskera. I wondered if this political life was connected to the cooperative phenomenon, and I set out to examine the links between the two. What I found was a complicated set of political, social, and ideological relationships that touch the core of the Basque nationalist dilemma of class-based versus national identity. Therefore, a central task of my "demythification" of the Mondragón system is to situate it in its political and ideological contexts. I am also interested in why the Mondragón myth was created in the first place.

Pragmatism over Ideology

The Mondragón cooperatives are portrayed as having overcome labor–management conflict and as free of the twin burdens of ideologies and political involvements. Whyte and Whyte explain:

> For many years, the field of economic organization and management was locked into the intellectual prison of the two-valued orientation: the choice between private versus government ownership and control of the means of production. . . . Over the years, this dogmatism has been fading in the face of experience. . . . This shift away from absolutist ideologies has accompanied the sudden rapid growth of worker cooperatives and employee-owned firms. Abandoning formerly popular ideologies, increasing numbers of people around the world are experimenting with unorthodox ways of organizing and controlling economic activities. . . . *It is in support of this more pragmatic and pluralistic view that we turn to Mondragón* to learn what it can teach us about social and economic development. (1988, 7 [emphasis added])

The idea that the cooperatives represent an ideology-free pragmatism, both within the Basque region and as they are replicated in other countries, is an important aspect of the myth of the Mondragón. The argument is twofold: that the Mondragón system does not emanate from a political project and that the model derived from that experience is also apolitical. The implication of this argument is that economic justice is brought about by a form of business rather than by social classes engaged in political action.

Yet the argument itself is embedded in a political discourse. Distrust for politics has become a defining feature of the cultural climate of North America and Western Europe. Over the past decade, and especially since the fall of communism in Eastern Europe, we have become accustomed to hearing that labor movements and left/labor parties can no longer represent the interests of working classes. Some on the left have postulated alternatives to working-class politics, such as new social movements (e.g., Habermas 1986; Touraine 1985). They believe that movements based on specific issues and identities, such as environmentalism, feminism, and gay and lesbian rights, tap more deeply the concerns and allegiances of the working and middle classes and thus are more relevant than unions or political parties. Others have, in an effort to be pragmatic, eschewed ideologies in favor of concrete and winnable projects, such as workplace democracy and employee ownership. Pragmatists and new social movement theorists believe that unions and parties cannot achieve the goals of working classes, something they think that workplace democracy can do (see Boggs 1986, 129–69). They find workplace democracy and worker ownership attractive because both seem to offer workers a degree of equity and control over their jobs without political activism and union struggles.

The task is to transform the workplace, and that task appears to be facilitated by the increasing willingness of corporations to sell stock to their employees and to institute forms of worker participation in management. The management initiatives of ESOPs, the team concept, quality circles, and total quality programs suggest that capitalism is evolving and that it may become a more democratic system (see Bradley and Gelb 1983; Whyte and Whyte 1988, 3–7). Governments have also supported worker ownership. The Chrysler Loan Act, passed by the U.S. Congress in 1975, granted Chrysler guaranteed loans on the condition that the firm establish an ESOP (Rosen 1981, 7). Several years later, under the conservative governments of Reagan and Thatcher, legislation was passed in both the United States and Britain to promote worker ownership. Cooperatives were encouraged by enabling legislation in Britain and the United States. So, too, were tax breaks granted to companies that sold stock to employees. Ronald Reagan himself spoke in favor of transferring ownership to workers:

> Could any country be a land of free men and women, where the pride and independence of property ownership was reserved to [*sic*] the few, while the majority existed in dependency and servility? It should be clear to everyone that the nation's steadfast policy should afford every American of working age a realistic opportunity to acquire the ownership and control of some meaningful form of property in a growing national economy. (Quoted in Rosen 1981, 67)

Politicians seem anxious (for political and ideological reasons) to extend ownership to workers. It seems, then, that what is required of scholars, business consultants, and managers is to map out a strategy to seize the opportunity.

Those concerned with reforming the workplace have before them the best model for worker ownership under capitalism—the Mondragón cooperatives. The Mondragón system has overcome all of the standard obstacles to growth faced by cooperatives: lack of investment capital, inability to attract and retain expert managers and engineers, and a failure to focus on research and development. Moreover, the cooperatives are reported to have avoided the major pitfalls of worker ownership by preserving democracy in the face of economic success. (The most common failure of democracy is the transformation of members' shares into standard, dividend-paying stocks and the breakdown of democratic decision making.)[2] Furthermore, they have reportedly done so without (apparently) entering into the political domain. For these reasons, Mondragón has the attention of a broad range of people—both critics and supporters of capitalism, from the political right and the political left. The cooperatives appear to be the best test case for how far workplace reforms can go toward achieving what unions and parties are thought to be unable to do. This is considered a particularly impressive accomplishment given the highly political environment in which they are found.

Eschewing Politics

Euskadi is renowned for its movement for national independence, which has been described as "the most active popular movement in Western Europe today" (Chomsky and Aske 1991, 105). It also has a history of labor militancy dating to the early twentieth century, when heavy industry developed in the area. More recently, an active labor movement was revived in the mid-1960s, and struggled against the Franco dictatorship. Mondragón itself had a particularly strong syndical movement early in this century and is currently a politically active place with a visible and effective Basque nationalist left. This radical nationalist movement is comprised of the member organizations of Movimiento de Liberación Nacional Vasco (Basque National Liberation Movement). The town's medieval gates and the walls of local buildings are plastered with an ever-changing array of posters and painted with graffiti from many radical groups. If one visits for several days, chances are one will witness a demonstration, perhaps in solidarity with political prisoners or in protest of a plant closing. These political facts have not, however, been a part of the analysis of the co-ops.

William Foote Whyte and Kathleen King Whyte, who have written the most important English-language book on the Mondragón cooperatives, devote only a few pages to a discussion of Basque politics. They tell the reader who might be interested in the armed nationalist organization ETA that ETA has had very little to do with the cooperatives (1988, 17). Morrison makes a similar claim (1991, 55). Indeed, much of the international interest in the cooperatives lies precisely in their reportedly autonomous, apolitical, and nonideological nature: "Mondragón is of interest for pragmatic, rather than purely ideological reasons" (Bradley and Gelb 1983, 3). Furthermore, none of the existing literature examines the relationship between local syndicates and the cooperatives, despite the fact that labor activism is obviously an important feature of the Basque landscape.

The fact that no serious consideration of Basque politics or syndicalism has been undertaken makes the literature on the Mondragón cooperatives utopian. Nineteenth-century advocates of cooperatives, such as Fourier and Owen, were called utopian by their critics not because cooperative business ventures were tenuous nor because cooperatives could not be made to turn a

FIGURE 1

"Open the way to freedom. . . . Amnesty." Demonstration in support of Mondragón's political prisoners. Marchers are carrying enlarged photographs of ETA prisoners from Mondragón. Credit: Arrasate Press.

profit; rather, what made them utopian was their retreat from politics and, thus, the whole question of power (Hobsbawm 1962, 277–99). Early promoters of cooperatives were followers of the philosopher Saint-Simon, who, as Eric Hobsbawm argues (1962, 277–99), was both a rationalist and an idealist and was convinced that simply by conceiving of a more just and rational economic form he could usher in social change. Saint-Simon believed that by exposing the inability of liberal political economic theory to achieve the central goal of capitalism—maximizing individual happiness—he could make a case for socialism. The cooperative experiments undertaken in Europe and the United States in the 1800s would show capitalists, political economists, and governments that cooperative societies could do the work of capitalism better than privately owned factories could. Therefore, advocates of cooperativism did not think it necessary to link their projects to working-class activism; unlike (and counterposed to) their Blanquist contemporaries, they considered the problem of political power to be irrelevant. They believed, instead, that cooperatives would generate socialism through private enterprise without involving the state; consequently, they saw no need for political organization or action (Hobsbawm 1962, 277–99; Mendizabal 1989).

FIGURE 2

Mondragón's main gate (the portalón) with political posters.
Credit: Sharryn Kasmir.

This analytical point is also rooted in shifts in the relationship between political movements and cooperatives. It has historically been the case that both consumer and producer cooperatives spring up in association with workers' organizations but break that affiliation over time. For example, in Oldham, England, consumer cooperatives first appeared in 1808, when they grew out of the working-class organizations of their day. However, in the 1850s, the radicalism of the local working class was compromised by a series of middle-class programs aimed at intervening in and restructuring workers' lives. Among those programs were a conservative adult-education program, the temperance movement, and new cooperatives that were autonomous business forms detached from older working-class organizations. As these new co-ops grew, they created a stratum of managers that had more in common with the town elite than with the working class (Foster 1974, 220–24).

Owen himself provides another example. In 1833, he attempted to unite the newly legalized British trade unions with his cooperatives. This new association was called the Grand Moral Union of Useful and Productive Classes and later became the Grand National Consolidated Trade Union. The organization was short-lived, in part because Owen and the trade unionists could not overcome their differences, the former favoring reformist strategies and the latter favoring class struggle (Cornforth et al. 1988, 12). After losing their link to mass movements, these cooperatives may have been able to offer economic opportunities to some workers, but they could no longer be considered working-class organizations.[3]

The Mondragón system is likewise estranged from local working-class movements. Other authors take this as an indication that the cooperatives stay out of politics. However, the evolution of cooperatives without a link to mass movements does not demonstrate their neutrality; rather, it represents their political character. How did cooperators become distant from political organizations? Has this distance been beneficial for cooperators, or has it hampered the exercise of their rights on the shop floor? How have the cooperatives reshaped working-class politics in Mondragón?

The presumed neutrality of the cooperatives (a stance that co-op managers also claim) has never been questioned by those studying Mondragón. For example, Morrison's commitment to postmodernist arguments about the futility of politics leads him to overlook the implications of his own data. He writes:

> Mondragón and its development is part of, and a commentary on, the post-modern condition—it is essentially an experiment in social reconstruction through cooperative community. Although spawned amidst the historical context that produced both Carlistas and militant Basque separatists, the Mondragón cooperators have chosen a radically different

path, one that helps them begin to transcend the general conditions of industrial modernism and the more particular forces of Spanish history (they have, for example, *avoided entanglement with the politics of Basque separatism while successfully advocating Basque autonomy*). (1991, 55) [emphasis added]

In the context of the Basque Country, advocating autonomy while rejecting separatism is, to the contrary, to engage in partisan politics of a very traditional sort. In particular, it signals support for the conservative nationalist party Partido Nacionalista Vasco (PNV) over the radical Basque nationalism of Herri Batasuna (HB). Clearly, to understand the cooperatives it is necessary to enter into the arena of Basque nationalist and working-class politics as they are played out in Mondragón.

The Town of Mondragón

Mondragón is located forty-five kilometers inland from the Bay of Biscay, in the southwestern corner of the Spanish Basque province of Gipuzkoa (Guipúzcoa). Like other Gipuzkoan towns, it sits in a narrow valley surrounded by the Cantabrian mountains. Yet it is not isolated. After traveling some twenty to thirty kilometers on heavily trafficked or mountainous roads, one reaches the cities of Bilbo (Bilbao) and Gasteiz (Vitoria) in about forty minutes. One can get to Donosti (San Sebastián), the capital and commercial center of Gipuzkoa, by highway in a little more than an hour.

Like many other Basque towns, Mondragón is neither wholly urban nor wholly rural; rather, it belongs to a category of settlement common to the Basque Country that is best described as a densely populated, industrial town. Approximately seventy small to medium-sized factories, both privately and cooperatively owned, and twenty-five workshops and construction firms exist within its boundaries, employing approximately seven thousand people (Arrasateko Udala, n.d.). With a population of approximately twenty-six thousand, the largest part of the labor force works with its hands in an industrial setting. Mondragón is a working-class town.

The industrial and class character of Mondragón is reflected in its built environment. Architectural monuments of note are few relative to neighboring towns. Its landmark architecture includes a fourteenth-century Gothic-style church, the wooden facade of the house of Bañez dating from the sixteenth century, the eighteenth-century Palace of Monterrón, the nineteenth-century town hall, and the *portalón*, an eighteenth-century stone archway that is the main entrance to the town center. The dominant monuments are instead factories, which occupy much of the flat and easily urbanized land in the narrow valley. Apartment houses climb the sides of hills and mountains, revealing the fact that the town is desperate for space that it will never find. Certainly, the rapid and unplanned growth associated with the industrial boom of the 1960s still marks Mondragón, like other industrial Basque towns, with a lack of housing, poorly designed roads, and inadequate parking. This phase of unregulated growth, a legacy of the Franco regime, also left the town with serious pollution problems. The air is often heavy with smoke from the factories, and not infrequently one sees the Deba (Deva) River run the most unnatural of colors, from purple to orange to iridescent green. The industrial and proletarian character of Mondragón is at the heart of its local identity.

Mondragón is also the scene of an active Basque nationalist movement and is considered to be a solidly *abertzale* (Basque patriotic) town (Heiberg 1989, 136). The visitor to Mondragón is immediately struck by the salience of nationalist politics in everyday life. The radical version of Basque nationalism, expressed by ETA, MLNV, and the electoral coalition Herri Batasuna (HB), pervades the town. HB has held the mayorship since 1987 and won over 24 percent of the vote in the 1991 municipal elections. HB regularly wins an average of 18 to 20 percent of the vote throughout the Basque Country. While it is autonomous from the illegal organization ETA (necessarily so or it, too, would be outlawed), HB evolved from the political wing of ETA and has a relationship to the organization similar to that of Northern Ireland's Sinn Fein to the Irish Republican Army. HB is the only major Basque party to refuse to publicly condemn the group; given the historic popularity of ETA, this fact accounted for some of its electoral success (see Chomsky and Aske 1991; Clark 1990).

In Mondragón, the presence of radical nationalism is visible on the facades of factories, stores, and banks, which are covered with murals as well as graffiti and posters. Not even churches are left clean in the search for public space in which to debate the issues of Basque independence, environmental destruction, women's equality, sexual politics, the draft, and deindustrialization. Political messages and art are informative, timely, and elaborate, making the street a major arena for political communication (see Chaffe 1988). Indeed, "the street" is an important concept not only in the political domain but in the social domain as well.[4] Geographically, "the street" refers to the center of Basque towns or neighborhoods where bars are clustered, away from rural areas and excluding homes. Socially and culturally, it refers to the ambience generated inside and spilling out from the bars. Working-class social life often centers around pubs and taverns where workers are "beyond the meddling control of 'bosses'" (Cumbler 1979, 155) and are free to elaborate their own style of conviviality and to discuss union activity and politics (Kornblum 1974; Halle 1984). Just as the pub functioned as a social institution linked with working-class identity and union politics in Lynn, Massachusetts, from 1880 to 1930 (Cumbler 1979, 155),[5] so it does in contemporary Mondragón, where bars are

FIGURE 3

Wall of building covered with posters announcing two political demonstrations.
Credit Sharryn Kasmir.

simultaneously working-class and Basque cultural establishments, frequented
by both men and women (Kasmir 1992a, 1992b).

It is estimated that the province of Gipuzkoa has more bars than any other
place in Europe (Hacker and Elcorobairutia 1987, 358). A wide variety of
townspeople spend hours each day making *vueltas* (the rounds of bars) with
their *cuadrillas* (friendship groups), stopping for small glasses of wine or beer
in a ritual called the *poteo* or *txikiteo.* Their choice of which bars to patronize
is based largely on the political tenor of the establishments. One knows the political commitments of a bar immediately upon entering. Bars that sympathize
with radical nationalist politics prominently display pictures of the town's political prisoners, close down during demonstrations, and sell t-shirts and lapel
pins decorated with political slogans and logos. Those that cater to young
people also play *radikal rok basko,* radical Basque punk music. Basque bars are
a center for political discussion and mobilization; they are loci of ekintza (taking action [Kasmir 1992a, 1992b]). An American observer wrote:

In the bars—many with an atmosphere of a well-lit, old fashioned American kitchen—business is transacted and news messages exchanged.
The main purpose is social and political, not sexual and alcoholic. For

FIGURE 4

Posters of ETA prisoners from Mondragón and gay pride banner, "You should make love as you like."
Credit: Sharryn Kasmir.

FIGURE 5

Radical nationalist bar with Basque flag. Credit: Sharryn Kasmir.

example, I felt it would be impossible to organize a demonstration overnight. Who would do the calling, the organizing? And only about half the homes have telephones anyway. My comments were simply ignored. A faster form of communication existed in the bars. The demonstration was attended by thousands (Hacker and Elcorobairutia 1987, 362).

These demonstrations might also be different from those imagined by Americans: Children, young adults, and older men and women board buses together to go to Bilbo or Donosti for Euskadi-wide mobilizations, and gather in Mondragón's town center to particate in local marches. Activism pervades most arenas of the town, including factories, the local press, and the town hall, yet this has not been told as part of the story of Mondragón.

The Development and Structure of the Cooperative System

At the close of the Spanish Civil War, a young Catholic Action–oriented priest named Don José María Arizmendiarrieta was appointed to Mondragón. He organized a Young Catholic Workers study circle for teenage apprentices in a local factory. His passion about social action and work influenced them to reconceptualize factory work. In 1955, these young men completed their technical educations and opened a small factory called Ulgor in a nearby city, where they produced kerosene stoves. They moved the operation to their hometown in 1956 and, along with sixteen co-workers, reorganized the firm into a cooperative. In the next few years, they shifted production to gas stoves, which were in high demand. Following their successful lead, others opened cooperative ventures: an agricultural co-op; the consumer cooperative Eroski; the social security and health insurance cooperative Lagun Aro; and the cooperative bank the Caja Laboral Popular. All of the cooperatives were loosely integrated into one system called the Mondragón Cooperative Group.

In the last four decades, the Mondragón system has grown to employ approximately twenty-one thousand worker-owners in some one hundred fifty cooperatives. These co-ops are located throughout all of the provinces of the Basque region, but they are concentrated in Mondragón and the surrounding towns of the *comarca*[6] of the Alto Deba, where about 50 percent of the total work force is employed in the co-ops. The industrial cooperatives emphasize state-of-the-art, high-tech production and are strong in the sectors of machine tools and numerical-control systems as well as refrigerators, washing machines, and stoves for homes, restaurants, and hotels. Turn-key plants have been exported to Chile, Argentina, Libya, Egypt, and other countries (see Caja Laboral Popular 1990).

The cooperative group has become a key financial player in the region. It is the single largest employer in the Basque Country, and the cooperative

FIGURE 6

Caja Laboral Popular and Lagun Aro Central Offices. Credit: Arrasate Press.

bank is the largest savings bank in Euskadi and the seventeenth largest of seventy-one banking entities in all of Spain. In 1989, the co-ops completed their first buy-out of a major private corporation; with the purchase of Fabrelec, they claimed 30 percent of the Spanish market in consumer durables and became the dominant market force in that sector within the Spanish state. In 1990, they purchased majority stock in a second private firm, Luzuriaga, and created a stock-holding company for the purpose of gaining controlling shares of firms in key market niches. In 1992, the cooperative group consolidated these developments by incorporating the holding company as a standard stock company—in Spanish a *sociedad anónima,* as opposed to a *sociedad cooperativa* (cooperative firm). For now, the only shareholders in the holding company are the cooperative bank and the social security co-op, but, as some people warn, the juridical structure allows for capitalist investment in the future, which would mark a definitive break with cooperative values.[7]

Obviously, the Mondragón group does not fit the image of cooperatives as small, economically tenuous, and capital poor. Greenwood's work (1992; Greenwood and González et al. 1989) correctly portrays them as sophisticated business entities with astute and flexible management strategies. The structure of the system is also ingeniously crafted. Each cooperative is linked to the bank

FIGURE 7

Worker in cooperative refrigerator factory. Credit: Sharryn Kasmir.

FIGURE 8

Home appliances produced in the Mondragón cooperatives. Credit: Sharryn Kasmir.

through a contract of association, which limits the autonomy of the individual firm in matters of product line and capital investments but also gives the small firm access to a wide range of business and financial services, including investment counseling and accounting assistance. Associated cooperatives borrow from the Caja at interest rates that are lower than those for commercial loans at regular banks. The close ties between the producer co-ops and the Caja has insured that the banking decisions remain responsive to industrial development. Whereas other banks are tempted by speculative strategies—for example, favoring real estate over industry—the integration of the bank with economic development is one of the signal features of the system, and is considered to be a crucial element in its success (Ellerman 1984; Mendizabal 1989, 539–40). In the 1980s, the bank grew at a faster rate than its member firms and so sought out other investments, such as vacation villas, but it also put money into business development. In 1991, the Entrepreneurial Division of the bank became an independent consulting cooperative, with the goal of business creation (Whyte and Whyte 1991, 199–200).

In the past decade, the cooperatives have responded to the twofold challenges of entry into the European market and worldwide recession by strengthening their internal links. Sectoral groups were created to pool capital, labor, and managerial expertise (Weiner and Oakeshott 1987). The most important of these is the Fagor Group, which unites thirteen industrial cooperatives in three divisions: consumer products, industrial components, and engineering and machine tools, most of which are located in the town of Mondragón (Whyte and Whyte 1988, 157–69).

The cooperatives survived most of the economic crisis without laying off workers, though they encouraged early retirement and transferred workers to other cooperatives. Even in the midst of crisis, the cooperatives have had lower levels of unemployment and significantly higher levels of job creation than other Spanish firms. In the 1980s, job losses were reported for only two years—562 in 1980 and 44 in 1983—but the losses were recovered by job creation in each of the following years (see Whyte and Whyte 1991, 206). This is an economically and politically important fact, given the disturbingly high unemployment rate in the Basque Country, which was between 20 and 25 percent for the first three years of the 1990s. In 1985, only 0.6 percent of cooperative workers were unemployed, while the unemployment rate in the Basque Country was 27 percent (Whyte and Whyte 1991, 234). Since Spain undertook a massive industrial restructuring in preparation for entry into the European Market, regions that hosted heavy industry declined while new industrial zones emerged, for example, in the area surrounding Madrid. Many sectors that were mainstays of the Basque economy have been severely cut back as a result of central government-led initiatives to renew Spain's economic base; Basque shipbuilding has nearly been wiped out, and steel production has dramatically declined. From 1976 to

1986, the cooperatives created 4,200 jobs, while there were more than 150,000 jobs lost in the Basque Country (Whyte and Whyte 1991, 204; see also Moye 1993). In Mondragón, two medium-sized firms faced closure in 1990, and both cut back their work forces, resulting in the loss of hundreds of jobs. Meanwhile, no local cooperative has closed, and cooperators are transferred between firms to avoid layoffs.

Deindustrialization and the sale of local factories to multinationals (which promptly downsize) have plagued the Basque economy since the late 1970s, yet the cooperatives have stayed put, securing for themselves a central place in two important sectors of the restructured economy: machine tools and white-line appliances. This fact is singled out by researchers from other deindustrialized regions, such as the northeastern United States, who see Mondragón-style worker ownership as an alternative to capital flight. They reason that since workers are interested in maintaining their employment rather than maximizing profits, they will be committed to preserving capital investment in their region even if they are forced to accept pay cuts or to lose their health or pension benefits (see Bluestone and Harrison 1982, 257–62; Schweickart 1984). Worker ownership of the Mondragón cooperatives can be partially credited with preserving the economy of Euskadi (see Mendizabal 1989).

The individual firms that make up the Mondragón system are fully worker owned. By contributing the total of about one year's salary upon joining a cooperative (a sum that can be borrowed at a low rate of interest), a member opens an individual capital account with the Caja Laboral Popular. A share of the co-op's yearly profits or losses is credited or debited to this account, which accrues interest at the standard rate for savings banks. The distribution of net profits is decided by the General Assembly of each co-op in accordance with minimums established by Spanish law. At least 10 percent goes to the social fund, used for community projects such as education, housing, and publications. A minimum of 20 percent goes to the reserve fund, a capital fund belonging to the cooperative. The remaining profit, at a maximum of 70 percent, is deposited directly into members' individual capital accounts, which are held as savings accounts in the Caja. The precise division fluctuates with the business climate and the financial accounts and needs of individual firms.

In the 1980s, when cooperative business plans and crisis-induced profit losses required higher levels of investment, those co-ops that manufactured home appliances invested half of their profits into the reserve fund (Whyte and Whyte 1988, 43). Similarly, members of those co-ops made contributions to the Caja's development fund and extra payments to their social security fund (Lagun Aro) to cover the pensions of members who retired early or were laid off. The distribution of collective and private capital is considered by Gui (1982) to be an excellent balance between the two forms of property, because it both ensures that the cooperatives have operating capital and gives workers material incentives to contribute to the firm.

Part of the profit distributed to members is paid as salaries. These are called *anticipios* to indicate that they are advanced payment in anticipation of end-of-year profits. The rest of the payment to members remains in the bank, in their individual accounts, available to the system for investment. The bank has access to these monies, just as deposits are part of the investable monies of any bank. Anticipios as well as payment to individual accounts are based on job ratings. Ratings are numerical rankings given to each job depending upon skill level, responsibility, and such personal attributes of the worker as seniority and pace of work. Job ratings increase by increments of .05, from a low of 1.0 to a high of 3.0. These indexes are then converted into a pay scale in which the highest-paid director earns 4.5 times the salary of the lowest-paid production worker. Such a slim difference between the earnings of workers and managers is considered one of the most egalitarian attributes of the system.

In 1990, while I was living in Mondragón, a delegation from the Soviet Union toured the cooperatives. A daily newspaper reported that delegation members were impressed with the system, but they thought that the 1:4.5 margin should be increased.[8] This struck a nerve among cooperators, for the pay differential was one of the most fiercely contested issues between managers and workers. Two years earlier, the Caja Laboral Popular voted to increase its job index to 1:6. This vote affected only the bank; nonetheless it set a powerful example. In 1989, Fagor management called a meeting to propose a widening of the salary spread there. Workers organized against the management proposal and defeated it before it was taken to a vote. Managers argue that they are not sufficiently remunerated for their work. A study by the Caja Laboral Popular (1988) showed that the highest-level engineers in production co-ops, to pick one example, earn 30 percent less than comparably skilled engineers in private firms in the province of Gipuzkoa.

Managers believe that since they can easily find work elsewhere, the cooperatives should provide more incentives for them to stay. Until recently, though, they were unable to bring this pressure to bear, because they also promoted an ideology that wedded the managerial role to the cooperative project. Over the past few years, however, managers have shed their cooperativist ideology in favor of an "efficiency" ideology; they argue that the cooperatives won't survive unless more economistic or capitalistic changes are made (see Taylor 1994). Among those changes are managerial salaries that are competitive with those in the private sector.

The valuation of managerial expertise over the productive knowledge of workers is a trend that characterizes the post-1973 period throughout Europe and the United States. Workers in Mondragón, however, continue to view the 1:4.5 salary ratio as a central democratic feature of the system. Indeed, the question of salaries almost spontaneously mobilized workers to take collective action against management. This show of activism and combativeness by cooperators marked a distinct departure from the past. The other feature of the system that has always marked it as democratic is the internal organization of the cooperatives. When we are presented with an organizational map, we see a well-thought-out structure, with a clear procedure of checks and balances and for distributing rights and responsibilities via the following committees:

General Assembly. At least once a year, the entire membership of each individual cooperative convenes as a body, the General Assembly, to attend to the broad concerns of managing the firm. It votes on the annual business plan, allocates earnings, decides on mergers and acquisitions, votes on the admission of new members and the punitive expulsion of members, and elects the Governing Council and monitors its performance. Each cooperative member has one vote in the Assembly, regardless of his or her position in the firm. Beyond the regular meeting, an extraordinary meeting of the General Assembly can be called by collecting signatures. This means that workers, like managers, have the right to organize a meeting of the entire cooperative if they feel it is warranted; however, it is usually management that exercises this right.

The Governing Council. The president, vice president, and secretary of the General Assembly, along with several other members of the cooperative, make up the Governing Council. All are elected by the General Assembly. The Governing Council is the closest thing the cooperative has to a board of directors, but, unlike a board of directors, only co-op members can be elected; no outside person sits on the Governing Council. This body prepares annual plans, proposes the distribution of profits for the approval of the General Assembly, appoints and oversees managers, determines job classifications, and presents annual reports and accounts. Members of the Governing Council hold office for four years (Whyte and Whyte 1988, 35–37).

General Manager. The General Manager is appointed by the Governing Council and is accountable to that body. The manager is also accountable to the General Assembly, which can vote to dismiss a manager who is not performing well (though this rarely happens). Managers preside over department heads who are also appointed by the Governing Council. The manager is appointed for four years and can be reappointed with the approval of the Governing Council. As Whyte and Whyte note, chief executive officers of major corporations are not subject to predetermined limits to their terms; in this respect, the position of General Manager is inherently more democratic (1988, 37). Typically, a co-op has departments of engineering, marketing, and personnel; the head of each department is appointed by the General Manager.

Management Council. A Management Council is a consultatory body to the General Manager and is made up of department heads and other executives who are nominated jointly by the General Manager and the Governing Council.

Social Council. Workers are represented to management by the Social Council, which is elected directly from the geographic sections of the shop floor. This council brings grievances to management on behalf of workers. In this regard, it operates like syndicate delegates in a private factory who are concerned with health and safety, job ratings, work pace, job assignments, and internal promotion. However, the cooperative Social Council differs from a syndicate in that it functions not only to exert pressure upwards from the shop floor to management but to communicate managerial decisions and convey information downward as well. In recent years, this has been the focus of a great deal of criticism, as the Social Council increasingly is viewed as an organ that does not represent workers to management but convinces workers to accept the dictates of management. Further, local syndicates are prevented by co-op by-laws from presenting lists for Social Council elections in the cooperatives.

Audit Committee. As required by Spanish cooperative law, the Audit Committee (sometimes called a "watchdog committee") is charged with inspecting all documents brought before the General Assembly.

Clearly, in all of the above organs there is a difference between rights and the power to exercise those rights. One development that limits the powers of the various committees is the juridical organization of the new sectoral groups like Fagor. Groups typically consist of six to twelve co-ops in similar lines of production, such as furniture or kitchen appliances. This centralization of management, marketing, and financing has gone a long way toward staving off the effects of economic crisis and the implications of Spain's entry into the European Economic Community. The central offices of the Fagor Group, for example, have unified marketing strategies, consolidating Fagor's leadership in the home-appliances sector. The group structure also allows for maximum flexibility in allocating resources according to demand, orders, and market potential (Greenwood 1992). From the point of view of democracy, however, the centralization has been destructive. Each group has a Governing Council, Social Council, and General Assembly, to which delegates are sent from each cooperative (Ormaechea 1991, 120–22). There is increasing dissatisfaction with this arrangement; workers and plant-level managers feel that important decisions are made outside of their control as the groups become more powerful.

A parallel development is the Cooperative Congress, which was created in 1987 to bring together representatives of all of the cooperatives into one body. There are more than three hundred delegates; given the high-powered nature of the Congress, these delegates tend not to come from the ranks of manual workers. The Congress also has a president and a permanent commission, made up of representatives of the cooperative groups. The Third Congress, held in 1991, was undoubtedly the most important to date. There, many of the changes that the Mondragón system had been undergoing were formalized into proposals for rewriting the cooperative by-laws, including the new organization of the co-ops into twenty-five sectoral groups that, in turn, are organized into nine divisions. What was previously the loosely affiliated Mondragón Cooperative Group became the Mondragón Cooperative Corporation. The Corporation has its own Governing Council, comprised of a president, vice president and representatives from the member co-ops (Greenwood and González et al. 1992, 162–68). Proposals to form the sectoral groups and the Cooperative Corporation were ratified in the individual cooperatives, even though there was a sense that the centralization of management and committees represented a dissolution of democracy. But other decisions taken by the Congress were soundly defeated, most notably a proposal to increase the salary ratio to 1:9 or 1:10.

These no votes signaled a shift in the political climate inside the cooperatives, and some cooperators are now building relationships with local syndicates to deepen their ability to challenge management (developments that are discussed in chapter 7). In order to fully understand this shift and to evaluate its implications for the Mondragón model, we must broaden our view to encompass the ethnographic context of the cooperative system, and we must turn to an analysis of its historical development.

Conclusions

In my field experience in Mondragón and in the experiences of many townspeople, politics were a constant feature of daily life. Even those who don't participate in vigils, demonstrations, or elections hear and see political discussion and events every day. Mondragón is an active place where conflict is palpable.

Thus, the absence of politics in the literature on the cooperatives is a significant ommision. I argued in this chapter that this exclusion echoes the utopianism of nineteenth-century socialism as well as recent calls by academics and policymakers for pragmatism over ideology: The Mondragón cooperatives were crafted as a pragmatic, "post-political" industrial model. I also showed that this depoliticization of the cooperatives is an aspect of the myth of Mondragón, a story that tells us that worker ownership offers workers equality, democracy, and job satisfaction without having to involve unions or political parties. As we shall see, this claim overlooks the relationship of the cooperative system and of cooperators to the local labor movement, and it ignores important ties between cooperativism and Basque nationalism. Moreover, the declaration that the Mondragón cooperatives are apolitical obscures some of the most dynamic and participatory aspects of the town itself.

2

The History of Mondragón as a Working-Class Town

Mondragón was "a difficult town and one of the most brutal. I remember going around with body guards."

—(An executive of one of Mondragón's leading private firms, in the early twentieth century, quoted in Whyte and Whyte 1988, 26)

Early in the twentieth century, Mondragón was described by business leaders as a brutal town and a place where local identity was intimately linked with being working class. This characterization contrasts with contemporary portrayals of a town without labor or class strife. In this chapter, I explore this contrast by reconstructing the history of class formation in Mondragón. Since the thirteenth century, the nature of artisanry and industry as well as local politics have made Mondragón different from nearby towns. I suggest that Mondragón was a place where artisans, rather than elites, created local identity. My ethnohistorical research shows that in the years just prior to the founding of the cooperatives, Mondragón's workers were more class conscious and more politically active than their neighbors in surrounding towns. This historical portrayal is relevant for two reasons. First, it is an element of a contemporary identity that townspeople embrace for themselves. Second, within this historical setting, the founding of the Mondragón cooperatives in the 1950s looks different from the politically neutral way in which it is usually represented. Instead, questions about the political character of the cooperatives become consequential. The historical picture of Mondragón I create in this chapter is based on census records and secondary sources as well as interviews I conducted with townspeople. It is also based on Mondragón residents' invented stories about the past, which are contemporarily invoked to explain class relations and identity. Thus, I offer this history in the contingent way in which it is lived and interpreted (cf. Zulaika 1988).

History, Myth, and Identity

In reviewing the history of Mondragón, I encountered two historical myths that shape the construction of the past. One is a legend that imagines that Mondragón gained its independence from a ferocious dragon through the labor and ingenuity of the town's iron workers. Centuries old, this legend is central to the contemporary popular recounting of Mondragón's history, because it confirms an identity that townspeople currently embrace for themselves; in its present telling, it affirms the strength of Mondragón's working class. A second myth is that of Basque egalitarianism. Originally articulated in the sixteenth century, Basque egalitarianism depicts Basque society as emerging from a kin-ordered mode of production without ever fully developing feudalism. This myth is also popularly embraced, since egalitarianism distinguishes Basque history from that of feudal Spain and Europe, thereby providing historical and cultural legitimation for claims to independence. Moreover, various Basque nationalist parties interpret it differently making the myth an active part of contemporary ideology and a contentious part of political agendas.

The Slaying of the Dragon

Mondragón has two founding dates for its transformation from village to incorporated town—one mythical, the other historical. Both are associated with the development of industry. Late one night, after making the rounds of our usual bars, Iñaki,[1] a friend of mine who works on the assembly line in a Fagor cooperative, recounted the legend of Mondragón. I had already read the legend in accounts of local history (see Caro Baroja 1972, 26–27; Letona 1987). So had Iñaki. But as he told me the story that night, I understood that the retelling itself was significant; the legend was a dynamic part of his identity as a townsperson.

> For generations, villagers were terrorized by a dragon who guarded
> Mount Murugain [Iñaki pointed in the direction of the mountain]. Every
> year, the dragon demanded the sacrifice of a virgin. In exchange, people
> were permitted to mine the iron ore within the mountain, which contained
> particularly rich veins. But the artisans were determined to free them-
> selves from the rule of the dragon. One year, they got together and made
> a wax figure, which they offered instead of the maiden. When the dragon
> realized that he was tricked, he came after the iron makers, who tore out
> his insides with an iron rod they had prepared for the battle. They killed
> the dragon.

This legend is a thinly veiled allegory of town-dwelling artisans' challenge to an oppressive rural regime, symbolized by the dragon. As Caro Baroja notes

(1972, 26–27), the heroism of the iron makers is a critical dramatic element of the story, which credits industry and artisans, rather than agriculture and rural elites, with freeing Mondragón. The tale is also a text which champions town-based organization and collective action over the hierarchical and tributary social relations of the countryside.

A similar myth is told in the Bolivian mining community of Oruro (Nash 1979).[2] The Bolivian tin mine, like the iron deposits in Mondragón, represents both danger and wealth, and the Bolivian myth similarly recounts the violent transition from an agricultural to a mining economy. In Oruro, the spirit of the hills fell in love with the daughter of the sun god; the sun god, defending the old religious order, hid his daughter from the hill spirit. The hill spirit sought revenge by proselytizing a new religion, which worshiped material wealth and work in the mines over agriculture. After embracing the religion, along with the wealth and the vices of the mines, the people were visited by the daughter of the sun god and were inspired to fight for their old way of life. The hill spirit fought back with three plagues, including an attacking serpent that the villagers slew with a sword. A chapel now stands on the site of the slaying.

Structurally, both myths cast the mines as being ruled by nonhuman creatures that are conquered after they display the human emotions of love or lust. In both myths, the maiden mediates between the creature and her community. In the Bolivian myth, the community rebels against the avarice associated with the mines, which is seen as opposing rural life. However, in Mondragón, the defeat of the dragon represents the victory of industry over rural life, a transition that is associated with freedom and the triumph of popular will. Both myths are part of contemporary understandings of the character of the community, what Nash considers to be the fusing of the past and the present.

The myth of the dragon has its historical parallel in the social processes that began in 1260. In that year, the village known in the Basque language of Euskera as "Arrasate" was given the Spanish name of "Mondragón" and granted the status of a free town by Alfonso X, King of Castile (Caro Baroja 1972, 13–40; Letona 1987). The renaming is significant, because naming always carries with it a heavy symbolic load, especially when a centralizing language replaces a regional one (a language shift took place in Bolivia, too). The names themselves also indicate the consolidation of the economic base of the town and the shifting power relations between town-based classes and the rural elite, represented by the dragon, which prohibited the free mining of ore. In Euskera, *ate* means door or gate, suggesting that the village of Arras*ate* was probably a place of transit along trade routes (Caro Baroja 1972, 30). The name Mondragón, "dragon mountain," instead referred to the mythical victory of the artisans and the liberation of the iron ore once guarded by the dragon.

Mondragón was declared a free town along with twenty-five other Gipuzkoan towns that were established by the Crown in the two centuries that followed the Castilian annexation of Gipuzkoa in 1200. (The Gipuzkoan towns had been ruled since the early eleventh century by the Kingdom of Nafarroa [Navarre].) In an effort to secure a dependable northern border and to consolidate its power vis-à-vis competing local elites, Castile created allies by privileging Gipuzkoan towns (Arizaga 1990, 3–35; Clark 1979, 118–25; Heiberg 1989, 20–21). All newly created towns were granted privileges and *fueros,* a combination of custom and law that limited the Crown's power by guaranteeing self-governance in many areas of town life. The town was governed by elected councils called *hermandades* that regulated important areas of daily life such as dowry and inheritance practices. Free towns were exempted from Crown taxes and permitted to levy their own. They were also free from military conscription and conceded the right to raise their own armies.

These processes parallel the social transformations that occurred throughout Europe in the thirteenth century. Craftsmen who had escaped the seigniorial manor founded free settlements where they practiced their crafts and traded with a nascent commercial class. In the twelfth century, European monarchs began to grant legal status to these urban communes in order to consolidate their own power over local feudalities. They used monarchial law to create a stratum of town dwellers, exempt from feudal dues and servitude, who were to be loyal to the Crown rather than to the local nobility. As urban craft economies strained feudal arrangements, new laws were devised to extend military, political, and juridical autonomy to the communes. The assembly, or the hermandad, was created as the body politic of the new towns that united property-holding free males, artisans, and feudal elites alike (Anderson 1974, 15–43; Poggi 1978, 34–59). While undergoing some of these transitions, Basque towns and the surrounding countryside are thought to have diverged in their class structure, and the extent of this difference and the precise nature of Basque class structure of this period are the topics of a much politicized historiographic debate (e.g., Monreal 1980; Otazu y Llana 1986; Urtiaga 1962). The second myth lies at the heart of this controversy.

The Myth of Basque Egalitarianism

Some claim that the Basque Country maintained a democratic and egalitarian society—organized in patrilineal clans—while the rest of Europe developed feudal regimes. Castile seemed to recognize this egalitarianism in the sixteenth century, when it granted collective noble status, called *hidalguía,* to all Basques. This collective nobility and juridical equality is at the heart of the concept of Basque egalitarianism. Some historians argue that this version of the past, elaborated in various forms since the sixteenth century, is essentially an invention for the purpose of producing an image of a Basque society free from internal conflicts and inequalities. It appears to have been employed at historical junctures that are most rife with social and class tension (Monreal 1980;

Otazu y Llana 1986). Contemporarily, Basque egalitarianism is part of a nationalist discourse that seeks a differentiating characteristic for Euskadi to legitimate its claim for independence (Azcona 1984, 165–71). Euskadi is not
Spanish or French, it is reasoned, because social relations and class patterns are
significantly different: Euskadi should be left free to construct (and reconstruct)
its own society. Radical nationalists, who advocate socialism as well as national
independence, take the argument one step further: Euskadi is primordially com-
munistic; class equality was imposed by the centralizing states of Spain and
France. Independence for Euskadi necessitates class struggle and the fight for
socialism. As we will see in later chapters, these arguments and the various interpretations of egalitarianism have contemporary salience for how cooperativism is viewed and for who is deemed the modern agent of egalitarianism. In
its present interpretation, egalitarianism is considered to be Basque, to express
autonomy, and is an ideology that must be embraced, manipulated, and fought
for by all parties and groups.

Beyond this political competition, there is some historical evidence for
Basque difference. The Basque Country, especially the coastal provinces of
Gipuzkoa and Bizkaia, largely escaped Roman, Nordic, Celtic, Moorish, and
other invasions that contributed to the development of feudalism throughout
Europe. Moreover, at the time of the founding of the free towns, rural Basque
society was ruled by clan-based elites called *parientes mayores* in Spanish and
buruzagi in Euskera. According to Caro Baroja (1974), these elites came from
the most powerful agnatic lineages. Their military role was clearly feudal-like.
Buruzagi could organize successively larger spheres of kinsmen, the largest
grouping being a band, thereby extending their territorial capacity. However,
the nature of the social and economic relations between clan chiefs and their
kinsmen—specifically, the question of tenurial rights—was less clear. There is
evidence that Basque buruzagi were democratically elected by their kinsmen to
protect the town and that this position was not inheritable, lending credence to
assertions of communal and democratic relations. On the other hand, records
of property transmission testify to the economic and political power wielded by
clan heads who controlled cultivated lands, pastures, and woods as well as
roads, churches, commercial businesses, mills, and iron works. Among their
sources of income were rents, tithes, and tolls (Arocena 1980, 1–15).[3] Otazu y
Llana (1986) concludes that buruzagi were, in fact, a feudal nobility, but Urtiaga (1962) insists that Basque property forms were more communal then feudal during this period.[4] In Mondragón, the ruins of the castle of Santa Barbara
suggest a noble presence. However, while the building date is unknown, it is
thought to have been constructed before 1200 for the King of Nafarroa, suggesting that it pre-dated the founding of the free town. Furthermore, the castle
was destroyed in 1457 (Letona 1975), reflecting the anti-elitism of the period.
(Suggestive, perhaps, of contemporary anti-elitism, the ruins of the castle are

buried under centuries of growth and are rarely marked in townspeople's emic geographies of their town. This point merits further research.)

The Band Wars

Regardless of how they characterize class structure, historians agree that from the thirteenth to fifteenth centuries, the Basque Country was in a state of endemic warfare between two agnatic bands—the Gamboinos and the Oñacinos. The fighting was destructive of the countryside and ruinous for many towns, especially Mondragón. Monreal claims that it was these band wars that led Gipuzkoa to seek a "civilizing" power in Castile. He argues that villagers sought in the Crown the wherewithal to end these conflicts that lasted until the late 1400s (Monreal 1980). However, the direction of causality between the band wars and the creation of towns is not clear, and is itself a politically contentious topic with contemporary implications for Basque independence. If Castile tamed the Basque Country once, perhaps it should save Euskadi today—this time from the political violence of ETA.[5] Another interpretation is that the growing power of the town-based mercantile classes, and the usurious credit they extended to the lineage heads (who consumed luxury goods they could ill afford), sparked the conflicts. According to this view, band warfare resulted from efforts at territorial expansion in order to increase revenues from rents to pay their debts (Ortzi 1978, 13–16).

The creation of towns was the first step toward dispossessing these lineage heads/feudal elites of their political powers. In the fourteenth century, there was heavy fighting between the bands and the king, who was allied with the hermandades. Mondragón was almost completely destroyed in 1448 by a fire set during conflicts between the local branches of the Gamboa and Oñaz bands. (This fire looms large in the contemporary consciousness, and its current meaning deserves further study.) The arsonists were eventually found and forced to pay property damages. This punishment and the ability to enforce it was an indication of the growing power of the king and the townspeople over the bands. In 1463, the towns prohibited lineage heads from holding local office (Caro Baroja 1972, 13–40, 51–57; Letona 1987; Ortzi 1978, 13–17).

The defeat of the bands and the suppression of the rural regime allowed for the development of urban crafts and town-based proto-industry. This is the historical lesson of the legend of the dragon. As the fueros (legal codes) were drawn up to outline property rights in the newly founded towns, proto-industrial development was codified. In Mondragón, it was declared in 1262 that the ore taken from the mines could be forged only within the town, thus protecting the growing artisan class. Use rights were established for the woods, where kindling was gathered and charcoal was produced; both were necessary fuels in the transformation of ore into iron. Mondragón's workshops were also an important object of legislation and social control. The fueros specified one hundred lashes and a fine for leaving the iron works before the end of a contract and the death penalty for intentionally breaking a bellows. There were severe penalties for competing with or defying the iron masters (Caro Baroja 1972, 49). Far from providing a picture of egalitarian relations between Mondragón's artisans and apprentices, these codes nonetheless indicate the growing juridical power of artisans in a legal environment previously dominated by rural elites.

Colonialism and Class Transformations

By the time of its founding, due to its mines and workshops, Mondragón had the largest population among the surrounding towns (Caro Baroja 1972, 22 fn.). In the period after the political defeat of the clans in the late fifteenth century, Mondragón became yet more exceptional in the local landscape.

Throughout Europe in the sixteenth century, there was a new phase of class stratification in urban communes as a nascent mercantilist bourgeoisie began to buy feudal offices from monarchs, displacing feudal elites (Poggi 1978, 60–85). In Euskadi, this new class was called *jauntxo* and was economically tied to the conquest and colonization of the Americas. In Basque towns where this class was vibrant, there are surviving examples of a change in architectural style dating from the early 1600s. Renaissance-style, multistory buildings with balconies appeared. Buildings from this period are plentiful in Mondragón's neighboring town, Oñati. Popularly, Oñati is seen as having been inhabited by a traditional nobility (indeed, these nobles repeatedly sought to conquer Mondragón) that was later invigorated by a new class that made its fortune in the Americas. Basques went in large numbers to the Americas, and they were heavily represented in the Crown's administration, in the clergy, and in business. When they returned home, sent remittances, or bequeathed their estates to their home towns, they transformed the Basque Country. Jauntxoak particularly benefited from the Crown's sixteenth-century declaration of hidalguía (collective nobility) for all Basques. Upon returning home, Basques who had been colonizers in the Americas purchased noble titles and invested in land and homes befitting their new status (Otazu y Llana 1986, 380–90).

While people from Mondragón also went to the Americas (Caro Baroja 1972, 57–64; and Letona 1975, *ad passim*) and no doubt sent back remittances, the town does not appear to have been similarly transformed by them. Although scores of Mondragonese sought official recognition of their status in the seventeenth century,[6] Caro Baroja points to only two surviving examples of elite architecture in Mondragón: the house of Bañez and the Palace of Monterrón (1972, 66). The relative absence of elite architecture is all the more notable when we remember that Mondragón was nearly fully destroyed by a fire in the mid-fifteenth century; even with the opportunity to rebuild, elites did not shape the town with class-appropriate style and design. Mondragón appears to have stood out as a town of artisans whose political and economic interests lay in the development of a craft economy. Partially mythical, partially real, this reputation became an important part of townspeople's identities.

As an important iron-producing town, Mondragón clearly benefited from Spanish colonialism in other ways. It produced armaments, naval instruments, and agricultural tools that were used for conquest and expansion (Caro Baroja 1972, 57–66; Monreal 1980). Mondragón thrived from the fifteenth to eighteenth centuries. At the end of the fifteenth century, there were five workshops in town (Unión Cerrajera n.d., 11). According to the sixteenth-century historian Garibay, the Mondragón of his day had three large forges and three smaller shops. Iron smelted there was sent for arms manufacture to neighboring Bergara and Placencia and as far away as Toledo (Caro Baroja 1972, 41–70). The number of shops remained at six in the seventeenth century. Eighteenth-century Mondragón was known as a center of experimentation in metallurgical methods.

In Mondragón, refractory bricks were used in the furnaces and quartz was employed; both were significant innovations. The rest of the Gipuzkoan metal sector was in a state of stagnation and was quickly falling behind the more innovative iron industries in Sweden and England. In 1783, Basque intellectuals studied Gipuzkoan metallurgy and concluded that there were too many small shops, and they were too geographically dispersed. Many of these firms did not survive the century (Ferrer 1966, 140–41). While Mondragón was better off than the rest of Gipuzkoa, crisis eventually hit, and the late eighteenth and nineteenth centuries were difficult. By 1794, the number of workshops had fallen to four, and the ore veins that had supplied Mondragón for centuries were exhausted. In 1856, there were only two shops left; these survived by shifting production from long arms, for which the market had been destroyed, to agricultural and domestic tools. One shop was located in the neighborhood of Zigarrola, in the (then) outskirts of Mondragón, and manufactured agricultural tools. The other, located in Zaldibar just outside of the town center, made residential locks. The two enterprises merged in 1906 to form Unión Cerrajera, S.A. (Oktubre Taldea 1987, 14–21).

The Carlist Wars

The merger of the Zigarrola and Zaldibar shops and the creation of the modern corporation Unión Cerrajera was indicative of broader business and economic changes that took place after the Carlist Wars. The Carlist Wars were fought twice, first from 1833 to 1840 and again from 1873 to 1876. These wars were, in a sense, Spain's only, if limited, experience with bourgeois revolution and first experience with national integration (see Nadal 1976). Formally, they began as a contestation of the legitimacy of Isabella's right to inherit the throne; Carlists claimed that Don Carlos was the rightful heir (hence the name *Carlistas*). In actuality, the pivotal issue was that Isabella and her advisors were re-making Spain in the liberal tradition of the French Revolution. The 1812 Constitution gave Spain a modern and liberal juridical character. The final disentailment of public lands took place in 1823, and the mines were disentailed in 1854.[7] Modern borders were also mapped out.

For the most part, the Carlist Wars were fought in the Basque Country, by and between Basques. The tensions between the ancient regime and the French-inspired liberal state were most pronounced there, and Basque sovereignty was at stake. Liberal programs brought state-level centralization and ended the economic and political privileges and legal autonomy provided by the fueros. A primary economic question of the Carlist Wars regarded the location of the border; this was a Basque question. Under Isabella, Spanish liberalizers set out to move the customs collection house from the inland Ebro River (which separates the Basque provinces from Spain) to the coast, thereby incorporating the Basque provinces within Spain for the first time in history and creating a national border separating southern (Spanish) Euskadi from the (French) Basque provinces to the north.

Beyond its implications for autonomy, moving the border threatened the Basque mercantile class, the petty nobility, and the peasantry, who lived better than their Spanish counterparts—due, in part, to the availability of duty-free goods in the region. By the time of the first Carlist War in 1833, peasants had already lived through a century of population growth, which intensified demands for already limited lands. They were further stressed by the shift from in-kind to cash taxes legislated by the 1812 Constitution. Rural landowners also began demanding rent in cash, and reduced the length of tenancy. Cash rents allowed agricultural profits to be shifted to commerce and industry, thereby transforming a segment of the old rural elite into a town-based bourgeoisie.

Basque peasants responded to the resulting decline in their standard of living with two popular revolts. In 1718, an earlier attempt to move the border to the coast sparked a riot among peasants who worked part-time in iron-shops or as charcoal makers. According to Ortzi, five thousand of these peasant-workers descended from the countryside and went after local elites, pulling them from their homes. Rioters forced the deputy general to sign a declaration forbidding the transfer of the border, and after he signed, they killed him (Ortzi 1978, 19–21.) In 1766 there was a rebellion over the price of wheat. The emergent elites (both agriculturalist and mercantilist) were stockpiling grain in order to drive prices up while peasants went hungry (Otazu y Llana 1986, 265–355).

In this context, downwardly mobile elites, along with the Church, were able to successfully organize the peasantry on the side of the Carlists. While it is generally thought that this alliance grew out of peasants' interest in the preservation of the fueros and thereby the autonomy of the Basque Country, Heiberg refutes this idea. She argues that in the town of Elgeta, peasants sided with the Carlists not to defend the fueros, of which she says they were largely ignorant, but to defend the Church and to reclaim their common lands, of which liberalization had deprived them (Heiberg 1989, 174–75).

The emergent Basque industrial elite sided with Spanish centralizers on economic questions. Liberal policies were indispensable for the expansion of mining and industry. Under Isabella, the Spanish state enacted legislation to construct railroads, to free ore for foreign export, and to form modern stock companies. Moreover, the Basque industrial elite favored the coastal border over the inland one, since the further development of industrial capitalism depended upon creating a tariff-free internal market. In the years between the first and second Carlist Wars, the sympathies and economic status of the popular classes shifted. After losing ground in the years following the first war, more peasants went to work in the mines and shops. This time, the bourgeoisie found an ally in popular classes whose livelihoods were more closely tied to industry than to the land (Beltza 1978; Carr 1966, 246–57; Clark 1979, 25–32; Ortzi 1978, 20–25). After the final liberal victory in 1876, the fueros were abolished, putting the Basque provinces fully under the control of the Spanish state for the first time in their history. The 1876 law read:

> The duties that the Constitution has imposed on all Spaniards to present themselves for military service when the law calls them, and to contribute in proportion to their abilities to the expenses of the State, will be extended, as the constitutional rights are extended, to the residents of Alava, Vizcaya and Guipúzcoa, in the same way as to the rest of the nation. (Quoted in Clark 1979, 35)

Furthermore, the dismantling of the fueros eliminated the last of the legal fetters on the export of ore. Technological developments in steel processing coincided with these events, bringing an influx of British capital to Euskadi.

As it happened, Basque ore was nonphosphorous. It was precisely this scarce ore that the British-pioneered Bessemer converter required. Since its invention in the 1850s, the Bessemer converter facilitated the mass production of steel and secured Britain's dominance in that sector. Nonphosphorous deposits were rare, and British steel makers invested heavily in the Basque Country. Basque industrial elites were able to tap this investment, using it to develop home industry, rather than simply watch the export of natural resources. They parlayed foreign investment into a banking structure that would soon become the most powerful in Spain. In these ways, they consolidated their power as an industrial-financial oligarchy with ties to and influence in Madrid. In 1906, Spain had the highest protective tariffs in all of Europe, guaranteeing Basque manufactures a home market (Chilicote 1968, 1–27; Clark 1979, 31–37; Flinn 1955).

Unión Cerrajera and the Making of a Modern Working Class

In Mondragón, Carlism was not the dominant force it was in the surrounding countryside and some nearby towns, and liberals were able to consolidate their position early. Several years before the Carlist Wars ended, the liberal manager of the Zaldibar factory set out to modernize that firm. He organized a group of investors, including a family that owned properties in Oñati, to buy the factory. This was the first step in a process of modernization that gained momentum after the Carlist defeat in 1876. The new company, named Vergarajauregi, Resusta, and Co. for its owners, began to purchase small shops in other towns; in 1894, they employed 550 workers in the Mondragón plant. Several years later, when they needed capital to build a large and modern plant in Bergara, they changed the legal status of the firm to a stock company, and sold shares (Oktubre Taldea 1987, 14–15; Unión Cerrajera n.d., 11–17). Owned and managed by liberals, Vergarajauregi, Resusta, and Co. was hated by the Church, which encouraged a boycott against it.

Backed by the Church, a group of Carlists resuscitated the Zigarrola factory to manufacture domestic locks in direct competition with the liberal firm; by 1905, the Carlists employed one hundred workers (Oktubre Taldea 1987, 14–21; Unión Cerrajera n.d., 11–20). Economic competition between the two groups found the Carlists at a disadvantage. The liberals had more capital and a larger base of operations and were better able to compete in the iron and steel sector, which was undergoing a phase of concentration led by the new Basque financial-industrial oligarchy (Heiberg 1989, 41). The Carlists were thus forced into the unhappy position of proposing a merger with their political foes.[8] The resulting firm, Unión Cerrajera, S.A., became the economic and political center of Mondragón until the 1960s, when the cooperatives replaced it in importance (Oktubre Taldea 1987, 14–21).

From its founding, Unión Cerrajera radically transformed Mondragón, intensifying older points of distinction to create a political and class structure that was significantly different from that of neighboring towns. Demand for labor in this large firm brought two groups of new workers to town. First, the already dwindling peasantry was further proletarianized. According to the 1900 census, there were approximately 380 peasants in Mondragón, just over 10 percent of the population. Of the 380, sixty-two men worked in factories, while an uncounted number of peasant women took in piecework to their homes, often

FIGURE 9

Unión Cerrajera, Credit: Arrasate Press.

pre-assembling parts. Neighboring Bergara, which had already surpassed Mondragón in population, had about 2,400 peasants, almost 39 percent of the population. By 1930, Mondragón's peasantry had fallen to 185, about 2.5 percent of the population, while in Bergara the percentage was about 9.3. The peasant population continued to decline in the next decade.[9]

A second pool of workers immigrated from surrounding towns. Residents of Gatzaga (Salinas), about ten kilometers away on the road to Gasteiz, transported their houses intact or brought the materials saved from houses they tore down to build anew in Mondragón. In 1900, Gatzaga had 128 structures; in 1910, 116. Over the same ten-year period, the population fell from 503 to 446 (Aranegui 1986, 222–24). Aretxabaleta, about five kilometers from Mondragón, had a 7.31 percent drop in population during this decade (Mancomunidad del Alto Deba 1982, 39). Mondragón absorbed these and other people, and the town more than doubled in size in thirty years (see table 2.1).

The modern, corporate nature and the size of Unión Cerrajera were crucial factors in the political and economic development of Mondragón. For the most part, Gipuzkoan firms were small scale and locally owned, and labor–management relations tended to be personalistic. Firms in Bizkaia, on the other hand, tended to be large scale and to draw in nonlocal investors. Bilbo is

TABLE 2.1

Population Growth in Mondragón, 1900–1930

Year	Population	Increase (%)
1900	3,713	
1910	4,706	26.74
1920	5,915	25.69
1930	7,720	30.52

Source: Mancomunidad del Alto Deba (1982, 39)

exemplary of the Bizkaian pattern (Ferrer 1966; Heiberg 1989, 45). Unión Cerrajera was a Bizkaian-like enterprise and created in Mondragón an opposition between capitalists and working classes that typically characterized Bizkaian rather than Gipuzkoan towns. Townspeople today have a sense of being different in this way, and they point to the effect of "the Cerrajera" on the town.

Unión Cerrajera was owned by 106 investors. Most did not live in town or manage the firm, and thus do not seem to have left a lasting imprint on Mondragón's social life or culture. The history of the firm, commissioned by the company on the occasion of its seventy-fifth anniversary in 1981, claims that Unión Cerrajera represented a form of capitalism that was different from the oligarchic variety that dominated Bilbo. Unión Cerrajera, it explained, was owned by Basque families, whereas large firms in Bilbo were held by financial elites, banks, or foreign investors (Unión Cerrajera n.d., 9–25). This version of history simply misrepresents the character of Unión Cerrajera: The firm was not the small-scale, family-owned firm that characterized Gipuzkoan industry. Of the 106 investors, one-half came from Mondragón, 20 percent from surrounding towns, and the rest from Donosti, Bilbo, and Madrid. Six families held more than 64 percent of the stock, and intermarriage among these families consolidated ownership still further. One of the most important of these families lived in Donosti (Unión Cerrajera n.d., 25–30). Despite the image the company wished to present in the 1980s, the owners of Unión Cerrajera were not paternalistic locals but were removed from the daily social and cultural life of the town. Unión Cerrajera stockholders and managers did control much of the formal apparatus of town-hall politics from the early 1900s until 1970, but this industrial elite did not create in Mondragón a vibrant social and cultural life for itself.

In contrast to neighboring Bergara, Mondragón does not have buildings that show off a resident bourgeoisie. In 1989, I attended a talk organized by the parish priest of the church of San Juan in Mondragón's central plaza. The priest made a plea for community support for a restoration project for the church. At the meeting, the architect hired to plan the restoration presented his proposal to townspeople. The talk was very poorly attended. There were a few artists in attendance whose interests were mainly aesthetic; only four townspeople came to support the renovation. The priest stressed that San Juan was the only surviving gothic church in all of Euskadi and the only distinctive building in Mondragón. He continued his appeal by arguing that while Oñati has the homes of its nobility and Bergara the homes of its bourgeoisie, Mondragón has only its factories. Only the church of San Juan could rescue Mondragón from its dreary industrial image.

Popular opinion in Mondragón holds that Bergara has a bourgeois air about it. Women's dress is considered an important point of distinction. It is said that since the eighteenth century, fashions made their way from Paris to Madrid via Bergara. Today, Bergarese women of all classes are considered to be more likely to favor bourgeois style—for example, expensive accessories such as belts, hand bags, costume jewelry, and high-heeled shoes—than do women in Mondragón, where the norm is a more working-class style—jeans, flat, sturdy shoes, and sweaters. A popular refrain mocks Bergarese women's emulation of elite style: "En Bergara la mujer de un obrero sale con un bisonte y él con el buzón." (In Bergara, a worker's wife goes out in a fur coat while he wears coveralls.) Moreover, Bergarese are known as the first people in the area to have taken up the upper class recreation of skiing (interview with archivist Pedro Uribareren).

Beyond intertown rivalries and stereotypes, there is historical evidence that Bergara and Mondragón had different class characters throughout the twentieth century. In 1930, Bergara was host to the fifth Congress of Basque Studies, an organization linked with the rational cultural planning strategies of the local and Basque bourgeoisie and professional classes (Enciclopedia Histórica-Geográfica de Guipúzcoa 1983; Ferrer 1966, 138; Urla 1989). Although heavily industrialized like Mondragón, and with a large working class, Bergara was a bourgeois town in the sense that this class lived there and was able to influence the town's image. This was not true of Mondragón.

Nor did Mondragón have a vibrant professional or shop-keeping class. Whyte and Whyte describe the class nature of Mondragón before the founding of the cooperatives in following way:

> Mondragón was a predominantly working-class town. A few families formed the upper crust, and a very small group of shop keepers, professionals, and office employees made up the middle class. A great gulf separated the masses of workers from the small upper strata. (1988, 26)

Mondragón lacked both a resident upper class and a moderating middle class. What resulted was a working class that was considered especially problematic.

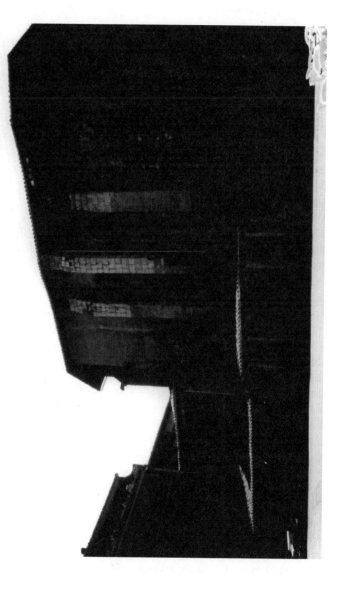

FIGURE 10

Church of San Juan. Credit: Sharryn Kasmir.

Politically, Mondragón's workers were more likely to be class conscious in their political commitments and affiliations than were the working classes of most other Gipuzkoan towns.[10]

A group of workers from Mondragón, calling themselves "Oktubre Taldea" (October Group, after the Russian Revolution), compiled the labor history of the town from the late 1800s to the Spanish Civil War in 1936. Their book, *Arrasate 1936: Una Generación Cortada,* documents Mondragón's first major strike. The strike took place in 1915, when the polishers at Unión Cerrajera walked off the job for two weeks to protest automation in their section of the plant. Workers in other sections showed support by staging slow-downs. The polishers won the strike and made other demands upon settlement, including equal pay rates for workers, stable prices for jobs, and a review of the responsibilities and jurisdiction of foremen (Oktubre Taldea 1987, 28–44). At a time when working classes elsewhere were losing similar strikes, and companies were becoming increasingly monopolistic in their business and labor practices (see, for example, Nash 1989, 59–65), this was an important victory.

The 1915 strike signaled the existence of, and served to further consolidate, a self-conscious working class that organized itself politically through two associations—Asociación Obrera and Sindicato Profesional. Asociación Obrera later became the syndicate Solidaridad de Obreros Vascos (SOV), tied to the Basque nationalist PNV. Sindicato Profesional became Sindicato Metalúrgico of the Unión General de Trabajadores (UGT), tied to the Partido Socialista de los Obreros Españoles (PSOE, the Socialist Party of Spanish Workers). Represented by their newly organized syndicates, workers struck for four months in 1916 over a change in work schedules.[11] This time management was prepared; they locked out workers and called in the Civil Guard in the third week of the strike. Civil Guardsmen violently broke up a solidarity demonstration of women, who were both supporting the male strikers and defending their own economic interests, since many were engaged in industrial homework for the factory. In the third month of the strike, syndicalists held meetings at the provincial level. By the fourth month, the strike had been broken (Oktubre Taldea 1987, 28–44).

Significantly, the town council, made up largely of the owners and managers of Unión Cerrajera, gave the Civil Guard a Spanish flag to show their gratitude for the officers' assistance in putting down the strike (Oktubre Taldea 1987, 32–34). Thus began the Civil Guard's career of repression in Mondragón, where the townspeople learned to fear and hate them. The Civil Guard was housed rent free on Unión Cerrajera property from the 1916 strike until 1979, when continuous bombings by ETA forced them out of town.

Thirty-one workers were fired as a result of the 1916 strike. Several of these workers opened small metal shops in the area, beginning a new pattern of industrial development. Workers forced out of Unión Cerrajera continued to open small shops into the 1970s. This is one way in which Unión Cerrajera spurred the growth of small firms in Mondragón. It further stimulated the metal-working sector by supporting the development of an industrial infrastructure—the railroad arrived in 1917—and by contracting out work to smaller shops.

Socialism versus Basque Nationalism

Heiberg (1989, 42) notes that in Bilbo from 1890 to 1930, large-scale operations run by professional managers and small–scale personalistic factories encouraged divergent political tendencies. With the growth of industry in the northern Basque provinces, laborers from poorer areas of southern and central Spain immigrated to Euskadi. There they worked in large factories, at low-skilled jobs and were likely to be Socialist in their syndical affiliations (UGT) and political sympathies (PSOE). Basques, on the other hand, often had personal ties to local, small-scale industrialists; they worked in these smaller firms and were more likely to be nationalists (PNV). Political differences, therefore, tended to coincide with ethnicity and factory regime.

In Mondragón, where the immigrant population from Spanish provinces was as yet minimal,[12] the size, ownership structure, and nature of work in Unión Cerrajera led to the class-based organization that was characteristic of Bilbo's large factories. A more widespread acceptance of socialist ideas and a more militant brand of socialism grew among Basque workers in Mondragón than in most of Gipuzkoa, where small-scale enterprises flourished. Still, Basque nationalism was influential among local workers.

PNV was founded in Bilbo in the late 1890s by the downwardly mobile children of small manufacturers and merchants who were pushed out of business and into the professions by the new industrial-financial oligarchy. The founder of the party was Sabino Arana. Sabino Arana formulated a nationalist stance on what it meant to be Basque; "purity" of Basque blood, as measured by Basque surnames, was considered by PNV to be the essence of Basqueness. This laid the foundation for a Basque nationalism that was hostile to southern and central Spanish immigrants who had come to Euskadi to work. Like Carlism, PNV's nationalism was a traditionalist ideology that sought the reinstatement of the fueros: Its slogan was "God and Old Laws." Sabino Arana was responsible for conceiving of the territorial and cultural unit of Euskadi that includes all seven Basque provinces, both French and Spanish. Unlike Carlists, Sabino Arana conceptualized Euskadi as a federation of provinces. During what was a heyday for nation-building in pre–World War I Europe, PNV was more like other contemporaneous petty-bourgeois nationalist movements than Carlism, which defended the ancient regime (see Hobsbawm 1990).

The enlightenment tradition ended there, however. PNV believed, for example that the primitive Basque democracy could be restored and that political rights need not be guaranteed constitutionally, since shared Basqueness would ensure egalitarian relations. This belief underlies PNV's position on class questions as well. PNV sought to direct labor conflicts away from class discourse and class-based organization in favor of social peace, which it thought Basques were uniquely capable of promoting. This was the political legacy for PNV of the myth of Basque egalitarianism. Its associated syndicate, Solidaridad de Obreros Vascos, later renamed Eusko Langileen Alkartasuna–Solidaridad de Trabajadores Vascos (ELA-STV), organized workers at the point of production but rejected the class rhetoric of PSOE and UGT as anti-Christian and anti-Basque (Heiberg 1989).

In the towns, PNV was well organized. In Mondragón, it played an important role in cultural, social, and political life. The PNV social club, the *batzoki,* was inaugurated in 1910. A branch of the women's organization Emakumeak began in 1931 with sixty members, and youth and mountain-climbing clubs were organized (Oktubre Taldea 1987, 76–88).[13]

The militance of the Socialists and the size of their constituency nevertheless marked Mondragón as different from the Gipuzkoan pattern (with the exception of Eibar). This made Mondragón a place where the central tension in Basque politics between class and ethnic-based identity and the compatibility of socialism and nationalism would play out in unique ways. The Basque working class everywhere suffered from a kind of ideological and political schizophrenia. They were torn between the class identification but antinationalism of PSOE, and the nationalism but antisocialism of PNV. This tension was acute in Mondragón, where workers were clearly class conscious and socialism was strong.

Socialism was in evidence in Mondragón from 1910, when Socialist candidates were first presented for the Spanish Parliament. After the military coup of General Primo de Rivera in 1923, Socialists became important political and social actors in town. As proponents of a nonreligious social life and vehemently anticlerical, it was over religion that Socialists came into the most conflict with PNV. They demanded a civil cemetery, the removal of the statue of the Virgin Mary from the town hall, and the replacement of religious holidays with secular ones. In Mondragón's first municipal elections of the Second Republic in 1930, the Socialists won two seats in the town council and PNV won three. Shortly thereafter, Mondragón had its first civil wedding. During this period, the most heated arguments (which sometimes came to blows) were those over the use of the municipal band for civil versus religious celebrations. On the eve of the Spanish Civil War, the Socialist-affiliated and PNV-affiliated syndicates claimed an equal number of members, with seven hundred each (Fusi 1984; Oktubre Taldea 1987, 98–158).

The competition between socialism and nationalism for the allegiance of Mondragón's working class accounts for the electoral success of the Acción Nacionalista Vasca (ANV), the first party to attempt to bring together both ideologies. ANV was a liberal, republican party which formulated an anticlerical nationalism and rejected the anti-Spanish chauvinism of PNV. For the most part, it did poorly in Basque industrial towns, but Mondragón was an exception. When ANV appeared in Mondragón in 1930, it counted fifty affiliates and was able to open a social club. In the 1931 elections, ANV won a seat in town government (Granja 1984; Oktubre Taldea 1987, 96).

When the Second Spanish Republic was declared in 1930, PSOE and ANV participated. PNV did not, distancing itself from the democratic coalition and remaining outside of the Republican sphere. But four years later, there was a short-lived revolution in Spain. This 1934 Revolution pushed PNV into unwilling political allegiance with the Republic. The events of this unsuccessful revolution were more serious in Mondragón than in other Basque towns. Concurrent with the worldwide depression of 1929, Unión Cerrajera had moved yet further from a paternalistic style of management and intensified the exploitation of labor. In 1933, a new manager, Marcelino Oreja, took over the firm and developed a reputation for being authoritarian. During the revolution, Oreja was executed by Mondragón's Socialists.

In Mondragón, as elsewhere, PNV stayed clear of these events. Officially, it declared itself neither in favor of nor opposed to the revolution, but the Spanish right was convinced that PNV supported the uprising. This distanced PNV from the right, with which it otherwise shared a powerful bond as a defender of the Catholic Church.

Furthermore, there was the issue of the autonomy statute. The right wing of the coalition government defended the unity of Spain. It was only in 1936, when leftists controlled the coalition government, that the Spanish Basque Country was granted its autonomy (Fusi 1984). The statute established a Basque government, and PNV's Aguirre was named the first president.

On the eve of the Spanish Civil War, PNV was in the political company of the Republicans and wound up, therefore, on the Republican side of the fighting. This marked a decisive break with the traditionalism of the Carlists, who sided with Franco. Rural and conservative Nafarroa, historically a bastion of Carlism, became a fascist ally, as did rural Araba (Fusi 1984). If we consider that a similar kind of social conservatism on the part of Breton nationalists in France led them to ally with the fascists during the Vichy regime (Maynard 1991), we can see the importance of the events of the 1934 Revolution for the future of the Basque nationalist movement: PNV was positioned as an opponent of the Franco regime.

Post–Civil War Mondragón

With the outbreak of the Civil War in 1936, Mondragón came out squarely in support of the Republic but fell to the fascists only a few months later. Approximately two hundred Mondragonese, from ANV, PNV, and PSOE, formed the Batallón Dragones (alluding to the dragon) and joined Republican forces elsewhere (Oktubre Taldea 1987, 169–321). When the Republicans were defeated in 1939, Basque towns were left to rebuild under conditions of severe repression. Because they were so solidly Republican, and because they had achieved some independence through the autonomy statute, Gipuzkoa and Bizkaia were doubly punished by Franco as traitorous provinces. In Mondragón, the consequences were serious. War casualties and the imprisonment and exile of those who fought with the Republicans caused what older townspeople recall as a notable decline in population. The parties and syndicates that supported the Republicans were criminalized, and there were public humiliations and executions of Republicans, in part by fascist troops but also by local Carlists (forty of whom were counted after the war [Oktubre Taldea 1987, 231]). There was generalized terror, and people remember hiding in their homes. There were also food shortages caused by wartime destruction of farm land, and people vividly remember going hungry. Euskera (the Basque language) was outlawed—this fact was reported by most of the young townspeople I knew, suggesting that the historical memory of the Civil War for those who did not live through it is distilled as a repression of Basque identity.

For José Antonio Etxebe the political events and repression of the Civil War were integral to personal identity. José Antonio was forced into exile in the French Basque Country in 1947; his exile seems to have made the events of the war all the more salient. With Juan Ramón Garai and Geoffrey Bate I crossed the border to interview José Antonio in his home in Hendaia. José Antonio told us that upon their return from the war or from fascist prisons, most of Mondragón's men went back to their jobs in Unión Cerrajera, despite their Republican sympathies. However, one group was blacklisted; "reds" were not hired back, though PNV affiliates were. At the same time, Spain was in severe economic crisis, and there was considerable unemployment in the Basque region. In some towns, people who had fought on the Republican side were ordered to work without pay to rebuild roads and houses that had been destroyed during the war (Heiberg 1989, 201). In Mondragón, "reds" who were locked out of Unión Cerrajera were employed at a very low wage by the Donosti-based firm Olasagasti and Co., not to build houses but to enlarge private factories, including Unión Cerrajera. José Antonio described the labor conditions at Olasagasti and Co.:

The bosses, . . . with the impunity that they enjoyed (we didn't even have syndicates) and with the reign of terror that was in the air, didn't even show us the most basic kind of respect, human respect. Due to the abuses, very hard work, and deplorable conditions, many of us who worked in construction would get a simple flu or something like that and in our weakened state, without any resistance left, would simply die. You can't forget that at that time food was scarce (except for those who could buy it on the black market) and on top of that, we didn't have proper work clothes or shoes, which was especially bad in the winter and when it was damp.

In the years just after the war, there were still resistance fighters in the mountains, and commando units were being trained along the French border. But under conditions of severe repression, only limited military resistance was possible. ELA-STV and UGT were outlawed and replaced by the fascist-controlled vertical syndicate. Labor struggle and political resistance were also difficult. In Mondragón, political resistance came dramatically: In 1944, shortly after being released from prison, José Antonio and five others who had been active in the UGT before the war formed a Communist Party cell in Mondragón. Most Gipuzkoan towns had no Communist Party, nor was there one at the provincial level. While its concrete impact was negligible, the fact of its existence is testimony to Mondragón's pre- and postwar exceptionalism. Also striking is the fact that Mondragón's Communist Party was able to reorganize and gain control over the local UGT, which had always been PSOE's syndicate and elsewhere remained in PSOE's hands. Most importantly, José Antonio and the others propelled a historic collaboration between UGT and ELA-STV, drafting and circulating a joint manifesto condemning the Franco regime. Since UGT and ELA were illegal under Franco, and the writing and distribution of this document were imprisonable offenses, this manifesto was no small act of rebellion.

According to José Antonio, after the two syndicates produced the manifesto, Mondragón's Communists proposed a second document to be drafted, this time by the two parties. In an initial meeting, it was agreed that local members of the Communist Party would draft a leaflet. A second meeting took place in which the PNV representatives accepted the document on the condition that it was approved by their party leadership. Provisionally, they planned to print two thousand copies and distribute them illegally throughout the area. José Antonio remembered that the leaflet expressed "the parties' struggles and yearnings for democracy, liberty, and political change." A clash between the parties resulted, however, over the closing words of the document. José Antonio thought that he remembered verbatim the ending written by the Communist Party: "We close this manifesto in remembrance of all of those who gave their

lives in the war as well as those who died in Franco's jails." The Catholic PNV
wanted to insert: "We ask you to pray for the souls of the dead." The Communists could not accept this call to prayer and suggested that the document remain as it was, adding only "and to those believers who read this we ask for a
prayer for their souls." This was not acceptable to PNV, and the party leadership directed the local branch to terminate discussions. Although the effort was
thwarted, the attempted coalition was a historic step toward confronting the
central conflict in Mondragón—that of class versus nationalist organization
and struggle.

Conclusions

Since the thirteenth century, the class character of Mondragón has
evolved in distinctive ways, earning the town its early-twentieth-century reputation as an unruly proletarian stronghold and producing a working-class identity that is part of contemporary collective identity. Unlike other Gipuzkoan
towns where small factories dominated, Mondragón was dominated by a single large factory, which was responsible for proletarianizing the local peasantry
and consolidating the working class. The scale and ownership structure of
Unión Cerrajera contributed to the development of socialism in Mondragón (in
terms of both affiliation with PSOE and nonaffiliated socialist sympathies),
which took root more firmly than in other Gipuzkoan towns. Comprising only
a small portion of the population, elite and middle classes left little mark on the
town's culture and social life. An industrial and working-class image is conjured up in myths and intertown rivalries that are daily confirmations of Mondragón's identity.

3

Cooperativism and Middle-Class Reforms

In the early part of the twentieth century, Mondragón's work life was centered in Unión Cerrajera; older townspeople still refer to themselves as *cerrajeros* (lock makers). In 1994, Unión Cerrajera narrowly escaped closure. Fewer than two hundred workers remain in what used to be the town's largest firm. Instead, it is the cooperatives that give life to the town. The cooperatives have created relative prosperity despite nearly two decades of economic crisis. Mondragón's young people are more likely than their contemporaries in other towns to find at least temporary work in co-op factories, and their parents are less likely to have experienced layoff. Today, people from nearby towns refer to the people of Mondragón as *los cooperativistas* (the cooperators), conveying their simultaneous disapproval of and distance from those who seem to "have it easy" as well as their envy for Mondragón's relative security.

But the presence of the cooperatives has more than an economic effect. The glass and steel complex of the Caja Laboral sits on a hillside overlooking the town. The consumer cooperative chain Eroski (a maxi-mart that is a combination of KMart-like store and a suburban supermarket) attracts shoppers from Mondragón and neighboring towns. Smaller Eroski co-ops dot the neighborhoods. The Polytechnical and Professional School occupies a two-square-block area just below the bank, and co-op language centers offer English and Basque courses. The clinic that was originally constructed as a private medical center by the cooperatives (cooperators do not participate in the national health system) is now the town's public hospital. From education to shopping, the cooperatives are prevalent in daily life.

This integration of services is considered by many Mondragón scholars to be a strength of the system. Education produces well-trained managers and engineers for the cooperatives. In recent years, investments in Eroski have been far more remunerative, and have generated more jobs, than have investments in industrial cooperatives. And providing services to members is believed to solidify the cooperative spirit and serve the town as a whole. But some townspeople express frustration that the cooperatives that seem to be "everywhere."

When I was still relatively new to Euskadi, I visited a small town about forty miles from Mondragón. As I was walking along the street, I stopped to ask directions of three middle-aged people who were sitting quietly on a bench. They sent me to ask in the local Eroski, and one woman motioned toward the store and said offhandedly, "They know, they're the bosses." I was surprised by this response, because the directions I sought required no special knowledge and because there was no reason they could not have helped me. I was taken aback by their passivity, which was so at odds with the control I was used to seeing Basques express. This event stayed with me, and while it seemed unusual, some aspects paralleled a sensibility that was also common in Mondragón. This was the perception that the cooperatives represented authority and that this authority was estranged from ordinary townspeople. The purpose of this chapter is to explore this perception.

Gramsci's Concept of Hegemony

John Foster has noted that cooperatives can be perceived as forces outside of the community, or as distant from the social world and interests of local working classes. Such was the case in nineteenth-century Oldham, England. In his social history of Oldham, Foster shows that the middle class promoted consumer cooperatives in order to reform working-class life. Along with the temperance movement and adult-education programs, cooperatives were advocated by middle-class reformers who spared no energy in bettering the patterns of consumption and association of workers. While no doubt beneficial to some segments of the local working class, these interventions ruptured the social fabric that the workers had created for themselves. Within their own institutions, workers had previously commanded an arena where they developed political consciousness and organizations. By taking control of that social world, Oldham's middle class was able to curb working-class radicalism and pave the way for the Tory dominance that was to characterize Oldham by mid-century (Foster 1974).

The struggle over social institutions and the creation and imposition of control over social organizations is a familiar theme in ethnographies and social histories of industrial towns. In one of the first ethnographies of a working-class European town, Frankenberg (1990) showed that the village choir, dramatic society, and football club were central to collective identity in the North Wales community he studied. These institutions were controlled by local workers who surrendered leadership only after village tensions strained club relationships; seeing the signs of trouble, working-class leaders handed over club offices to upper-class individuals whom they later blamed when the institutions dissolved. Workers set out to organize new leisure activities. Similarly, in Pittsfield, Massachusetts, General Electric was able to dominate town life from the 1930s partly because it was able to shape the social sphere (Nash 1989). In Jay, Maine, the transition from independent working-class forms of socializing to those dominated by International Paper was a decisive factor in depoliticizing unionized workers (Carbonella 1992). These cases show that voluntary associations, social clubs, and leisure activities are often the objects of class conflict and that control of these social arena by middle classes, upper classes, or corporations constitutes hegemony over working-class life.

In his essay "Americanism and Fordism," Gramsci (1971) elaborated his concept of hegemony to explain this subtle phenomenon of social, cultural, and ideological control. He argued that the Fordist regime was powerful because it went beyond control of workers in the factory (through a mental–manual division of labor, the routinization of jobs, and strict managerial oversight). Ford's vision was to make his workers into new social and moral beings. To Gramsci, Fordism implied the nuclear family structure made possible by the family wage: male authority; the construction of the home as the physical and emotional site of social reproduction; women repairing male workers for the next day in the factory (including sexually); and the socialization of children to become industrial workers. Fordist hegemony also operated through social-reform movements. Christian temperance movements and YMCAs channeled working-class amusements away from drink and toward reputable pursuits (cf. Peiss 1986). What distinguished hegemony from brute force (e.g., when factory owners called in state police to suppress strikers or fired workers who did not comply with work rules) was consent. Fordism created desire among workers for consumer goods and family life. While Gramsci understood that this desire was real, he also argued that when these new social forms were introduced, workers experienced them as an imposition, an affront to more organic patterns of behavior.

In pre–Spanish Civil War Mondragón, the working class led its own social and cultural life. As I showed in the previous chapter, Mondragón lacked a sizable resident elite, and it did not have a middle class that would have been capable of imposing its values on the town. This made Mondragón different from neighboring towns. In this chapter, I argue that like the interventions of Oldham's middle class, the cooperatives represent an effort on the part of reformers to regulate Mondragón's workers. Chief among those reformers was Father José María Arizmendiarrieta, the priest who is credited with founding the cooperative movement. My argument runs counter to the standard interpretation of Arizmendiarrieta as a nonpolitical, nonideological figure (e.g., Whyte and Whyte 1988, 239). I believe this interpretation is part of the myth of the Mondragón cooperatives. Rather, I suggest that Arizmendiarrieta set out to create a middle class and a middle-class identity among workers through education and through cooperativism. I also show that his project was an expression of the larger political project of the Catholic Partido Nacionalista Vasco (PNV) to build a stable, socially conservative, and technocratic middle class for the Basque Country.

In his book or Basque nationalism and social class, Beltza (1976, 59–62) suggests (in a footnote) that the Mondragón cooperatives correspond to the political mentality of a native and "Basque-patriotic technocratic class" (see also Nuñez 1977, 119–35). Exploring this proposition, I show that from the outset, the cooperatives were embroiled, alongside PNV, in a political struggle over the organization of Basque society; this political project represented an attempt to impose a hegemonic set of values on the town.

The suggestion of social distance between the cooperatives and the town diverges from a common story told about the cooperatives. To raise the capital for the first cooperative, the founders used

> an old and well established custom, the *chiquiteo* [txikiteo]. Every day after work groups of friends gather on the streets of Mondragón and move along from bar to bar. . . . Through these informal channels, [they] spread the word that they were planning a cooperative firm and they were looking for the help of the community in the form of loans. . . . [A]bout a hundred people in the community responded with pledges. (Whyte and Whyte 1988, 34)

I heard this story in Mondragón's working-class bars, sometimes told snidely, as if to mock a story that had been heard too many times, other times told sincerely, to demonstrate that the cooperatives were based on an idea that was "*muy maja*" (very nice). Indeed, individuals often alternate between expressions of alienation, when they argue that the cooperatives were flawed from the start, and near-sentimentalism about the past. Here I consider the historical roots of this alienation. In later chapters I discuss recent changes in the cooperatives that have exaggerated the alienation and popularized the discourse of social distance but have also transformed this sentimentalism into a political argument.

Father José María Arizmendiarrieta

Newly ordained, Father José María Arizmendiarrieta arrived in Mondragón in 1941 and found working-class organizations still active. "Leaders of the political opposition and of militant unions had necessarily gone underground, but the spirit of political radicalism and social-class remained alive in ,the minds of the working people" (Whyte and Whyte 1988, 26). In the context of this activism, Arizmendiarrieta fashioned himself into a community priest, taking an activist approach in his parish. While the Spanish Catholic Church collaborated with the Franco regime and Spanish clerics often represented the Church hierarchy in the local arena, many Basque priests were different. They maintained a close and sympathetic tie to their parishioners and shared the political sympathies of their communities. Arizmendiarrieta identified with this traditional of the liberal Basque priest. He was a PNV-style nationalist who served as a journalist on the side of the Republicans during the Civil War. Early in the war he was captured and jailed (though he was quickly released). Arizmendiarrieta was influenced by Catholic social doctrine, which directed its practitioners to be concerned with problems of social justice in economic life and to question the moral basis of private property. He was trained in the tradition of the Catholic Action movement that was pioneered in Belgium in the early 1900s. In the European social context of the rise of industrialism and the spread of communism and socialism among workers, Catholic Action pioneered an apostolic religious philosophy that saw the activism of the apostles as a model for daily life, including for lay Catholics. Priests were supposed to encourage action among the laity. This philosophy emerged from two central concerns of the Church: the increased secularization of the masses and the church's political dilemma. On one hand, the Church abhorred Bolshevism, and on the other, it opposed the abuses of capitalism. Hatred of Bolshevism usually won out. In Italy, for example, Catholic Action formed an alliance with Mussolini (Quigley and Connors 1963; Poggi 1967).

Arizmendiarrieta brought these ideas about social justice and activism to Mondragón, where he organized a Catholic Action cell and other social projects (Azurmendi 1984, 13–26). Considerable attention has been paid to documenting the evolution of Arizmendiarrieta's thought (e.g. Azurmendi 1984; CLP 1983; Larrañaga 1981). The British sociologist Oakeshott, who first brought Mondragón to the attention of the English-speaking world, was instrumental in creating a mystique about the man (1975). Arizmendiarrieta died in 1976 after the cooperatives had achieved considerable success. Oakeshott attributed this long-term success of the cooperatives to the intellectual and spiritual guidance provided by Arizmendiarrieta. Oakeshott also noted an ideological parallel between Arizmendiarrieta and Mao Zedong, and the story he recounted has gained something of the status of folklore in the literature on Mondragón. The vignette is that when Oakeshott met Arizmendiarrieta, he suggested the similarity with Mao. Father José María discreetly unlocked a desk drawer and produced a copy of the "Little Red Book" (Oakeshott 1978a). The image created is one of a clever and committed subverter of fascism.

Resolving the issue of the centrality of Arizmendiarrieta's intellectual contribution to the development and success of the Mondragón cooperatives is not a trivial problem. Since the goal of most of the research on the coops is to assess their transferability, an overemphasis on the importance of Arizmendiarrieta's influence leads to the conclusion that Mondragón cannot serve as a model for industrial transformation. For this reason, Gutiérrez-Johnson and Whyte (1982) offer a corrective to Oakeshott's work and qualify the centrality of Arizmendiarrieta (see also Greenwood and González et al.

1989, 55). Moreover, given that much of the cooperatives' international appeal is in their purported political neutrality, there has been a tendency to portray Arizmendiarrieta as an eclectic or nonaffiliated thinker (see, for example, Whyte and Whyte 1988, 239).

Intellectual histories of Arizmendiarrieta which stress his idiosyncracy or individuality preclude a serious analysis of the more ordinary and common aspects of his project and of its intersection with larger political movements and ideologies. Arizmendiarrieta's thinking must instead be evaluated within the spectrum of Basque political views and the political environment of Mondragón. No matter how visionary his ideas may have been, they would not have gained popular support had they not resonated with a larger political ideology and social project.

Arizmendiarrieta was ill at ease with the class conflict that was demonstrated in the Spanish Civil War. In and of itself, this was not an uncommon position. As Zulaika shows for the Basque town of Itziar, the effects of the war were so disturbing that the reaction of many people was to vilify conflict itself (1988, 20–35). However, Don José María went further: He undertook a social and political project to overcome class struggle.

The beliefs that class conflict had to be ameliorated and that one should adopt an activist approach toward the working class were positions Father José María would have encountered during his seminary days. Lannon's (1979) research on the transformation of the Gasteiz Seminary, where Arizmendiarrieta studied, provides an important insight into the formation of Arizmendiarrieta's thought. From the 1870s (after the Carlist defeat), the Spanish Church, and the Carlist Basque Church with it, was on the defensive against the liberal state and civil society. It saw the problems associated with industrialization as sins against which the Church must be on guard. The areligiosity of the workers was seen as evidence that the working class should be avoided; thus, strict seclusion of monks was enforced. Monks were taught with traditional texts (the Scholastics and St. Thomas Aquinas dominated their studies), and they were instructed to renounce positivism and subjectivism as worldly philosophies.

The Gasteiz Seminary went along with these Church positions until 1910, when it began to teach nonreligious subject matter and employ new methods, including collecting sociological data and carrying out studies of working-class neighborhoods based on research—a radical departure from the Church-held view that texts were the only valid sources of knowledge. Ethnography was a key research method, especially for the study of the Basque language, popular religion, and literature. Father José Miguel Barandiaran held the chair of the department of ethnology, geology, and prehistory at the Gasteiz Seminary.[1] His students studied the social problems of Basques, especially of the working class. One study was a demographic and sociological study of a working-class neighborhood of Bilbo (Lannon 1979).

Trained by Barandiaran, Arizmendiarrieta would likely have taken a problem-solving approach to the question of class conflict. His biographer Azurmendi (1984) notes, however, that the priest never developed a concrete analysis of the class struggle, even though he recognized its existence. Azurmendi characterized Arizmendiarrieta's views in the following way:

> At the root of the class struggle can be found the myth of revolution, faith in violence, etc., that in the opinion of Arizmendiarrieta characterize the twentieth century, and that he summarily rejects. The question of the class struggle is phrased, for Arizmendiarrieta, as the question of how to overcome it, urgently. (1984, 694–95)

Overcoming class struggle was also the historic project of PNV; to Beltza, the "mentality of social peace" characterizes both the cooperatives and conservative nationalism (1976, 60). As I discussed in chapter 2, Basque nationalism was a traditionalist response to the rise of a Basque banking and industrial oligarchy and the proletarianization of the peasantry; it projected a retreat into a mythical past where it was imagined that class antagonism did not exist. Sabino Arana and his followers saw class struggle as a foreign concept, for which the greed and lack of ethnic solidarity of Basque oligarchs were largely to blame. PNV also saw socialism as a foreign movement that must be prevented from corrupting Basque workers.

PNV envisioned the patrimony of Basques as egalitarianism. As I noted earlier, the ideology of Basque egalitarianism has a long history. Its first political expression came in the sixteenth century, when the Castilian Crown declared the collective nobility of all Basques. Basque egalitarianism was institutionalized in the nineteenth century by what Otazu y Llana (1986) sarcastically calls the "egalitarian historical method," that is, simply disregarding evidence of social inequality in the towns, especially in the province of Gipuzkoa, which was named the guardian of Basque equality. This egalitarian myth has the peculiar history of appealing to and being used by different classes and political groups at various political moments. Otazu y Llana argues, for example, that it was first used as a legitimizing strategy by a rising bourgeoisie which sought to redefine its mercantilist wealth through a decree of nobility. Later, peasants called upon Basque egalitarianism during the 1718 and 1766 revolts (Otazu y Llana 1986, 7–16). In late-nineteenth-century PNV circles, egalitarianism served two functions: differentiating Euskadi from Spain and discrediting modern socialism as unnecessary for the naturally egalitarian Basques. PNV nationalists elaborated an egalitarian ideology in support of a native capitalism. Heiberg explains the relationship of the egalitarian myth to the nationalism of Sabino Arana:

In Arana's interpretation of Basque history his idea of Basque original
sovereignty played a pivotal role. Original sovereignty was an innate attribute of Basques and conferred an eternal right to and drive for independence. The Basques had never been subjects of a personal ruler.
Political authority was symbolized by the egalitarian *boina,* the Basque
beret. . . . Original sovereignty was intimately tied to original nobility, *hidalguía originária.* The latter, like the former, was an inalienable part of
the Basque condition. For Arana, the grants of collective nobility were a
public acknowledgement of Basque original nobility, independence, purity of blood and, on the local level, Basque egalitarianism. (1989, 55)

For PNV nationalists a major political and ideological task was to express
egalitarianism while maintaining political distance from socialism. The Mondragón of Arizmendiarrieta's early days was a town with a small bourgeoisie
and shop-owning class and a combative working class. Arizmendiarrieta said
of Mondragón; "This was an active and restless town even before the war and
there was a considerable socialistic orientation. There had also been serious tensions" (quoted in Whyte and Whyte 1988, 26). Arizmendiarrieta undertook to
transform Mondragón's working class into small-property owners. At the same
time, he was offended by Unión Cerrajera's economic dominance in the town.
Catholic Action philosophy told him that aggressive capitalism was as harmful
to society as was class struggle waged from below. Father José María was re-
markable in that he found a vehicle for eliminating both sources of class conflict in two social movements: technical education and industrial cooperatives.

One of Father José María's first assignments was that of spiritual adviser
to the boys in the apprentice school of Unión Cerrajera. Sons of Cerrajera workers attended the school from the age of fourteen as a precursor to their full-time
employment. The proceedings of Arizmendiarrieta's spiritual exercises were
recorded in a notebook from August 1940 to November 1948. They reveal that
Arizmendiarrieta introduced the ideas of Catholic Action, which embraced not
only religious considerations but social concerns as well, such as human respect, study and action, dating mores, and social justice. The study circle was
linked to the local branch of the Catholic Action Youth group, Juventud Obrera
de Acción Católica (JOAC). Records of meeting attendance indicate that the
group became increasingly popular, with an average of thirty-five to forty participants but sometimes as many as ninety.

Arizmendiarrieta's experience in the apprentice school convinced him of
the need to establish a technical school that would be independent from Unión
Cerrajera. Since the apprentice school limited enrollment to the children of
Unión Cerrajera workers, it discriminated against a whole sector of Mondragón's children. Arizmendiarrieta called upon townspeople and local businesses to make donations to build a new vocational school. The cooperative

Escuela Politécnica opened in 1947.[2] In the postwar period there was a general shortage of trained technicians and engineers in Euskadi, and a number of private vocational or polytechnical schools were opened by the joint efforts of business and religious leaders (González and Garmendia 1988, 54–56). In this regard, the Escuela Politécnica was not unique, but it was nonetheless a great accomplishment. Researchers as well as many who live in Mondragón credit Arizmendiarrieta with training working-class boys and breaking Unión Cerrajera's grip on technical education—that is, for democratizing education. The school he founded is now considered one of the best technical colleges in Spain, and a significant number of Euskadi's engineers are educated there.

In an important sense, Arizmendiarrieta set out to introduce middle-class values to the working class. By stimulating social mobility through education, he sought to create the stable middle class that Mondragón was missing. This effort was not unlike the social and moral projects that Gramsci considered to be at the heart of hegemony. By the 1940s, the working class of Mondragón was already disciplined in many of the ways Gramsci (1971) highlighted. Women no longer did industrial homework for Unión Cerrajera as they had at the turn of the century; instead, they became dedicated largely to the domestic sphere where they daily replenished the labor power of their husbands and sons. Unión Cerrajera had already built its model houses outside the factory gates, complete with garden and picket fence, where family life was to be developed. The work force was accustomed to the schedule of industrial production. Nevertheless, Mondragón's workers were not disciplined in key ways—for example, alcohol consumption was high (see Ortzi 1978, 23). Moreover, the working class still maintained control over its own social institutions; there remained class-based identification and organizations. Like other devoted reformers, Arizmendiarrieta sought to rechannel the energies and better this working class.

Arizmendiarrieta wrote extensively on education. Azurmendi commented that these writings "invariably had a character we could call propagandistic. Arizmendiarrieta dedicated himself to convincing the people of Mondragón of the urgency of promoting professional education" (1984, 197). Repeatedly, Arizmendiarrieta expressed the view that men are civilized through education. He also believed that education was a better way to express social responsibility to one's people than was political action. He wrote:

> The emancipation of a class or of a people must begin with the training of those who make it up. We have said many times that we must struggle against social injustices, against the exploitation of the wage laborer, against the excessive accumulation of wealth, etc., but have we understood that the central servitude, that the first and gravest slavery is intellectual poverty? We consider that the saddest inheritance of the world is

FIGURE 11

One of the homes built by Unión Cerrajera. Credit: Sharryn Kasmir.

the lack of educational opportunities and not economic inequality. (Quoted in CLP 1983, 84–85)

Arizmendiarrieta was also passionately devoted to promoting social mobility for Mondragón's working youth, and he was instrumental in sending the first sons of town workers into higher education. Several of his students from the Unión Cerrajera study circle went to Zaragoza to earn the equivalent of an associate's degree in engineering. These young men later returned to Mondragón. They were the founders of Ulgor, the first industrial cooperative.

The second phase of Arizmendiarrieta's social and political project to reform the working class was the promotion of entrepreneurship. The Basque Church is known for producing dissident priests (see Zulaika 1988, 36–73). An older man I interviewed who knew Arizmendiarrieta and other priests told me that during Arizmendiarrieta's time, these priests were of two types. First, there were those tied to the labor movement, many among them syndicalists. Second, there were those who promoted Basque nationalism, which they believed was expressed through the creation of small businesses. (Remember that, for PNV, "good" capitalism was built by small Basque-owned businesses rather than by large firms with links to foreign capital.) This group of priests believed that small-business-mindedness characterized the Basques as a people. Arizmendiarrieta is representative of this entrepreneurial tendency.[3] Azurmendi interprets Arizmendiarrieta's theory of the relation of business and nation:

So that there may be men who are entrepreneurs, who are indispensable so that nations may progress, steps must be taken "such that those who have capabilities cultivate them in an environment of work and excellence with a social sensibility and a social project." (1984, 198)

Arizmendiarrieta's entrepreneurs were cooperators; they would transform Basque society through enterprise. Arizmendiarrieta believed that cooperators, who were drawn from the working class, should remain in solidarity with their fellow wage earners. However, his suspicion of working-class organization and class consciousness led him to take cynical positions regarding class politics: "We live in the heart of a community and of a town of people and not of proletarians" (CLP 1983, 21). The cooperative project itself progressively transformed the town of Mondragón and distinguished cooperators from the rest of the working class.

The Cooperatives and Corporativism

The existence of the cooperative movement under fascism often strikes scholars as enigmatic or contradictory. Greenwood and González et al. write:

If we think of the public image of anthropology as the study of exotic cultures, it seems surprising that an anthropological study of the industrial cooperatives would have been so long in coming. What could be more unusual than a group of industrial cooperatives, economically prosperous, organized and managed democratically and founded in the midst of the Spanish dictatorship by a priest and a few engineers in a valley of the Basque Country? (1989, 11)

Some authors believe that the cooperatives were founded because of, not despite, political repression, and they claim that if political parties and syndicates had been legal under Franco, political energies would never have been channeled into so unlikely a project as cooperativism (Oakeshott 1978; Milbrath 1986, 10). Other writers point out that in organizing the cooperative project, Father Arizmendiarrieta was careful to stay within the letter, if not the spirit, of the law. This gave the appearance of acceptability to what might have otherwise been seen as a subversive movement.[4]

For example, the Franco regime strictly limited the right of free association. Sports clubs were among the few legal organizations as were parents' associations, which fit Franco's scheme for municipal government that was composed of council members representing the municipality, the vertical syndicates, and the family. Parents' associations were organized in towns throughout Euskadi, and, although they were forced to take on the organizational form prescribed by Franco, they were of the Basque *pueblo,* meaning they had popular support (Heiberg 1989, 198, 204–5). In the early 1940s, Don José María founded two organizations: a sports club for young people and a parents' association. Both were legal forms of association, and both served as bases to raise money for the Polytechnical School Arizmendiarrieta was to found in the coming years (Whyte and Whyte 1988, 29–30; Ornelas 1980). Further, in order for the school to gain official recognition, it had to allow social sciences and physical education to be under the control of the fascist Falange Party (Ornelas 1980, 76). In these ways, Arizmendiarrieta conceded to the legal limits imposed by the regime, ensuring that the co-ops would meet with little opposition, while creating valuable associational forms for the town.

Undoubtedly, there was a good deal of clever maneuvering on the part of the priest, and this made him popular in Mondragón. Priests like Arizmendiarrieta who commanded local followings, especially among youth, were often accused of engaging in political activities and were consequently transferred to other parishes (Zulaika 1988, 45). Like many of his colleagues in the Basque Church, Arizmendiarrieta might have attracted the hostility of Francoist officials, but he did not.

To the degree that the cooperative movement supported Basque nationalism, it would not have been tolerated by the regime. Outlawed were the Partido Nacionalista Vasco, the *ikurrina* (Basque flag), and Euskera. However, there were ways in which the cooperatives could fit, at least from the perspective of the regime, within a fascist framework. The Catholicism of PNV and Arizmendiarrieta's Catholic Action roots would have made the project acceptable to the Spanish right, which was closely linked to the Church. Furthermore, cooperative philosophy and structure could be seen as corporativist by the Falange Party, which was making economic policy for the regime.

The Falange was the political party that introduced fascism to pre–Civil War Spain. It was vehemently pro-Spanish and pro-military. The Falange backed Franco's military insurrection and was rewarded with the administration of the state after Franco's victory. Though common sense may tell us they are antithetical, cooperativism does share with fascist ideology the negation of class struggle (Milbrath 1986, 60). Ornelas explains that the Spanish state was not hostile to the Mondragón co-ops because the cooperative form of enterprise, though it questioned the foundations of capitalist economic structure, was compatible with the dominant Francoist ideology regarding the nonexistence of social classes (Ornelas 1980, 79).

Cooperatives and fascist regimes have coexisted elsewhere. The case of Italy is instructive; it shows how cooperatives can be appropriated by and accommodated within a fascist discourse. Italian fascists were initially hostile to the cooperative movement, which emanated from the Socialist- and Communist-controlled factory council movement of the post–World War I period. Fascist bands terrorized, sacked, and burned co-ops in the early 1920s. In 1922, the cooperative movement, organized as the Lega Nazionale di Cooperativa e Mutue, sought official recognition from Mussolini, who granted it on the condition that the Lega purge Socialists and Communists. It did, and from then on, cooperatives flourished under Mussolini's rule. In 1927 there were 7,131 cooperative businesses, a number that grew to 14,576 in 1942 (Earle 1986, 21–33; Lloyd 1926, 107–11; Sarti 1971, 79–113).

Ideologically, the Italian cooperatives benefited fascist propaganda. Mussolini pointed to them as examples of the ideals of corporativism. They embodied worker participation, nonconflictual relations between labor and management, and the withering away of class identifications. Large corporations, despite the imposition of vertical, cross-class syndicates, could not bear the entire propagandistic burden of this ideal because structural hierarchies and status differences in the factories were too great, and managing their large work forces was too complex (Earle 1986, 21–33; Sarti 1971, 79–113). The ideal of the classless factory was central to Falangist propaganda in Spain as well. One high-level manager of a Mondragón cooperative recognized similarities between the *jurado de empresa*—the body that represented workers to management within the fascist-organized factories—and the cooperative social council (Whyte and Whyte 1988, 39–41). Both organs resolved conflicts internally without recourse to outside political forces such as syndicates or parties. Both rejected the legitimacy of organizations that based their politics on class interests. Small businesses and cooperatives demonstrated that capitalism and stratification were not necessarily linked, and that independent unionism was irrelevant.

In Spain, the first cooperative law was enacted during the Second Republic in 1931. This law was replaced in 1942 with one that brought cooperatives more fully into the fascist orbit by requiring co-op members to affiliate with the vertical syndicate. Just as Mussolini accepted and encouraged cooperatives after they had been purged, so, too, in fascist Spain co-ops were favored with legal and economic advantages after the 1942 law linked them to the state-controlled syndicates. In 1954, a law was passed that exempted these businesses from corporate taxes; in 1962 they were granted low-interest loans from the state (Milbrath 1986, 51–66).

Opus Dei and Industrial Development

The initial stage of cooperative growth also coincided with a shift in state industrial policy. In the first years of the regime, Falangists presided over all aspects of government, including economic planning. This made for a conservative and stagnant approach to economic problems—for example, ignoring the long-time Spanish problem of a nondynamic southern, land-owning elite and the low productivity of southern agriculture (see Martínez-Alier 1971). Until the late 1950s, Falangists dominated Franco's government and promoted an approach to industrial development that was classically fascist. They nationalized financial and major industrial interests under a corporativist state and organized factories with vertical, state-controlled syndicates.

However, the Falangists were not capable of dealing with the economic problems of the post–Civil War years in Spain. Heavily industrialized areas such as Euskadi fared somewhat better than rural areas, since they benefited from Spain's noninvolvement in World War II by selling armaments and other manufactured goods to Germany and Italy. This produced a short and minor boom in long-standing metal-working towns like Mondragón, Bergara, and Eibar, but the spurt was temporary and too insubstantial to bail out the problem-ridden Spanish economy, which was further damaged by the international isolation of the Spanish government after World War II. While other capitalist countries were experiencing a postwar boom, Spain was not (Albarracín 1987, 39). By 1958, inflation was out of control, exports had fallen, and investment dropped off. There was a high rate of small business failure, workers were being laid off, and the country was close to bankruptcy (Payne 1961, 262–63). A strike began in the mines of the province of Asturias and spread in the form of sympathy strikes to Barcelona and Euskadi. Though broken up violently by the police, these strikes indicated that the economic situation had escaped the control of the military-minded Falange. "Franco's time-worn economic system had finally run out of gas" (Payne 1961, 264).

By the 1960s, Franco had replaced the Falangists in many of the top cabinet positions with a new cadre of economists and technocrats who were members of Opus Dei, a Catholic lay organization (not linked to Catholic Action) that encouraged its members to demonstrate their faith by excelling in business or the professions. Members kept their affiliation secret, lending a mysterious and even sinister air to the organization. Opus Dei government appointees sought to institute a more classically liberal market economy and encouraged private rather than state-led investment. Under the reformed regime, the Spanish economy experienced the postwar growth that characterized the rest of Europe (Albarracín 1987, 39; Clark 1979, 190–96; Clark 1984, 3–28; Pimentel 1987). The revitalization of the Spanish economy was also propelled by aid from the United States. After years of isolating fascist Spain, the United States changed its position in the 1950s in order to pursue a new cold war policy in Europe. It paid millions of dollars for the right to build military bases in Spain, and encouraged the rest of the world to trade with and invest in Spain and welcome it into the international community.

But more than anything else, it was the 1959 Stabilization Plan—and the cluster of monetary, budgetary, and investment policies it implied—that was responsible for overhauling the economy. The Stabilization Plan was supported by the International Monetary Fund (IMF), which imposed conditions for Spain's economic development, including currency devaluation and other measures to attract foreign investment. The peseta was devalued by 30 percent, with the dual effect of increasing exports and cheapening tourism in Spain. Americans, for example, began to vacation there, spending $10 billion annually. The devaluing of the peseta and the freezing of salaries also encouraged foreign investment in industry. These policies both impoverished the Spanish working class and encouraged emigration of workers to northern Europe. Between 1959 and 1962, seven hundred thousand Spaniards left to find work in France, Germany, and Switzerland. The remittances they sent back home were an important source of income for Spain. Finally, the IMF required a cap on public spending (Bruni 1989, 24–26; Clark 1979, 190–96; Clark 1984, 3–28).

The Plan had devastating effects for Euskadi. Basques believed that international pressure on Spain might bring the downfall of Franco (for example, the United States had fought to keep Spain out of the United Nations). However, the development of a cold war strategy that included Spain as an ally and brought foreign investment to the country made it unlikely that there would be any diplomatic outcry over Franco. After the 1959 Plan, Basque hopes for American help were dashed (Bruni 1989, 24–26; Clark 1979, 93–102).

Of further consequence to the Basque population was the industrial policy spelled out by the 1959 Stabilization Plan. According to Clark (1979, 227–44), Franco had before him two alternative strategies for industrialization. The first was to further develop already-industrialized areas like Euskadi and Catalonia. The second was to bring industry into rural areas, which were to become known as development poles. These plans were meant to be mutually exclusive, but Franco chose to pursue them both. Herein lay disaster for Euskadi. Investment in industry in Euskadi, which was heavy throughout the next decade, was not backed by spending for infrastructure or services. This meant that southern Spanish peasants and agricultural laborers who were pushed off the land into northern industrial cities and towns entered environments that were not prepared to receive them.

Anthropologists studying Europe since the 1960s have been concerned with the wholesale shift of labor from agriculture to industry (see Cole 1977), which resulted from a combination of Marshall Plan reconstruction policies and the economic strategies of the newly formed European Community (EC). While Spain was outside of the EC and was therefore not affected by the agricultural policy it imposed on member nations (see Marsh and Swanney 1980, 11–20, 30–48), it nonetheless shared the same fate. Anthropological studies of the 1960s and 1970s document the effects of the shift in Spain's economy on rural populations (e.g., Aceves and Douglass 1976; Brandes 1976). In Euskadi, where farmsteads had previously been economically secure, and conveyed prestige to the child chosen as the single heir, they came to be seen as a burden for the inheriting child (Douglass 1971; Douglass 1975; Etxezarreta 1977; Greenwood 1976).

Industrial centers were crowded with Basque and Spanish immigrants. From 1940 to 1970, the population density in Bizkaia rose 103 percent, to 471 people per square kilometer. In Gipuzkoa, population increased 90 percent to 316 people per square kilometer. There was no housing for immigrants, hospitals were inadequate (in 1979 there were still only four thousand beds for a population of 2.5 million), and there were too few schools, parks, and mental health facilities. Also, the concentration of industry in a mountainous area like Euskadi, where valleys are narrow, meant that air pollution was extreme, yet the government did not step in to regulate air quality (Clark 1979, 227–44).

Spanish immigration to Euskadi was popularly understood by Basques to be politically motivated and tantamount to a Franco-engineered attack on Euskera, Basque culture, and Basque nationalism. Spanish immigrants symbolized the repression of the state. Not surprisingly, ethnic tensions between native Basques and Spanish immigrants resulted. Immigrants were discriminated against in employment and marginalized from the social rituals of town life. They tended to find low-paying, unskilled or semiskilled jobs in large factories, while Basques were given work in small, personalistic factories. Basques called the immigrants *maketos,* a derogatory term for foreigners that implied that they were to be mistrusted and kept at a distance. Some Mondragón residents I talked to remember locking their doors during this time, for the first time in their lives.

At the same time, Spaniards were also chauvinistic. Basques were ridiculed and reprimanded by teachers who came from Spain and represented the authority of the state. The issue of language is exemplary. When Euskera was banned after the Civil War, Basques were forbidden to give their children Basque names or use Basque salutations, instruction in Euskera was illegal, Basque-language street signs were changed, and gravestones were destroyed. Language oppression is remembered as being brutal and violent. Immigrants, who were in other ways low status, made fun of Basque peasants for speaking Euskera, which they along with the fascist clergy, called the "language of the devil." Language became one of the battlegrounds of ethnic tension in industrialized Basque towns.

Industrialization in Mondragón

Mondragón was dramatically affected by the 1959 development plan, more so than other towns. From 1950 to 1970, the population more than doubled. In 1950, there were 10,014 residents; in 1960, 14,168, and in 1970, 22,421. The rate of growth was much higher than that of neighboring towns, and by 1960 Mondragón surpassed Bergara as the largest town in the comarca, a position it had not held since the Middle Ages (Mancomunidad del Alto Deba 1982, 39). The town was unable to absorb so many people (either ecologically or culturally) so quickly in any kind of rational way. By 1970, only 45.8 percent of the population was native to Mondragón; 7.4 percent came from the co-marca, 4.2 percent from the rest of Gipuzkoa, and 8.7 percent from the other Basque provinces. Non-Basque immigrants constituted 33.9 percent of Mondragón's population (see table 3.1.) This amounted to an attack on Euskera in Mondragón, where nearly 47.3 percent of the population had no knowledge whatsoever of the language (SIADECO 1972, 27). Throughout the 1960s, Basque immigrants were welcomed, but Spanish immigrants were not accepted into the community (SIADECO 1972, 30–31).

Many working-class immigrant families were shunted into largely immigrant neighborhoods, where they were ghettoized, making an already-strained situation all the more difficult. Often they were housed in poorly constructed apartments thrown up quickly to meet the extraordinary demand. The town center is a small prestigious neighborhood, and homes there tend to be passed on within families, offering little opportunity for newcomers to take up residence. It is not surprising, then, that it remained largely Basque. From 1946 to 1961, Unión Cerrajera constructed several four-story

TABLE 3.1

Origin of Non-Basque Immigrants Living in Mondragón, 1970

Place of origin	Percentage of population
León	9.9
Old Castile	8.5
Extremadura	7.2
Andalucía	2.5
New Castile	2.2
Galicia	1.9
Other	1.7
Total	33.9

Source: SIADECO (1972, 27)[5]

blocks (275 apartments) for its workers in Musakola, Mondragón's first planned working-class district (Unión Cerrajera n.d., 260–61). This new construction housed some Spanish workers, but it was still a Basque neighborhood. San Andrés was built for new immigrants, and it is not popularly considered a very desirable place to live. However, it is not nearly as undesirable as Santa Marina, which has some of the shoddiest apartments in town. The segregated nature of Mondragón's neighborhoods is shown in table 3.2.

Rural farmsteads located on Mondragón's outskirts in small neighborhoods called *auzoak* were low prestige in economic terms, but they were still off limits to Spanish immigrants (see table 3.2.) The few successful farmers specialized in beef, dairy, and vegetable production, with high profit margins, requiring hefty capital investments (Greenwood 1976). Others simply gave up farming and turned large tracts of land over to pine trees for the

TABLE 3.2

Neighborhood Composition, 1969

Percentage of population

Neighborhood	Mondragón born	Non-Basque immigrant
Center	61.8	16
Musakola	48	28.2
San Andrés	36.2	47.4
Santa Marina	32.6	57.8
Rural areas	73.1	15

Source: SIADECO (1970)

growing furniture industry. Mountainsides previously covered with maple and oak (oak is the national symbol of Euskadi) were covered with pine trees, uniform in size, betraying their nonindigenous origins. While the majority of farmsteads were no longer economically remunerative, they began in the late 1960s to regain cultural and political clout as fortresses of Basque identity (a notion promoted by ETA). Spanish immigrants were not welcomed in these rural neighborhoods.

Segregation in housing most severely affected transplanted Spanish women. This is an aspect of Mondragón's past that deserves more attention. In the factories, immigrant men had an opportunity to form friendship groups within which they could partake of some of the social life of the town, although the high-status male social institution of the *sociedad* (the eating club) remained off limits (see Heiberg 1989, 205–8). Francoist ideology frowned upon married women working outside the home. In the language of the regime, the state was to "liberate" women from the factory, and there were legal impediments to women remaining in the workforce after marriage (Moreno 1977, 27–28). Most immigrant women stayed home. The male world of the bars was off limits to Basque and immigrant women alike (a situation that did not change until the 1970s, when younger women of both groups began to partake of bar culture). The work and social lives of women were centered in the home, but immigrants lacked the friends and family that visited in Basque homes. Some immigrant women were reunited in Mondragón with women from their natal villages. Many, however, were without their preexisting networks and found it difficult to create new ties. These women lived isolated lives in an unfamiliar and unfriendly town.

María Elena, a pensioner, recounted to me the story of how she first came to Mondragón from Barcelona in the 1940s:

> I met my husband in Barcelona. He was Basque. We were married there, but about six months after our wedding, we came to Mondragón to live in my husband's *baserri* (farmstead). I was lonely and bored and I went back to Barcelona to my mother. But I was pregnant so I came back to Mondragón after my son was born. But I wasn't going to stay at home alone anymore. I insisted that my husband take me out with his friends, at least on Saturdays. This was a brazen request for that day and age since there were no women in the bars. My husband and I fought, but eventually he gave in.

María Elena was not so "brazen," however, as to drink alcohol on those Saturdays, and remembered having as many as eight to ten cups of coffee a night while the men drank wine. María Elena lived this way for decades, having made few close friends.

FIGURE 12

Apartment blocks in San Andrés. Credit: Sharryn Kasmir.

FIGURE 13

Apartment blocks in Musakola. Credit: Sharryn Kasmir.

In addition to lack of housing, segregation, and ethnic tension, there were many other urban problems, some of which trouble Mondragón until this day.'Until recently, when the water table was low, water could not reach the higher floors of the new apartment buildings. Families living in the neighborhood of San Andrés sometimes found themselves without running water for days. Pollution of the air and river is still horrendous. Factories were given building permits for the scarce flat land primarily on the banks of the Deba River, and they bought up the most valuable farmlands, leaving only those *baserriak* located high up the sides of hills and mountains. Urban planning for traffic flow, parking, and parks was simply nonexistent. It is with full consciousness of these problems that a study of Mondragón was commissioned in 1970. Sociedad de Investigación Aplicada para el Desarrollo Económico (SIADECO), a group formed in the 1960s to apply social science to social reform, undertook the project. Urla (1989, 192–202) offers an insightful analysis of the SIADECO group. For our purposes, that these urban problems were identified and that there was general concern to intervene are further indications of the seriousness of Mondragón's industrial dilemmas (SIADECO 1970, 1972).

Comparable problems of urbanization plagued all industrial Basque towns. In Elgeta, which is situated in a particularly narrow valley, farmsteads sit on such a steep mountain that it is almost impossible to imagine that the land could be worked at all. Of course, machinery cannot be used on many of these plots. Entering the town of Zumarraga, one is welcomed by clouds of orange smoke that spew from a metal-working factory. In each town, the culprit is the unplanned growth that took place during the Franco regime; however, in each case, local businesses carried out the industrialization. In Mondragón, these were the cooperatives.

During the period of rapid industrialization in the decade after 1959, the growth of the cooperatives was phenomenal. In the 1960s, the cooperative group began to expand throughout Gipuzkoa and into Bizkaia but remained concentrated in Mondragón. In Mondragón in 1971, the cooperatives employed 41.5 percent of the total of 6,399 factory workers. Of 65 industrial firms, six were cooperatives; cooperatives tended to be larger, on average, than private firms. Only two co-ops had fewer than one hundred workers (SIADECO 1972, 58). Additionally, Mondragón was the administrative center of the cooperative movement, housing the central headquarters of the bank, the social security cooperative, and the Polytechnical and Professional School. The cooperatives did in Mondragón what private firms did in other towns. It is not the case that the cooperatives were agents of the Franco regime nor that they purposefully engineered the urban-planning disasters that befell Mondragón. Rather, they were the bearers of these ills simply because they were the most dynamic economic force during this period.

Some private firms pursued immigrant labor actively; for example, the personnel director of the metal-working firm Polmetasa told me the factory's owners sent buses to southern Spain in search of workers. In 1989, 65 percent of Polmetasa's work force was from Spain. In Aranzabal, another local firm, 60 percent were immigrants. While the cooperatives do not gather data on the ethnic breakdown of their membership (and personnel managers could not give me estimates), they were known for employing a higher percentage of Basque workers than many private firms. Bradley and Gelb estimated that in the 1980s, between 17 and 28 percent of the work force was non-Basque (1983, 41). Whyte and Whyte (1988, 255) estimated 25 percent.[6] This was due partially to the entrance applications, which gave additional points to applicants who were related to members; thus, the screening process tended to reproduce an ethnically Basque work force. Ninety-one percent of the cooperators in Bradley and Gelb's study said they had friends or relatives in the cooperatives (1983, 64–66; 75–82). Nonetheless, as the largest and fastest-growing firms in the area, the cooperatives attracted immigrants and brought environmental and social change that was not welcomed by many of Mondragón's residents.

Txema came from a baserri (farmstead) that was bought by the town so that it could be torn down to make room for apartment houses. He worked in the personnel offices of a cooperative from 1969 to 1973 and developed the following analysis of the impact of the cooperatives on the town:

During the economic boom in the 1960s, when Ulgor stopped making kerosene stoves and switched to gas, they had a domestic market that could absorb as many stoves as they could produce. They were faced with the opportunity to expand the plant. A thousand more workers were needed [if they decided to expand]. Rather than study the human resources they had in town, rather than see who was available to work in Bergara, Eskoriatza . . . they just made their decision based on profit. They decided to hire a thousand people and bring them in from Spain. They also did not decide to hire married women. [Though this would have been controversial in Francoist Spain.] This in a town of fourteen thousand was a real strain on Basque tradition.

Significantly, both Txema's mother and wife are Spanish immigrants. His analysis suggests the anti-Spanish sentiment of the 1960s, but it also reveals how anti-Spanish feeling was intimately tied to criticisms of unplanned growth. Txema considered Ulgor's business decisions to be assaults against the town. He was not alone in his views. Andoni, who works full time in the local office of the syndicate ELA-STV, told me:

The cooperatives have created jobs, yes, but without planning. If the cooperatives hadn't been created, there probably would have been the same number of jobs created. This area has a certain industrial potential that would have been reached anyway, more or less. But without the co-ops, maybe there wouldn't have been so much immigration without planning.

Although the effect of the cooperatives was ameliorated by their provision of services (including the school and hospital), the cooperatives engendered the frustrations expressed by Txema and Andoni. The cooperatives transformed the town through industrial growth and pursued objectives townspeople perceived as distinct from community goals.

The First Criticisms of the Cooperatives

An event that took place in 1965 gave a name to and solidified these vague anticooperative sentiments, which were emerging in the 1960s. In that year, Franco's minister of labor honored Father Arizmendiarrieta with the Gold Medal for Merit in Work. It must have been very difficult for Arizmendiarrieta to accept the award, given his antifascist and Basque nationalist past. Yet it would have been politically dangerous for him not to accept it. Franco's minister of labor made a visit to Mondragón to present the award personally in a public ceremony. The local branch of Catholic Action used the occasion to print a short and laudatory biography of the priest in the locally-published magazine *Mondragón*. But, the minister's presence was a symbol of state power over a town that hated the regime.

The award generated the earliest public criticisms of Arizmendiarrieta and the cooperative business form. The first was intended for publication in ETA's official organ of communication with its supporters, *Zutik,* which was printed by ETA leaders who were in hiding or exile in Bayonne (on the French side of the Basque Country.) The essay charged:

Franco knows whom to reward and whom to punish. To tell the truth, he is rarely mistaken. This is why José María Arizmendiarrieta, director of the Mondragón cooperatives, received a medal from Franco . . . he deserved it.

[T]he Basque worker is a compañero, a friend to his class. The problems of the workers are his problems. It is a disgrace to differentiate the problems of the working class and of cooperativism. What is happening is that each cooperative is converting itself into a closed world. Its workers do not want to have anything to do with other workers. When there is a strike, cooperative workers don't want to strike because they don't have problems. What kind of an attitude is this?

We are still forced to hear that cooperativism is the solution for Basque workers and will be the death of capitalism. This cooperativism that is built in the belly of capitalism in nothing more than selling oneself. It serves no other purpose than to break the working class, to intensify our isolation (we, in our corner, live well, the rest can go to hell), and to strengthen capitalism (ETA 1981, 4: 395–96).

The essay was the first analysis of the role the cooperatives had played in transforming the working class of the town. It was not well received. While townspeople like Txema and working-class organizations (including ETA) might have been suspicious of the cooperatives, this was overshadowed by the economic dynamism the industrial co-ops brought to Mondragón and to Euskadi, something that was dear to those committed to Basque nationalism. The essay was rejected for publication by the leadership of ETA. Though the article remained unpublished, its main thesis—that the cooperatives divided the working class of Mondragón—became more evident in the next decade, when a workers' movement was organized in Euskadi for the first time since the Civil War. In the context of this movement, the effect of the cooperatives on Mondragón's working class became the topic of fierce political debate. This is the subject of the next chapter.

Conclusions

The reforms initiated by Father José María Arizmendiarrieta are carried on today in a variety of ways. For example, there is a consumer committee, sponsored by the consumer cooperative Eroski, which is charged with educating the public on matters of nutrition, health, and safety. During my fieldwork I interviewed a member of the committee. I met Itxiar in a cafe just outside of the town center. The cafe was quiet, and the interview was more formal than the casual conversations I had with many informants in louder bars. Itxiar is about forty years old; she is a physical therapist by profession, and she volunteers on the consumer committee. Her husband is a well-placed manager in the cooperatives. During our conversation, Itxiar told me that Mondragón is an individualistic place where townspeople resist associating with each other. I was taken aback. I saw Mondragón as a highly associative place, where people spent hours together every day and took enormous pride in their collective forms. Itxiar explained:

In Mondragón when someone buys something and it turns out to be defective, they are reluctant to return it and would rather fix it themselves.

They don't think about how this will affect the next person who has the same problem. They're unwilling to demand better service.

Itxiar saw this as evidence of general apathy and of individualism; "they lack confidence in shop owners." To her, involvement and collectivity should be expressed by being a sharp consumer.

There are interviews that one conducts during fieldwork that are central in one's research—this was just such an interview. Upon reflecting on Itxiar's point of view, I understood that there is an essential tension in Mondragón between an identity that stresses consumption and one that stresses class affiliation. The consumer cooperative Eroski is involved in promoting the former. Despite the fact that Itxiar believed she was fighting individualism, the consumer identity she envisioned directly competes with that of class, one of the primary collective identities among townspeople. Eroski's philosophy, which can be seen in its magazine *Eroskide,* is that people must learn to consume correctly; this requires that they understand their rights (to return damaged goods, to be informed about what they are buying, to hold manufacturers and retailers responsible for misinformation). These rights are defined and articulated in this publication.[7] Eroski also offers courses that teach people that selection, service, and quality are their due in a consumer society.[8]

I interviewed the manager in charge of consumer education for Eroski. Telling me about Eroski's commitment to consumer education, she described an Eroski program for children:

> We give them a list of six items to buy and send them through the check-out line. We short-change them to see if they complain. Then we go on to discuss their shopping, why they bought a particular brand, why they bought yogurt with strawberry flavor instead of strawberries . . .

Itxiar is right. This level of consumer consciousness is not common in Mondragón; indeed, it would have been very much out of character for most of the people I knew. Itxiar and Eroski's worldview asserts that one's rights in society come from one's position as a consumer rather than as a producer (worker) or citizen. Stephanie Coontz draws a similar connection between consumer identity and political identity among U.S. women in the 1920s. "The prominence of women in consumerism coincided with the depoliticization of their drive for autonomy and the eclipse of an activist women's political culture" (1992, 170).

Since middle classes are created in part through patterns of and attitudes about consumption (see Bourdieu 1984), the retail cooperative Eroski's aims parallel the middle-class reformism that was integral to the cooperative

FIGURE 14

Inside of Eroski in Mondragón. Credit: Sharryn Kasmir.

project from its inception. The cooperatives were an attempt to generate middle-class values within the proletarian milieu of Mondragón; consumerism is the most recent expression of this effort. In the remaining chapters, I will show how the working class was transformed in other ways by cooperativism.

4

Remaking the Basque Working Class[1]

In this chapter, I analyze how the Basque working class made the passage from a "class in itself" to a "class for itself" in the decade spanning the mid-1960s to the mid-1970s. E. P. Thompson (1966) defined this process for the English working class as the expression of a common identity through cultural, social, and political forms. This collective expression constituted the English proletariat as a class for itself and was possible (though not inevitable) only after workers had shared a collective experience inside the factories and mills of eighteenth- and nineteenth-century England—that is, after industrial conditions made the proletariat into a class in itself. The Basque proletariat became self-conscious in this way at the end of the nineteenth century, after the development of a modern steel industry, when workers formed social and cultural clubs and joined syndicates and political parties. They also began to bridge class and national identities, especially in Mondragón, where the socialist and nationalist party Acción Nacionalista Vasca was strong.

However, as E. P. Thompson reminds us, the making of classes is a historical phenomenon; once made, they can be unmade or remade. This was the case in Euskadi. The political repression that followed the Spanish Civil War and the industrial transformation that resulted from the 1959 Stabilization Plan undid Basque working-class institutions and changed the composition of the working class. In the mid-1960s, workers undertook the task of remaking themselves as Basques and as a proletariat. This process was simultaneous with the emergence of the radical Basque nationalist movement. Labor activism increased, cultural and language organizations flourished, there was a sea change in what it meant to be Basque, and ETA became a socialist organization (socialist in ideology but unaffiliated with, and in opposition to, PSOE). In Mondragón, where a large segment of the labor force worked in the cooperatives, the events of this decade presented particular complications. As I show in this chapter, cooperators were less involved than were other workers in many of the labor struggles that contributed to the remaking of their class. This indicates the existence of a rift between cooperators and the rest of the working class.

In Mondragón, the political developments that characterized the period culminated in a walkout at the Ulgor cooperative in 1974. Townspeople remember the Ulgor strike as one of the most divisive events in recent history. Solidarity among cooperators eroded, and their political consciousness and experience became distinguished from the rest of the town's working class. The 1974 strike and its effects on Mondragón's working class are examined in this chapter.

From my reading on Mondragón I knew that some factions of ETA supported the Ulgor strike while others did not (see Azurmendi 1984, 617–19; Whyte and Whyte 1988, 91–93). When I set out to collect the relevant political texts, I found that several labor activists and cooperative workers had saved them. Partly these papers were mementos, but they were too hazardous to be ordinary souvenirs (people were arrested regularly during the Franco regime for possessing political documents). The ETA documents pertaining to the Ulgor strike had been saved because they contain an unfolding debate about the cooperatives that was as relevant when they were shared with me in 1989 as they had been fifteen years earlier, when they were put away. Since the early 1960s, ETA had carried on a dialogue about cooperativism that paralleled the debates I encountered during my fieldwork. For this reason, I determined that it was necessary to reconstruct what the various factions of ETA had to say about cooperatives, class, and politics. This dialogue on cooperativism was also an essential part of the political milieu in which the Basque working class remade itself.

Renewed Working-Class Militancy

A first indication that the Basque working class was remaking itself was the resurgence of labor militancy. The Opus Dei–led economic reforms of the late 1950s, which shifted Franco's government away from a strictly corporativist vision of the economy, introduced rational capitalist policies not only to business but also to labor relations. By the 1960s, the Stabilization Plan had generated a massive proletarianization in the Basque Country and throughout Spain, and this had political implications that could not be contained, even by severe and violent repression.

Growing working-class militancy forced the government to permit collective bargaining for labor contracts, although workers were still represented by delegates from government-controlled vertical syndicates rather than the independent syndicates (UGT and ELA-STV) they had formed before the war. Furthermore, rising prices and wage freezes triggered strikes. In 1965, the regime was forced to change the penal code to legalize strikes over wages, contracts, and other economic issues, but political strikes remained illegal. This was the regime's attempt to accept that conflict-ridden labor relations went hand-in-hand with a rational capitalist economy, yet it became clear that even strikes over strictly economic concerns were difficult to control. In 1967, all strikes were once again outlawed, but by then a new workers' movement had already developed (Clark 1984, 205, 252, 258–60; Colectivo Unitario–LAB 1989).

During the Asturian coal miners strike in 1956, an ad hoc committee, Comisiones Obreras (CCOO) was formed. From 1962 to 1964, during a wave of strikes, CCOO committees sprang up elsewhere in Spain. Under the control of the Spanish Communist Party (PCE), CCOO was popularly seen as the vanguard of the workers' movement. In Euskadi, where the Communist Party was never strong, ETA was a driving force in the development of CCOO (Colectivo Unitario–LAB 1989, 25–27). The developing of Basque workers' consciousness and the rebuilding of working-class organizations took place alongside political and cultural activism that was tied to ETA (Gurruchaga 1985, 255; Unzueta 1988, 160). In Euskadi, nationalist and class organizations were simultaneous and interconnected.

The Early Years of ETA

ETA originated in the 1950s, when a group of students from the prestigious Deusto University in Bilbo formed Ekin, a Basque nationalist organization independent of the Partido Nacionalista Vasco. They were convinced by PNV to affiliate with the party's youth wing, but their association was short lived. In 1959 they broke with PNV and named their new organization Euskadi ta Askatasuna (Basque Homeland and Freedom). The members of ETA distinguished themselves from PNV's nationalism by proclaiming themselves aconfessional (a move that foreshadowed the widespread rejection of the Church by young Basques beginning in the late 1960s and still prevalent at the time of my fieldwork). They also declared themselves to be "revolutionary," and they emphasized activism. ETA was organized into five fronts: the promotion of Euskera, education, political propaganda, legal actions, and military activity. When it drafted its principles in 1962, ETA condemned all forms of ethnic chauvinism—distancing itself still further from PNV—and began to differentiate its social-economic positions from the conservatism of PNV nationalists.

Identifying itself as neither Marxist nor explicitly socialist, the early ETA nonetheless called for the protection of the "primordial" socialist nature of productive property, alluding to Basque egalitarianism. It advocated a planned national economy, the socialization of basic resources, and the recognition of the supremacy of labor over capital. Like PNV, it conjured up an egalitarian past; but, unlike PNV, it did not believe that small-scale Basque capitalism was an expression of that egalitarianism. Nonetheless, it advocated cooperatives (Bruni 1989, 39–44). In its second assembly in 1963, ETA began to use the slogan "*Gora Euskadi Sozialista*" (Triumph Socialist Euskadi). The following year, ETA published "An Open Letter to Basque Intellectuals," in which it reiterated its positions regarding a planned economy and the nationalization of basic industries. However, its position on cooperatives changed./While ETA continued to advocate workers' control inside factories, it expressed doubt that cooperatives, along with worker-participation schemes proliferating in Europe at the time, could provide a viable solution to the central problems of capitalism—the dominance of values such as individualism, competition, and economism over humanism and solidarity. (Significantly, the issue was treated cursorily, and the Mondragón cooperatives were not mentioned.) ETA also declared that all workers had a right to affiliate with syndicates and that syndicates should play a role in the development of the national economy (Bruni 1989, 39–60).

This document moved ETA closer to a socialist program, but it was also conciliatory to Basque petty-bourgeois and middle classes, who, along with intellectuals, were its intended audience (Bruni 1989, 59). Though the letter stated that the agent of the national liberation of Euskadi was its workers, it invited "popular" or "revolutionary" Basque middle classes to join ranks with the working class. Between 1966 and 1967, ETA incorporated Marxism as a basis for its official ideology. At its fifth assembly in 1967 it declared itself a socialist organization, yet it continued to see nationalistic segments of the petty bourgeoisie as political allies. This cross-class alliance was also evident in the membership of ETA.

Unzueta's review of eighty-eight people who participated in ETA assemblies or actions from 1966 to 1970 showed that thirty-nine were students, nineteen were workers, fifteen had clerical jobs, thirteen were professionals, and two were farmers. Of the sixty-six who reported their family's class background, twenty-seven were children of workers, twenty-five were children of professionals, business people, or factory owners, and nine had peasant origins. In the 1970s the organization attracted more workers and others from increasingly modest family backgrounds (Unzueta 1988, 175–85). This cross-class alliance (both ideological and in its membership) is still nurtured by ETA and the organizations in its political orbit, and it was the cause of much of the early tension within the organization (Bruni 1989, 44–60).

Factionalism in ETA

Factionalism in ETA became evident after the fifth assembly. One faction was led by Txillardegi, who was the director of the cultural front since 1962. Txillardegi's group (known as the "culturalists") believed that the focus of Basque liberation should be to resist cultural and linguistic domination by rebuilding an Euskera-speaking population. Eventually, the group resigned from ETA to work in independent language and cultural organizations (see Urla 1987, 108–30). Another schism developed in the 1970s over the issue of armed tactics versus participation in the electoral arena. The splits were numerous and can best be followed in the sixteen-volume collected documents of ETA (1981), (see also Bruni 1989; Clark 1984). Here, I summarize the schisms that were most relevant to the debates about class.

The first of these splits occurred in 1967, when members of ETA's political front were expelled from the organization. The group formed a new organization called ETA-berri (New ETA) and criticized what it considered the petty-bourgeois character of ETA's nationalism and the watering down of its class analysis to fit a nationalist agenda. In 1971, ETA-berri voted to join the Spanish statewide Maoist party Movimiento Comunista de España (MCE). Over the next decade, Maoism would have a significant influence on factions within the left in Euskadi, and MCE would become one of the most influential of Spain's small factionalist parties. ETA-berri's decision to affiliate with MCE was based on its convictions that the focus of revolutionary struggle should be class and that ethno-nationalisms served simply to divide the working people of Spain. In the second edition of its magazine, *Komunistak,* MCE firmly rejected all nationalisms. The nationalist faction of ETA branded MCE members as *"españolista"* (pro-Spanish), a derogatory term that is still used today for political name-calling (Bruni 1989, 75–83). Later, MCE would be forced by the weight of popular political will to reconsider Basque nationalism as well as the linguistic struggle of many Basques. In the 1980s, they changed their name to Euskadiko Mugimendu Komunista (EMK), in recognition of the importance of Basque language revival in Euskadi.

Trotskyism brought further ideological and organizational turmoil to ETA. The first part of the sixth assembly was held in 1968, while many ETA leaders were in jail. In their absence, Trotskyists emerged as the majority faction within the organization, and marginalized the more nationalist elements. Like the Maoist groups, ETA-VI (so named because their positions were formulated in the sixth assembly) believed that the natural allies of Basque workers were not the Basque middle classes but Spanish workers. By 1972, ETA-VI had so fully rejected nationalistic, cross-class politics in favor of Spanish statewide working-class alliances that, according to Bruni, it lost its link with the historic goals of ETA and with the sentiments of the Basque people. In 1973, ETA-VI joined the Spanish Trotskyist party the Liga Comunista Revolucionaria (LCR) and soon after joined the Fourth International (Bruni 1989, 147–49). It, too, was branded españolista. Like MCE, LCR would later reconsider its positions on nationalism, including the culturalists' arguments about language, and change its name to reflect a Basque identity, becoming Liga Komunista Iraultza (LKI).

As ETA-VI lost credibility with a nationalist population, ETA-V (the faction that continued to hold to the positions of the fifth congress) consolidated its legitimacy among Basque working and middle classes in 1973 by assassinating Carrero Blanco, the newly named president of the fascist government and Franco's hand-picked successor. The events of the assassination were dramatic. The explosives used to blow up Carrero's car were so powerful that the car landed atop a nearby six-story building. That explosion is still celebrated in song at popular dinners, bus rides to political demonstrations, and in Euskadi's radical bars. Casanova (1983) credited ETA-V with contributing to Spain's transition to democracy, since it was ETA-V that effectively destroyed the mechanism, in the person of Carrero Blanco, for continuing the regime after Franco's death. There was a general awareness of this fact among Basques, and the action solidified ETA-V's position vis-à-vis the other factions of ETA.

In 1974, another major split took place in ETA when those favoring political action over military action left to form ETA político-militar, ETA(p-m). The group that remained was ETA militar, ETA(m). ETA(p-m) soon evolved into the political party Euskadiko Ezkerra and ended its affiliation with the organization. Today's ETA (sometimes called the "historic" ETA) is the descendent of both ETA-V and ETA(m) as opposed to any of the other factions.

ETA in Industrial Towns

The tensions over ETA's political line coincided with a geographical and class shift in its membership. As ETA began to move from its urban origins into the industrial towns of Gipuzkoa, the "heartland" of Euskadi (Clark 1984, 67–68; Unzueta 1988, 182–85), it confronted working-class concerns that influenced the nature of the organization. Zulaika provides an ethnographic account of the way in which Catholic youth groups in the town of Itziar mobilized young men into politics, most notably into ETA (1988, 39–73). The same was true in Mondragón, where young men's experience in the Scouts and Young Catholic Workers sparked their interest in politics. Zulaika suggests that the content of the discussions and the ideology of these groups, specifically that of *ekintza* (taking action), accounts for their political dynamism. Ekintza is a central concept in Basque culture and characterized Catholic Action groups as well as ETA, yet the Scouts and Catholic youth groups went beyond an ideology of activism and created vehicles for that activism within organized groups. These organizations contributed greatly to the remaking of the Basque working class.

Xabier is an ex-ETA member who I interviewed.[2] He remembers his affiliations with Catholic organizations as being important for the simple fact that they involved him in collectives. Since the right to assemble was strictly limited under Franco, the meetings of Catholic groups, whether for study circles, discussions, or to plan town fiestas, gave him and other young people a legitimate organizational form that they otherwise lacked. It was the only time they could safely come together. For Xabier, it was this fact of affiliation that influenced him most and led him to ETA.

ETA publicly introduced its version of nationalism in 1961, when it undertook its first armed action. The plan was to derail trains that were on their way to Donosti for the celebration of the twenty-fifth anniversary of Franco's military uprising. The attempt was not successful. Bruni wrote of the police repression that followed the 1961 action:

> In the factories and in the schools, the mood is very tense: the constant presence of the police, continuous, arbitrary arrests for the purpose of establishing police files on people, gratuitous abuse during police controls, etc. (1989, 40).

More than one hundred people were arrested and tortured. Most were jailed or sent into exile (see also Clark 1979, 157). Among them was J. J. Etxabe from Mondragón (several years later, Etxabe was killed outside his home by the Guardia Civil). From that point, ETA was known in town.

Xabier recalled that

> in the early sixties, young people in Mondragón were recruited [into ETA] only to carry out propagandistic actions, mostly to paint "ETA" on town walls, hang up the ikurrina [the Basque flag] and those sorts of things.

In 1964, a special unit of ETA called "las Cabras" was formed in Mondragón and nearby Oñati, and Xabier joined.

> Las Cabras carried out political education, mountain excursions (where police tortures and interrogations were simulated to prepare members for the worst), distributions of political propaganda, military training. . . . We also contemplated guerrilla warfare. We reviewed the mountains surrounding Mondragón from a military standpoint to evaluate the tactical advisability of waging a guerrilla war. We concluded that guerrilla war would be unwise.

But shortly after las Cabras was founded, tensions emerged between the student leadership of ETA living in urban centers, whose contribution was largely intellectual and ideological, and working-class militants from Mondragón, like Xabier. Urban leaders devoted themselves to producing texts that became cornerstones for the movement (most notably, Federico Krutwig's *Vasconia,* published in 1963). Xabier explained:

Meanwhile, members of las Cabras, most of us attended school only until age fourteen, and then we went into the factory. The students were removed from our reality, the problems of industrial life and the dangers of activism—arrest, torture, and imprisonment.

In 1966 las Cabras split from ETA and operated autonomously. By 1968, during one of many Madrid-imposed States of Exception to be declared in Euskadi— when all civil rights were suspended, allowing the government to make "preventive" arrests without specific charges, to hold detainees incommunicado, and to impose curfews—las Cabras was crushed by the police (see Bruni 1989, 73).

Las Cabras was not the only faction of ETA that developed in Mondragón. As a place where working-class identity made nationalist expression complex, workers founded a short-lived Marxist-Leninist faction of ETA-VI, and Maoist and Trotsktyist factions were stronger there than in many other towns.

The Cultural Work of Building a New Working Class

Under the dictatorship, it was illegal to use Euskera in public (including in church services); Basque cultural societies were banned, and some libraries and publishing houses that held Basque-language materials were burned (Urla 1987, 103). Many children watched their parents struggle in Spanish, a language in which they were not fluent, or risk humiliation and arrest for using their own language. These painful memories were vivid to many people I knew. Given these circumstances, they were anxious to engage in cultural activism. Its early attention to cultural activism popularized ETA's movement for national liberation in a way that politics alone could not.

In ETA's first assembly in 1962, the organization called for "the establishment of a government that is democratic and absolutely representative, in the political and socio-economical sense as well as in the cultural" (Bruni 1989, 41). ETA's goal was to encourage Basques to participate in the rebuilding of the social and cultural fabric of their nation. ETA encouraged a broad range of people to participate in cultural life and public celebrations and fiestas and to transform these events into expressions of the political, social, and cultural will and identity of the Basque people. In the early 1960s, simply overcoming the fear and shame of thinking politically, organizing, and taking action was a struggle. In Xabier's words:

People like me who came of age during these years felt the repression on two levels. First, the regime instilled pure fear [arrests and torture were common]. Second, after years of living under the dictatorship, we had internalized the belief that it was immoral and irresponsible to enter the world of politics because of the dangers it presented to our family and community. By the mid-1960s this stigma was being cast off, and we began to see resistance as moral and courageous.

This changing attitude about activism (fomented by ETA) was critical for a popular participation in social and cultural events that was unthinkable a decade earlier.

What is notable about the cultural movement is that it was not purely romantic or folkloric (although there were elements of both). Txillardegi, the leader of ETA's culturalists, remarked:

> We reject the excess of sentimentality . . . which to our way of thinking existed in 'official' nationalism and translated into such incomprehensible attitudes as denouncing the oppression suffered by Euskera but doing absolutely nothing to learn it. (Quoted in Gurruchaga 1985, 239)

ETA sought to create a generative cultural movement and avoid passive romanticism. The type and character of social and cultural expression established the basis for a social world that was imbued with politics, which could propagandize and motivate, but was also a means of personal and collective artistic expression. The intimate relationship forged in the 1960s and 1970s between politics and popular culture remains one of the most essential nexuses of Basque radical politics.

Much of the cultural politics of the 1960s centered around Euskera. The cultural front of ETA drew on anthropological theory, especially the Sapir-Whorf hypothesis, to develop their ideas about the relationship between language and culture. ETA believed that language shaped the cultural being. Urla (1987) reported that this position was accepted by much of the Basque-speaking population; peasants in rural villages were concerned that they not only spoke Basque but thought in Basque.

Language activists opened clandestine *ikastolas* (schools) to teach children in their own language. At first, ikastolas operated underground, and consequently there were very few. In 1960, only about three ikastolas existed in all of Euskadi. After 1968, ikastolas were tolerated by the Franco regime (though they were still officially illegal) and began to operate openly. Soon, an ikastola was started in nearly every Gipuzkoan and Bizkaian town. By 1974 there were 132 in Euskadi. The schools were run as cooperatives. Parents paid a modest monthly fee which covered their child's tuition and gave them a right to vote in the assembly that governed the school. Teachers (mostly young townspeople who were native Basque speakers) were also part of the assembly, as were local business people who contributed to the school (Gurruchaga 1985, 258–64; Urla 1987, 133–38). Gurruchaga argues that ikastolas not only taught Euskera under conditions of repression, they went beyond this initial goal to become "a key element in the meaning of the collective We" (Gurruchaga 1985, 260). Ikastolas were centers of dense social relationships between students, parents, and teachers. Teachers were important cultural referents for the town, and the ikastola itself was a symbol of cultural reproduction for the Basque nation (Gurruchaga 1985, 259–60). If Basques in industrial towns like Mondragón were remaking themselves, as a class and as a nation, then the ikastola was a core institution in this process.

The effort to construct the Basque nation led also to the project to unify the many dialects of Euskera into a single, official language. The project was undertaken in 1964 (not, of course, without the power struggles that tend to characterize language unification and often turn on the dominance of one dialect over others). The result was Euskera Batua, now the official Basque language (Urla 1987, 148–65). Euskera found a voice in poetry, fiction, and plays. Gurruchaga argues that a Basque poetry genre was developed: Poems were set in the city, they ruptured the dichotomy between purity and vulgarity, and they were social commentaries (1985, 257). The language movement went beyond simple language transmission to generate new art forms, and thus became more dynamic than a purely folkloric or sentimental revival of language.

There was a revival and infusion of politics into the traditional song dueling of the singing poets or *bertsolariak.* A *bertso* (verse) is spontaneously composed to a tune and rhythm chosen by the singer, and the bertsolari's opponent must respond in the same tune and rhythm. The rapidity, rhyme, use of language, humor, and emotional depth of the verses are the characteristics by which they are judged (see Zulaika 1988, 208–35). Most demonstrations and political events feature a berstolari.

Other musical forms were elaborated. *Txalaparta,* an ancient drumlike instrument thought to have been used to communicate from mountain to mountain, was discovered and revived. (Most political actions I attended in Mondragón began with the sounding of the txalaparta.) And a Basque folk-music movement that was contemporary with the New Music movement in Latin America became important; Mikel Laboa was a leading figure. Laboa's work is particularly interesting because, stylistically, it is often more experimental than folk, yet he uses traditional and sometimes sentimental poems and political messages for his lyrics (Gurruchaga 1985, 255; Urla 1987, 138–40; Unzueta 1988, 160). Significantly, he sometimes does not use lyrics at all; some of his songs are simply compilations of Basque sounds or strings of single words. In my estimation, Laboa's music represents Basque language revival as a central symbol of a renewed nationalism, since he suggests that language, being more than the direct transmission of vocabu-

FIGURE 15

Bertsolari performing at a political act in Mondragón. Credit: Sharryn Kasmir.

lary and grammar, requires the familiarity of sound and the development of sentiment.

Basque Fiestas

All of these cultural forms played a role in language revival and stood on their own as art forms that engaged people in cultural expression. They also became building blocks of popular fiestas that began to resurface in the Basque

FIGURE 16

Txalaparta students playing during winter fiestas in Mondragón.
Credit: Sharryn Kasmir.

Country. The resurrection and reinvention of Basque holidays and fiestas at the national and local levels were at the cultural core of remaking the Basque working class.

Aberri Eguna, the day of the Basque fatherland, was celebrated anew in 1964. First held on Easter of 1932, during the liberal government of the Second Republic, its revival in Gernika (Guernica) was an extremely important event. Politically, it showed the ability of the Basque people to organize despite twenty-five years of repression. Symbolically, Gernika resonated with meaning. Not only was it the ancient capital of the Basque Country, it had also been destroyed during the Civil War by massive bombings by Franco-allied German pilots—an air raid that was the subject of Picasso's famous painting named for the city (Clark 1979, 115).

Local Basque fiestas were also revived. Town fiestas were held during the dictatorship, but they had an official and authoritarian character; they were not considered either popular or Basque. Indeed, participation in the official event was often seen as collaboration. Greenwood (1977) writes about the local government's concern about the lack of participation in the ritual of Alarde in the coastal town of Hondarribia (Fuenterrabia). Although he does not suggest that nonparticipation might have been a political statement on the part of townspeople, he does note that the local Francoist government reorganized and manipulated the festival, thereby crushing popular participation. In Mondragón, boycotting fiestas was an explicit means of protest (and still is throughout Euskadi).

Throughout the dictatorship, fiestas were a source of conflict between townspeople and the Franco-installed local governments. In Mondragón, where the patron saint is San Juan, the first popular, Basque San Juan fiesta to be held under Franco took place in 1964. It signaled the resurgence and, in some sense, reinvention of a popular festival. Young people joined the Comisión de la Fiesta Vasca (the committee in charge of the fiestas) to participate in planning the events, and townspeople took part in the festivities, which included playing folk instruments, such as the *txistu* (a flutelike wind instrument), rural sports, and the performance of new art forms.

ETA was anxious for these fiestas to be successful. In its underground magazine *Zutik,* which was circulated clandestinely among townspeople, the organization communicated the following evaluation of Mondragón's first popular San Juan:

The abertzale [Basque patriotic] tone was high and people sang abertzale songs and talked about Euskadi. . . . Arrasate was bubbling with patriotism. A young girl spent the whole day playing the txistu and the drum. In this it could be clearly read 'Gora Euskadi Askatuta' [Long live free Euskadi]. The topic of conversation was the New Resistance [ETA]. . . . They are the best, when do we start, they are courageous, they are not afraid of anything. (ETA 1981, 3: 343)

While the tone of the congratulations to Mondragón's residents is clearly propagandistic, the salient point is that ETA engaged in a dialogue with townspeople about building fiestas. ETA intervened in popular culture, termed it political, and encouraged people to approach the fiesta from the same point of view. Townspeople were anxious to take back their fiestas, and they read in *Zu-tik* how this contributed to the Basque nationalist movement as a whole.

Redefining Basqueness

Social and cultural expression of this sort was not a wholly new phenomenon in Basque towns. Before the Civil War, PNV organized mountaineering clubs, social clubs, and town and national fiestas. What was new was the intermingling of social life with the radical politics of ETA and the effect this had on what it meant to be Basque. In the late 1960s and 1970s, taking part in social and cultural events became a more important condition of identity than was ethnicity. This marked a dramatic change in the nature of Basque nationalism, for it meant that one did not have to *be* Basque in order to *become* Basque. Rather, Basqueness was achieved by activism in radical nationalist culture and politics (Kasmir 1992a, 1992b).

This was of particular importance for Euskadi's working class, which was both Basque and Spanish. For the first time, Spanish immigrants could partake along with their Basque neighbors in social and cultural events. Moreover, as ETA's version of nationalism gained popularity, Basqueness was transformed. Spanish immigrants who were committed to the working-class-identified radical nationalist project could become Basque. For example, María Elena's (see page 81) children became Basque not only because their father was Basque and because they grew up on a farmstead but because they were part of the radical nationalist sphere.

Heiberg (1980, 1989) has written about Basque identity, analyzing the evolution of the PNV concept of Basqueness, from the blood-based definition espoused by Sabino Arana to the political conception of Basqueness PNV adopted some ten years later. As first set out by Sabino Arana in 1895, the core of being Basque was "purity" of blood demonstrated by generations of Basque surnames. Later, physical anthropology was employed to make Basqueness a scientific category. Anthropologists collected anthropometric data on body type, cranial size, and nose length, and their findings were used to support nationalist claims that Basques constituted a distinct type from Spaniards, French, and other Europeans (see Urla 1989). Basques were found to have a significantly higher incidence of Rh-negative factor blood than other populations (Moulinier 1949). However, when turn-of-the-century nationalists set out to transform their political ideology into a party (PNV), race was not sufficiently exclusive to demarcate the population. Not all racial Basques could be considered truly Basque. Since PNV was at the same time antioligarchic and anti-Socialist, the party excluded two groups from their newly conceived Basque community—financial and industrial Basque elites tied to Madrid, and Basque supporters of the PSOE. Furthermore, PNV successfully imposed the responsibility of political commitment on those who claimed the status of being Basque.

> Arana had to make race a politically operative category—not a static matter of once and for all biological inclusion or exclusion. Basque status was granted solely to those who faithfully and publicly adhered to . . . political behavior. . . . [A] real Basque could only be a Basque nationalist. (Heiberg 1989, 56)

Heiberg argues that one feature of Basque identity persists over time: the fact of inclusion in what she calls the "moral community," at first biologically and later politically defined. She considers the continued pattern of inclusion and exclusion to be more important than the shift from a race-based definition to a political one, and she states that the existence of a moral community today, albeit along different political lines, replicates the structure of earlier nationalism. The development of radical nationalism is, in her estimation, best understood as continuous with rather than a definitive break from PNV's socially conservative nationalism (1980, 1989). Heiberg's analysis is compelling, especially considering its parallel with poststructuralist theory that locates identity in the creation, often through language, of concepts of self and other (e.g., Butler 1990). However, Heiberg does not intend to make a poststructuralist argument. Rather, she means to note a historical continuity in the bounding of a Basque community even when the standard by which the community is defined changes.

This phenomenon is not particular to Basque conceptions of identity. Anthropologists have shown that ethnic or racial identity is typically about inclusion and exclusion (see Williams 1989). Nor is it exceptional that the content of Basqueness would change over time or in response to changed circumstances. What is significant about the Basque case—and I think this is missed by Heiberg—is the content of Basqueness itself. Basque identity was disarticulated from ethnicity and located in spheres that were accessible to Spanish immigrants. Even though PNV's version of Basqueness was linked to politics, it was still off limits to Spanish workers. In contrast, the radical nationalist concept of Basqueness made possible the integration of Spanish immigrants into the social life of Basque towns (Kasmir 1992a, 1992b). In so doing, it redefined the movement for national liberation as a multiethnic, working-class struggle. This was one of the most important ways by which the ethnically divided Basque working class remade itself.

By the 1970s, Spanish immigrant men and women who participated in the radical-nationalist world felt Basque and were accepted as Basque. This was simultaneous with the entry of large numbers of women, including married women, into the work force. Women in Mondragón told me that Spanish

women, along with Basque women, began to go to bars, where some of the informal political talk and organization took place and a new male and female social life was created. Both in popular consciousness and political writings, these
immigrant men and women were increasingly seen as "more Basque" than
Basque ethnics who were socially or culturally inactive or politically conservative (Kasmir 1992a, 1992b). In its "Open Letter to Basque Intellectuals"
ETA wrote:

> We have always been and always will be on the side of workers who,
> whether born in Euskadi or not, work for a true democracy in our coun-
> try. They are the basis of the future Basque society. We consider them and
> their children, without a doubt, rather more Basque than those capitalists
> with several Basque surnames who dare to call themselves patriots while
> they do not cease to enrich themselves at the expense of their own people.
> (Quoted in Bruni 1989, 58)

The following example from Urla's fieldwork in Usurbil indicates that ETA's
program reflected popular opinion and influenced daily life:

> As one of my Basque friends, the author of the article on race, told me in
> a heated discussion, even if Fraga Ibirane, (Fraga was born in Galicia but
> Iribarne is a Basque surname), had ten Basque surnames (and was thus
> "biologically" Basque), he would never be considered Basque. As head
> of the conservative Spanish party, Alianza Popular, his politics put him at
> odds with Basque identity—he was an anti-Basque. (1987, 118)

The process of the integration of Spanish immigrants into the radical-
nationalist community was not smooth—remnants of chauvinism were the subject of repeated critiques of the radical nationalist movement—but at least this
new conception of Basqueness was fundamentally more open to immigrants
than any that had come before.[3] In Mondragón, many immigrant workers found
the confidence (for it was difficult to take the first steps into a closed world) to
participate in the new Basque public life and to make their way toward being
Basque. This new identity not only allowed them to fit into their new environment (the story of what they lost in the process remains to be told), but also gave
them a vehicle for fighting the fascist regime.

I talked with many Spanish immigrants and their Euskadi-born adult children about becoming Basque. Mikel's story, which he told me one afternoon in
a bar, is fairly typical. Mikel is a thirty-five-year-old factory worker who
learned "about class from my red grandmother. She was a Communist before
the Civil War." Others told me similar stories (perhaps their parents or grand-
parents were anarchists). More commonly, older people were afraid to pass leftist politics on to their children and grandchildren, and kept silent about their

pasts. Still, these young people gleaned that their families had been "red." During the strikes of the 1960s, in which ETA and Comisiones Obreras began to tie together Basque nationalist and working-class concerns, Mikel said he "began to *feel* Basque."

At first, feeling Basque simply meant seeing a similarity of interest between himself and those who had been hostile to him when he arrived in Mondragón a decade earlier. He felt that "we were all oppressed in the same way, by the same dictator. We as workers. They as Basques." This vague affinity became more important to him in the early 1970s as the Franco regime seemed genuinely threatened by both workers and Basques: "It looked like together we were finally going to bring down this regime." On a deeper level, Mikel identified as Basque because he participated in radical political life. As more and more economic strikes included demands for amnesty for political prisoners or freedom for Euskadi, Mikel became involved in nationalist politics. He walked out of the factory along with fellow workers in solidarity with ETA members who had been arrested. In growing numbers, immigrants attended nationalist demonstrations, and there they suffered police violence and arrest along with ethnic Basques. This created strong affective bonds that began to integrate friendship groups and their daily round in the bars as well as dating relationships and marriages.[4] Mikel married an ethnically Basque woman, and they are both activists in radical nationalist causes. These ethnic and gender changes in social life are also reflected in ETA's composition.

By 1968, Spanish surnames began to appear on the lists of those arrested for involvement with ETA (Bruni 1989, 94–95). In the period of 1966–1970, an estimated 17 percent of ETA participants had non-Basque surnames. In the 1970s, 14.6 percent of full-time ETA militants had a non-Basque father and mother, and 12.6 percent more had one Spanish parent. (In 1975, 49 percent of the total Basque population had at least one non-Basque parent.) In 1980–1981, arrest records show 23.1 percent with two Spanish parents and 18.3 percent more with one Spanish parent. These numbers grew after 1980. Over the same period of time, the number of women participating in ETA increased from 9 percent to 17 percent (Unzueta 1988, 183–85).

Thus, by the early 1970s, the radical nationalist movement had built the basis for creating a unified working class that was Basque culturally, socially, and politically, regardless of older markers of ethnicity such as surnames or biological traits. With this broader definition of Basqueness, the working class became particularly combative.

Labor Activism

During the last years of the Franco regime there were intense labor conflicts throughout Spain. After more than three decades of dictatorship, the

workers' movement emerged stronger than it was in other industrialized countries. Activism and rates of affiliation with clandestine syndicates were high
(Albarracín 1987, 43–44). The Basque working class—of both immigrant and
Basque origin—was notable for its militancy. In 1973, Basques made up 10.9
· percent of the industrial wage labor force in the Spanish state, yet 37 percent of
the more than nine thousand labor conflicts in Spain occurred in the Basque
provinces. Gipuzkoa was particularly combative. From 1963 to 1974 there
were more than 1,600 labor conflicts (most of which were strikes) in Gipuzkoa,
18 percent of the total for the state (Núñez 1977, 189).[5]

In Euskadi, labor strikes coincided with the 1970 trial in a military court
in the city of Burgos of sixteen ETA members, including one person from
Mondragón. They were charged with the 1968 killing of a police official; they
were found guilty and condemned to death by execution. The Burgos trial was
a critical juncture in Basque political life. For the first time since the beginning of the cold war, the international community took a stand against the bru-
talities of the regime. Jean Paul Sartre (1975), for example, wrote an essay
supporting Basque people's right to self-determination and calling for the
commutation of the death sentences. And the arrest of so many ETA members
at once and the prospect of their executions was also a mobilizing force
among the Basque populace, who had by that time embraced ETA. (It also
created the vacuum in the organization that led to ETA-VI's majority position.) There was a general strike in Euskadi, and many people attended
demonstrations for the first time in their lives. In 1974 there was another general strike, combining economic and political concerns. The conjuncture of
political protest and labor activism made Euskadi a hotbed for the next several
years. There were ten general strikes in Euskadi from 1970 to 1977 (Núñez
1977, 185–215).

In Mondragón, several strikes shaped the experience of local workers
during this period. However, cooperators' experiences of these events differed
from those of the rest of the working class, and would set them apart from their
fellow workers.

The Labor Movement in Mondragón

Although independent syndicates were illegal under Franco, they continued to function clandestinely throughout the 1960s and 1970s. In Mondragón,
the PNV-affiliated syndicate ELA-STV (ELA for short) organized a twenty-day
strike in 1962 at Unión Cerrajera over the first contract that vertical syndicates
were permitted to negotiate with the association of business owners. Harassed
by management because of their participation in the strike, several workers left
Unión Cerrajera and went to work in the co-ops. Some even founded cooperative firms (interviews with strikers).

A syndicalist in Mondragón told me that, in retrospect, he believes that the 1962 strike was the moment at which cooperators left the labor movement. "When they went to work in the co-ops, they abandoned ELA." Although a handful of individuals affiliated over the years (in 1989, each syndicate counted several co-op members among their ranks) "as a group, cooperators were never active again." Another syndicalist told me that many early cooperative members were affiliates of ELA, but after several years in the co-ops they let their memberships lapse. "ELA was irreparably damaged when they left." Cooperators ceased to be part of any syndicate that could connect them collectively to the labor struggles that were to follow.[6] Cooperativist ideology may have been based officially on solidarity between cooperative workers and the rest of the working class, and Father Arizmendiarrieta may have written on the topic, but cooperators' actual record of solidarity was uneven.

ELA was a Basque ethnic syndicate, and it lost a primary source of its support in Mondragón—those who believed that a more local, egalitarian capitalism was an expression of Basqueness—when these people became cooperators. The decline of ELA in Mondragón left a vacuum in the labor movement that was filled by the young people who founded Comisiones Obreras (CCOO). In the late 1960s, a small group of workers comprising CCOO met regularly, often in the secrecy and safety of the mountains. One of their first efforts was a walkout in the Aranzabal factory (IFAM) in 1973, when 135 employees went on strike over salaries. After the first day of the strike, workers were locked out, and those who succeeded in entering were forcibly removed by the Civil Guard. CCOO of Mondragón called upon workers in other firms to express their solidarity with the IFAM strikers. In a leaflet written by CCOO, it was noted that, over a period of several days in three different factories, there were five work stoppages of an hour of so. Eight hundred to one thousand workers reportedly took part in these actions. This was the first cross-factory strike in Mondragón's history. Greenwood and González et al. (1989, 75) report that, in 1973, 264 individual cooperators stopped work for an hour in solidarity with strikers in a local private firm (presumably IFAM). This is an indication that some cooperators felt an allegiance to other workers. It is also the case that no single cooperative respected the strike by ceasing production. This directly contrasts with how the strike was carried out in private firms, where work stoppages were complete.[7] Reflecting on cooperators' lack of solidarity, a syndicalist from ELA said, "[their] form of solidarity is like a do-gooder or because they are doing a favor, but not because they see the problem as their own." These problems were not, strictly speaking, theirs. Cooperative ownership and democracy shielded cooperators from many of the pressures faced by workers under the fascist regime. There is little data regarding cooperative workers' attitudes at that time; the only study, conducted in 1965, showed that shop floor workers felt very integrated into their firms. (It also suggested that the rapid expansion being undertaken might compromise this fact [cited in Núñez 1977, 127–28].) But workers in private firms expected cooperators to show solidarity not because their salaries or job security were at stake but because those of their neighbors and fellow workers were.

In 1976 there was another strike in the Gamei factory.[8] The Gamei strike was also generalized throughout the town. Aitor, a CCOO affiliate, described the strike to me:

> Five people were expelled for trying to establish an independent union. There was a three- to four-month strike that was very popularly supported. Every day there were thousands of people in the plaza. The town was firmly behind the strike. Unión Cerrajera went out ten days in solidarity. The co-op workers talked about going out on strike, but the managers convinced them to wait, that they would talk personally with the management of Gamei to resolve the problem, that they knew the managers of Gamei personally and could get the workers their jobs back. . . . Finally, the [co-op] workers went out on strike, but it took a while. The rest of us were out, and they were still at work.

Aitor criticized co-op managers' policy of handling labor-management conflict in a private and personal way. He also condemned co-op workers' willingness to abandon the public conflict and retreat behind their managers' promise of personal intervention. Cooperators and regular workers—who often came together after work in their cuadrillas, were often family members, and otherwise were like each other—became divided along the lines of work regime.

The Ulgor Strike

The most significant strike of the 1970s was the walkout in Ulgor in 1974. The strike was the first (and, to date, last) mass protest of cooperators in Mondragón and a particularly divisive event in Mondragón's history. Ulgor was the largest of the Mondragón cooperatives, where refrigerators and stoves were manufactured (the present-day Fagor refrigerator plant and the Fagor Garagartza plant). The walkout spread quickly to the neighboring cooperative Fagor Electrónica, which produced electronic components.

Gutiérrez-Johnson and Whyte (1982) and Whyte and Whyte (1988, 91–103) chronicled the strike. According to them, a leading cause was the rapid growth of Ulgor, which had expanded in a few years to a membership of 3,500. Newly hired workers (both ethnic Basque and Spanish immigrants) were not given ideological training about the meaning of cooperativism. Moreover, the sheer size of the cooperative meant that the face-to-face relations, which were believed to make for better labor–management understanding, had been compromised. In this tense atmosphere, management in the major industrial cooperatives announced that new ratings would be assigned to jobs throughout the plant.

In the cooperatives, *anticipios* (anticipated share of earnings) are paid based on the rating assigned to each job. All jobs range in rating from one to three depending upon training and expertise required for the post, the level of responsibility involved, and job hazards. The project of reevaluating job grades and, therefore, redistributing earnings was initiated by managers concerned that engineering and managerial jobs had taken on increasing importance over the years but had not been reassessed in relation to assembly jobs. They appointed an evaluation committee to review all jobs in the plant. The committee recommended an increase in rates for engineers and a decrease for some assembly positions. Additionally, a merit system was introduced whereby individual performance, such as output, quality of work, and initiative could increase the rating by 0.15. Supervisors were given the power to evaluate workers and to recommend them or deny them merit points (Gutiérrez-Johnson and Whyte 1982; Whyte and Whyte 1988, 91–102).

Of the five cooperatives affected by the reorganization, it was at Ulgor where the most jobs were downgraded; 22 percent of the job classifications there were lowered. Individuals with complaints about their classifications were entitled to a review; more than one thousand petitions were submitted in the five plants, and the committee changed more than two hundred ratings (Whyte and Whyte 1988, 95–96). What was not subject to review, however, were the standards used to evaluate the jobs. Jaione worked in the co-ops from the time she was seventeen; she was one of the leaders of the Ulgor strike and did not see the size of the co-op or the acceptance or the dissemination of cooperative ideology as key issues. Rather, she had this to say about the events:

> The strike was over the system of evaluation. Management had been working on a manual for some time. It was then that I got my first surprise about the co-ops. They had the manual all developed, and the only thing that the workers could do was dispute their individual ratings. . . .
> The Social Council couldn't dispute the concepts they used to evaluate the jobs. They couldn't present an argument over the theory or ideology behind the evaluations. It was a professionalization.

Other strikers I interviewed saw the new evaluation system as an effort to "professionalize" the cooperatives by "valuing mental work over manual work." They interpreted this as a shift in class relations in the cooperatives, favoring more bureaucracy and hierarchy. Furthermore, the evaluation committee was appointed by management and composed of engineering and managerial personnel; thus, they argued, the review process was infused from the onset with a "technical bias" that they saw as reflective of a larger trend in the global economy.[9] Concretely, they wanted monotony to be a factor in the rating of a job, thereby increasing pay for manual work. They also wanted to introduce controls over the supervisors' discretionary role in rating individual workers.

The conflict began when a group of protesters demanded to meet with the Governing Council of Ulgor. The Governing Council refused, since the bylaws of the cooperative required that complaints be presented through the Social Council. The Social Council, in turn, was supposed to request a meeting with the Governing Council. Even though some of the protesters were themselves members of the Social Council (including Jaione), they were convinced that it was an ineffective organ, and they insisted on meeting with the Governing Council independently. They were turned away (Gutiérrez-Johnson and Whyte 1982; Whyte and Whyte 1988, 91–102). "That's when the strike began," Jaione told me.

> We walked around the factory in silence. And everyone knew that there was a strike. About half stayed. We walked out and stood in the street between Ulgor and Electrónica. The managers, meanwhile, went through the plant. . . . They told the workers who stayed that they'd have to fight us, that we wanted to destroy the cooperative system. They organized an antistrike picket line. [I asked Jaione who she meant by "they." She answered, "those in charge, heads of personnel," and she named some individuals.] The picketers encircled the strikers and would not let us enter the factories to get water or let us get our sandwiches. The picketers didn't want to let us bring water to the others. I said I'd hit them over the head with the water bottles if they didn't let me pass. They let me pass.

It was a hot summer day when seven hundred to eight hundred workers from Ulgor and Fagor Electrónica walked out. The strike and the picket lasted all day. The leaders were planning to hold an assembly inside the factory to vote on whether to continue the strike.[10] Jaione continued:

> The next day we arrived at the factory, like usual, in the buses. They had to let the buses into the factory gates because the people were mixed, both strikers and not. But already, management had prepared the first letters firing us. Some people got frightened and went back to work. Later, they saw that they lost, and everyone went back to work.

The strike lasted only one day and never fully stopped production. Since internal strikes (over work or wage issues within the cooperatives as opposed to external strikes over solidarity or political issues) were forbidden by a 1971 co-op bylaw, the Governing Council was free to sanction those who walked out. Twenty-four leaders from the two plants were fired.

Implications of the Ulgor Strike

Lembcke writes that "big strikes" have a tendency to insinuate themselves into the fabric of community relations (Lembcke 1991–1992, 425). The Ulgor walk out was just this kind of event. One reason was the firings. The co-op members who were fired were notified in the last days of June, but the firings were provisional, pending the vote of the General Assembly of Ulgor, which was not to convene until November. According to one of my informants, in the intervening months, cooperative managers held "informative chats" in the factory to influence the way in which people thought about the issue. Managers also went to the bars, including bars they did not normally frequent, to talk informally about the incident; strikers, too, went to the bars to tell their side of the story.

The social life of the bars became a battleground for the strike, and in this way it became a deeply divisive event in Mondragón and throughout Euskadi. Even the Church commented on the social upheaval caused by the conflict. The Secretary of Social Affairs of the Diocese of Gipuzkoa wrote a thirteen-page essay in response to the strike. He began by noting the strain on town life: "Mondragón is living through conflictive days, the consequences of which are being felt by individuals, families, and groups."[11]

Nevertheless, when the General Assembly of Ulgor met in November, it voted to uphold the firings. One person who was not involved but was sympathetic to the strikers told me that the General Assembly vote to fire the cooperators was a "tragic moment for Mondragón." To him, it was a dramatic expression of the lack of solidarity between co-workers in the cooperatives.

In the many illegal strikes taking place in private factories at the time, the first demand of striking workers was always readmission of workers who were typically fired when they initiated a strike. Yet in Ulgor, workers themselves voted to dismiss their colleagues.

About two-thirds of those fired were women. According to Morrison (1991, 180), women played an important leadership role because they worked at the lowest-skilled, lowest-paying jobs and were most directly affected by the technological bias of the new job ratings. Moreover, I learned from my informants that many of the women strikers had participated in a clandestine course in Marxism given by an economist who lived for a short time in Mondragón. Participants in this study circle developed theoretical tools for analyzing what they believed was the growth of a privileged and powerful class of technocrats in the co-ops. Some of them went on to join Movimiento Comunista de España (MCE), the Maoist-influenced party that had earlier been a faction of ETA. Thus, they were branded españolista.[12] Women also made up the vast majority (72 percent) of the group of 264 cooperators who stopped work in solidarity with the 1973 IFAM strike (Greenwood and González et al. 1989, 76). This relatively greater activism of women than men is an important area for future research.

The strikers believed that they were blacklisted throughout Euskadi, a claim the Church seemed to confirm.[13] They found it nearly impossible to get jobs, even in distant towns, and were forced to take the hardest and lowest-paying positions, a situation exacerbated by the general discrimination that women faced in the labor market. Jaione told me:

> We went all over Euskadi looking for jobs, to Navarra and San Sebastián, but we had been blacklisted. Each time we went to apply when they saw that we were from the cooperatives in Mondragón, we were turned down. . . . Many people took very hard jobs. One woman cleaned fish in a port. Many watched children. I went to work in a small shop, unloading trucks and lifting heavy loads. This went on for three and a half years.

The situation of the fired cooperators became a scandal. After Franco's death in 1975, workers and newly legalized syndicates fought for a general labor amnesty which they won two years later. All firms that had fired employees under Franco's antistrike law were required to give the workers their jobs back, a concession the postdictatorship government considered an essential feature of a new, democratic Spain. Not having applied Franco's antistrike law but its own bylaw, Ulgor did not have to readmit the workers, and it did not. To some, the co-ops began to appear worse than privately held firms which were willing to conform to the formalities of a democratic transition by rehiring workers. To others, including ETA-V and many local radical nationalists, the firings were just. Eventually, a campaign was launched for the rehiring of the Ulgor workers; they were finally readmitted in 1978.[14]

The fact that bitterness was so deeply felt, so widespread, and so persistent is an indication that there was something much more at stake than a simple labor conflict. Indeed, below the surface of the Ulgor strike were the splits in ETA and the struggle over the nature of the radical nationalist movement.

ETA and the Ulgor Strike

Though authors note that there were political aspects to the strike at Ulgor, no serious consideration of the political dimensions of the conflict has been undertaken in the literature on the cooperatives. In actuality, Basque nationalist politics were central to the conflict. According to Jaione, some managers accused the strikers of wanting to "destroy the cooperative system." Jaione and other strikers told me managers called them communists and españolistas. Most strikers, like Jaione, were born locally and had Basque parents, and there is no evidence (indeed, no one would make the argument) that among the hundreds of strikers there were more Spanish immigrants than native Basques. Managers also charged the strikers with "not loving Euskadi." Their language was taken directly from factionalist name-calling in ETA and reflected political claims to Basque identity and the manipulation of those claims.[15] The strike pitted cooperators against each other on the question that was dividing ETA: What is the relation of working-class concerns to a nationalist movement? The Ulgor strike, and cooperativism in general, was a canvas for this debate. Managers argued that striking over work-related issues in the cooperatives (what they would consider an extreme form of class politics) violated the national integrity of the co-ops.

On this point they agreed with radical nationalists. When radical nationalists gained enough control over the Basque social world in the late 1960s to delegitimize PNV's authority regarding Basque identity, radical nationalists also termed "ultra-leftists" anti-Basque. As splits in ETA became increasingly divisive, Maoists and Trotskyists who renounced Basque nationalism were branded españolista, regardless of their ethnicity. Cooperative managers, some of whom were known to be supporters of ETA-V and many of whom were PNV-style nationalists, overcame other political differences and jointly drew on this politicized notion of ethnicity to label the strikers, many of whom were Maoists, as anti-Basque. Managers were able to delegitimize the strike to non-striking cooperative workers, both Basques and Spanish immigrants, not so much because the demands were unimportant as because the politics were not correct. Strikers gave primacy to class rather than cross-class Basque solidarity.

From 1971 to 1975, several criticisms of the cooperatives were published. They came from all factions of ETA *except* ETA(m) and ETA-V (the predecessors of today's ETA), which maintained support for the cooperative system. As I discussed in the previous chapter, the first attack on the cooperatives was written in 1965 for *Zutik* but was not published, because the ETA of 1965, just as the ETA that survived after 1974, did not consider a criticism of the Mondragón cooperatives to be appropriate for a cross-class, nationalist movement (even if it had expressed doubt about cooperativism in general in 1963). However, when the various leftist factions split from ETA, they began to publish and distribute their own critiques.

In 1971, the Maoist ETA-berri published a copy of the newly instituted cooperative bylaw against internal strikes, asking sarcastically which was more "despotic": the fascist government, which outlawed strikes or co-op managers, who likewise forbade them. ETA-berri called upon co-op workers to "reflect upon an appropriate plan of action for organizing themselves."[16] A few months later the group wrote an analysis of the cooperatives, arguing that, in a capitalist mode of production, there was no possibility for cooperation between labor and management. They reasoned that the increasing integration of the cooperatives into the world market obliged co-ops to increase the number of contract laborers, making worker-owners an "aristocracy within the factory." The market further required cooperators to "produce according to profit motives rather than principles of social necessity and to reduce wages while work pace increased." They also referred to a recent survey in which 35 percent of co-op workers complained about the increasing pace of work. In this market-driven environment, ETA-berri argued, the possibility of self-management is taken from the workers and surrendered to a "new technocratic class." All of this, they concluded, is packaged in a cooperative ideology of paternalism, making it all the more difficult to fight.[17]

Azurmendi (1984, 617–19) cites another document distributed that same year, and he attributes authorship to ETA-VI. Entitled "An Analysis of the Cooperative Movement in Euskadi," the document raised two questions: What is cooperativism? And why is it concentrated in Euskadi? It answered that cooperativism is an effort by the state to defeat the working class of Euskadi.

In 1972, a three-page document entitled "What Is Happening in Mondragón?" charged the cooperatives with taking over the social life of Mondragón—work, sports, education, and the town hall. While the authors did not draw on Gramsci (and likely did not know his work) their argument parallels his analysis (1971) of the way in which corporations organized "appropriate" leisure activities for workers who were encouraged to give up their old forms of socializing to attend new activities that were planned for them. Applying a Gramscian framework, the leaflet emerges as a document that accuses the co-ops of stifling working-class cultural and social forms in favor of co-op institutions. The pamphlet further claimed that the co-ops had created in Mondragón an "island of peace and collaboration with the Franco regime" (Azurmendi 1984, 624).

In 1973, ETA-VI printed "Un Caso Particular: Las Cooperativas." The article laid out a plan for political action in the cooperatives, calling for grassroots groups to be organized to replace the Social Council, to struggle against management, and to ally with workers in other firms. The document further demanded the right to wage internal, economic strikes in the co-ops and to permanently fix the job differential at 1:3.[18]

In 1975, ETA(p-m) criticized the Social Council, writing that members of this body were apathetic, and it accused the General Assembly of a similar lack of interest. The document charged that, in meetings of the General Assembly, when the membership reviewed annual business plans and made other key decisions, rank-and-file cooperators had no consciousness of what they were voting for and simply rubber-stamped management's proposals. Moreover, ETA(p-m) argued that managers had real property in the co-ops while workers had only juridical property without corresponding powers. It also charged that work rhythms were faster in the co-ops than in other firms, that cooperators worked an enormous number of extra hours, and that their dehumanized work environment made them apathetic.[19]

In sum, the leftist factions of ETA observed that cooperative workers were isolated from the rest of the local working class and from the labor movement. They also charged that, as the regional economy became increasingly competitive, the cooperatives became more like private firms; thus, cooperators were subject to the same kind of exploitation as non-co-op workers. This critique became more forceful as the 1973 economic crisis impacted Spain, Euskadi, and the local cooperative economy. It is probably not coincidental that the Ulgor strike occurred over the issue of salaries, since, after accounting for the high rate of inflation after 1973, workers in Spain had not received a real increase in their wages since 1972 (Albarracín 1987, 50–51). Another criticism was that democratic organs in the cooperatives, especially the Social Council, were ineffective and unable to represent workers. Finally, cooperative management was accused of being paternalistic and of using the ideology of cooperativism to exploit workers.

The only faction within ETA not to criticize the co-op was ETA-V, the historic ETA (Azurmendi 1984, 625). Significantly, this was the faction of ETA that had the most popular support. In fact, ETA-V published an article in 1975 condemning the Ulgor strikers because the localism of the cooperatives counteracted the decapitalization of Euskadi, the centralizing nature of the Spanish state, and monopoly capital in general. ETA-V went so far as to applaud the solidarity of co-op workers with managers in upholding the firings of the strike leaders whom they perceived as agitators. To ETA-V, the co-ops represented the economic autonomy of Euskadi and the kind of cross-class, nationalist project they supported. Indeed, there were some ETA members and radical nationalists in high positions in the cooperatives. However, the article also implied that ETA-V understood that stratification in the cooperatives and the effects of the cooperatives on Mondragón's working class were more complicated. The article ended with a promise that ETA-V members would "devote themselves to a more profound study of the cooperatives in recognition of the great political importance of the Mondragón system for Euskadi." It called upon all of the "Basque socialists, patriots," to analyze closely the cooperative phenomenon.[20] In actuality, those in the orbit of ETA-V did not undertake this analysis, and remained silent on the issue of the cooperatives until 1989.

Over the next few years, radical nationalists founded several groups and parties in an effort to link political organization with military action and to create a socialist organization that could fit a nationalist struggle. Radical

nationalists confronted the problem of the organization and struggle of workers within the nationalist movement by founding the syndicate LAB (see Bruni
1989; Clark 1984). In 1975, the Basque Socialist Coordinating Committee (Koordinadora Abertzale Sozialista [KAS]) was formed, and in 1978, Herri Batasuna was founded to bring radical nationalism into the electoral arena (Bruni
1989, 289–94). All of these groups were part of the larger national liberation
movement MLNV.

When I interviewed cooperative workers in 1989 (chapters 5 through 7),
they were unhappy about many of the same things that the leftist factions of
ETA wrote about in the 1970s—especially the high-pressure work pace, their
lack of faith in the Social Council, and apathy among co-op workers. I often
heard the charge that the cooperatives were degenerating under the requirements of competing in a capitalist economy. But even if the charges made by
the factions of ETA rang true, their political conclusions—that the co-ops were
no better than fascism or that co-ops served *only* to fool the working class—
seemed extreme to most townspeople.

The historic ETA's reluctance to criticize the cooperatives meant that it
neglected these shop-floor concerns. Later, the syndicate LAB found itself in a
similar bind. Like ETA, LAB had a handful of affiliates who were managers or
engineers in the cooperatives. This reflected its dual character as a nationalist
and working-class organization, and contributed to its popular appeal. (It also
reflects a major difference between unions and syndicates, the latter encouraging individual membership among all levels of employees—and this membership is often politically motivated—while unions restrict membership to
workers in organized shops.) But it also made its position in the cooperatives
complicated, since it had to balance information and analyses from both management and shop-floor sources. As the situation in the cooperatives deteriorated throughout the late 1970s and into the 1980s, LAB repeatedly argued that
the co-ops were not as bad as private firms; at least co-op jobs were secure and
cooperative democracy held some (unrealized) promise. However, as we will
see in the next chapter, this response was inadequate to the lived experience of
the cooperative workers and the town.

Conclusions

In analyzing the local-level structure of Basque nationalism in the town
of Elgeta under the Franco regime, Heiberg shows that Basque nationalists built
a parallel universe to the official one organized by the regime. The elements of
this universe were ikastolas, Basque fiestas, cultural revival, and the cooperatives of the Mondragón system. Elgeta's cooperative furniture factory, Dormicoop, was part of what Heiberg calls the "Basque moral community"—the
world that was popularly seen as challenging the anti-Basque, pro-Spanish

world. She further claims that when the radical nationalist movement was consolidated in Elgeta in the 1970s, Dormicoop became part of that moral community (1989, 223–25).

> The Mondragón cooperatives had always looked to Basque nationalism for their political inspiration and ideological cohesion. Whereas the Mondragón cooperatives had openly propounded their cooperativist philosophy to the *socios* (members) of Dormicoop by 1975, the nationalist view of the cooperative movement was absorbed rapidly into the ideas the *pueblo* held concerning Dormicoop. Cooperativism was the Basque nationalist mode of production. (Heiberg 1989, 225)

The role that nationalist politics played in the Ulgor strike supports Heiberg's point. Managers were able to draw on the notion that the cooperatives fit within the Basque moral order, and, thus, to challenge them (as the strikers had) was anti-Basque. However, as I noted above, Heiberg does not adequately distinguish between conservative and radical nationalisms and the communities they bind. To accept the cooperatives into the Basque world was much more complicated for the radical nationalists than for PNV. As socialists, ETA and its supporters were committed to the class question in a way that PNV was not. Their silence on the co-ops is better understood as a compromise—the consequence of the cross-class nature of their constituency and the significance of the cooperative system to any concept of an economically sovereign Euskadi—than as a full-fledged embrace.

The silence was palpable in Mondragón. Radical nationalists routinely distinguish between their conception of Basqueness, which they call "euskaldun" (meaning Basque speaker, or Basque, and connoting authenticity), and PNV's Basqueness, which they derogatorily call "vasquismo" (a Spanish-language word conveying an ersatz, manipulated or sentimentalized identity). Given that radical nationalists dissected this difference on many issues, including cultural revival, they undoubtedly could have made a distinction between vasquismo and that which was euskaldun (truly Basque and radical) in the co-ops. But they did not. This silence may not have been a problem in Elgeta, but it was to have serious implications for Mondragón's working class, a full 50 percent of whom were cooperators.

After the Ulgor strike, cooperators had the reputation of not expressing solidarity with the rest of Mondragón's working class, and they were seen as increasingly isolated in their own privileged work world. While this did not translate into social isolation—friendship groups remained mixed, cooperators frequented the same bars as other workers, and families had members who were both cooperators and employees of private firms—cooperators became less and less interested in labor causes. The Church expressed concern over this issue.

In his essay, "Conflictos en el Movimiento Cooperativo," the Secretary of Social Affairs of the Diocese wrote that cooperators had grown "egotistical" and had become estranged from their fellow workers. He urged them to become more involved in the labor movement.

When the economic crisis grew serious in the 1980s, co-op workers were ill equipped to respond. They lacked internal organizations and alliances with outside syndicates that would have built a strong rank and file to confront the problems of automation, flexible work schedules, the hiring of contract laborers, and increased work pace that would come to characterize their work lives. Furthermore, LAB was weaker in Mondragón than it was in other, similarly industrialized towns, and the militants of Herri Batasuna were less involved in Mondragón's labor movement than they were in other working-class towns of Euskadi. That is, the radical nationalist movement was weak on labor issues, a situation that was a striking reversal from the Mondragón of the early to mid-century, when workers were more likely to be socialistic than their neighbors in nearby towns. The implications of this situation for workplace relations and shop-floor conditions are the subjects of the next chapters.

5

Comparing a Cooperative and a Standard Private Firm

Every year, Mondragón receives social tourists from all over the world; they come not for vacation but to experience the cooperatives. These visitors have read books, scholarly articles, and magazine accounts of the Mondragón system. They expect to find that working conditions in cooperative factories will be better than those in standard private firms, that cooperators will be actively involved in running their factories, and that cooperators will be more satisfied in their jobs than workers in private firms.

In 1990, I had the opportunity to join a tour for members of the World Sociology Congress. They were already in Madrid for a conference and made a side trip to spend three days in Mondragón. The tour included a trip to the headquarters of the cooperative bank, Caja Laboral; the research and development center, Ikerlan; the Polytechnical and Professional School; and the showcase Fagor refrigerator factory (previously called Ulgor). They also attended talks by several speakers on the history, organization, and economic profile of the system. Many congress members were surprised by the "efficiency" and "modernity" of the plants; the cooperatives were more automated than they had imagined. They had questions and comments about what they perceived as a speaker's emphasis on efficiency and production rather than the more human dimensions of work. Some were concerned about workers' health and safety and asked our tour guide about safety procedures in the plants. There were few questions, however, about the town beyond the cooperative complex.

Social tourists typically stay in a hotel outside of town and take their meals at Ikasbide, the management training center, which hosts many of the system's guests. Located in the nearby town of Aretxabaleta, Ikasbide is housed in a beautifully restored manor, with a library and modern conference facilities. The meals are exquisitely prepared Basque dishes. During their stay, most visitors see little of the town[1] and interact mainly with managers whose job it is to represent the cooperatives to outsiders. Not surprisingly, then, social tourists are offered a rather normative view of the cooperatives which tends to confirm their expectations about labor relations.[2]

When I first visited Mondragón in 1987 to carry out preliminary field-work, I had many of these same expectations. It was partly chance that redirected me. Not having made prior arrangements to stay in Ikasbide (and, in any case, not having a large enough research fellowship to afford to), I looked in town for a place to stay. I was truly fortunate to meet three young people who offered to put me up in their apartment. When I told them I had come to study the cooperatives, they decided to invite a friend of theirs to dinner. Begoña was in her late twenties and had been a member of one of the Fagor co-ops since she was eighteen years old. She had always worked on the assembly line. Over dinner, she told me that she felt exploited at work, "just like any worker in any firm."

"What about the fact that you share ownership of the firm?" I asked.

"It means nothing to me" she replied. Begoña also said she felt "apathetic" about the governance of the cooperative. "I only go to the annual meetings of the General Assembly because it's required. Everybody goes because they have to. If we didn't have to, we wouldn't go." What she resented more than anything was being told that she was participating in managing the cooperative and that "it is your firm."

As Begoña spoke, I began to hear the words "participate," "cooperate," and "your firm" in a new way; listening to her, they sounded imposing. Had I gotten the sense that Begoña was alone in her feelings, I would not have taken her complaints so seriously. However, she continually spoke for her fellow workers, implying that her experiences of alienation and feeling manipulated by cooperativist ideology were common. Furthermore, most of those at dinner had lived their entire lives among cooperators and did not seem surprised by what she said. To the contrary, they offered anecdotal evidence of instances of workers' apathy and frustration that they had heard from friends and relatives.

Begoña's words stayed with me as I designed my research. I decided that it was important to evaluate the Mondragón cooperatives from the points of view of those who worked on the shop floor as well as those of local syndicalists and political activists. I determined that an effective way to do this was to compare a cooperative and a standard private firm. When I returned to Mondragón in 1989, I undertook this comparison.

I chose the cooperative Fagor Clima, which manufactures gas water heaters. With 250 members, it was neither too large nor too small. Large size had been discussed as detrimental to the cooperative spirit (Whyte and Whyte 1988, 91), and, conversely, a small co-op would have made labor–management relations smoother than average. Finding a suitable private firm proved more difficult, but, in the process, I learned about Mondragón's business environment and the effects of the cooperatives on the labor relations in private businesses, which I discuss in this chapter.

In this chapter, I also consider whether cooperative democracy represents workers more effectively than standard conflictual labor relations. I first compare cooperative Social Councils with Workers' Councils in private firms at a normative level. I then compare the actual functioning of both councils and discuss two instances in which these normative rights are turned into powers.

In Search of a Private Firm

"How does the quality and extent of worker participation in the Mondragón cooperatives compare with the prevailing situation in private industry in Spain" (Whyte and Whyte 1988, 209)? As Whyte and Whyte note, there have been no large-scale surveys that provide the data necessary to answer this question.[3] Though the literature on the Mondragón system asserts that, for workers, cooperatives are better than private firms, the claim is largely ungrounded in comparative research.

The sole comparative study was conducted by Bradley and Gelb (1983). They surveyed 1,080 members of fifteen cooperatives, using 280 workers in two private firms as a control group. One of their control firms was Mayc's plant in Gasteiz (approximately 40 kilometers from Mondragón). The other was Unión Cerrajera in Mondragón. Their intention was to test the hypothesis that identification with the firm increased productivity in the cooperatives. They asked cooperative and noncooperative workers about their workplaces, and found that cooperators felt significantly less inhibited in voicing their opinions and grievances than did respondents from private firms, an observation other researchers have made as well (e.g., Greenwood and González et al. 1989, 119–50). They also found that cooperators perceived considerably less social division between workers and managers. Finally, they reported that fully three-fourths of cooperators did not support a "large" role for trade unions in the cooperatives (Bradley and Gelb 1983, 40–56).

Bradley and Gelb's study, however, misses the insights and confidences that come with longer acquaintance and a broader research strategy. As the authors themselves note, they decided to conduct a survey rather than interviews because Basques are "reluctant to discuss sensitive points with outsiders" (1983, 90). After completing the survey, they did conduct some interviews, but only with managers. These interviews provided them with more in-depth information but privileged managers' points of view over that of workers. Moreover, Bradley and Gelb did not draw on observation to strengthen, contradict, or interpret the survey data. I set out to undertake a more holistic and contextualized comparison.

I visited more than twenty cooperatively and privately held factories in the area. Typically, I began my visits to factories by completing an interview schedule with the owner or personnel manager (covering business history, labor relations, management style, demographic data, product line, market, and the productions process). He or she then gave me a tour of the plant.[4] I was looking for two firms that were roughly the same size, with similar enough product lines and production processes so that workers would have similar jobs, skills, and working conditions. Furthermore, both firms had to be fairly typical for the area. As Bradley and Gelb note, this task proved to be difficult (1983, 39).

Majority stock in Unión Cerrajera had just been sold to new owners who were decapitalizing the firm. Whole sections of the plant were closed or relocated and workers were laid off. The work force in the remaining sections was also reduced. By 1989, the plant employed 688 workers, half the number it had employed eight years earlier. All indications were that more jobs would be lost in the coming year, and workers as well as low- and mid-level managers were fearful and demoralized. (Indeed, more jobs were lost and the ailing company was finally sold to its employees.) These conditions would not make for a fair comparison. Other firms were too small, and still others had dissimilar product lines and production processes.

I also encountered a peculiar phenomenon in Mondragón. Two small private firms had adopted cooperative-like practices. These firms had weak Workers' Councils and low rates of syndical affiliation among workers. J. I. Uribari is the owner of one of these firms. He is in his sixties and a contemporary of the first generation of co-op members. He told me of his approach to business:

When I was first married, I lived in San Andrés [a less desirable neighborhood]. I have my friends from childhood. They work in stores, in factories, small businesses.

I went to the Polytechnical school; I follow Father José María Arizmendiarrieta's teachings. He molded me. I once went to Father José María and asked if it was moral to look for loopholes to avoid paying taxes, and he told me Yes, "but the money is not yours." You have to invest in sharing. Profit sharing is a good investment. The best patrimony is workers who work hard. . . . I could sell the business now and live wherever I want, but I have a commitment.

J. I. Uribari believed that his firm embodied the teachings of Father Arizmendiarrieta—egalitarianism, solidarity, and respect—as much as the cooperatives did. Each year at Christmas he gave workers envelopes containing a share of the company's profits. He said he learned from Father Arizmendiarrieta that personal relationships with workers were better than syndicalism; thus, he held meetings to keep employees apprised of business progress and future plans. While his workers have participated in solidarity strikes, he told me proudly that they have never waged an internal strike. I interviewed J. I. Uribari for nearly three hours (other interviews in private firms usually lasted an hour and a half). He wanted some of the recognition the cooperatives had gotten. He felt that he, too, was part of the cooperative movement.

The owner of the second firm is a contemporary of J. I. Uribari and also studied with Father Arizmendiarrieta. I interviewed the personnel director, and at the end of the interview I asked (as I usually did) how the cooperative experience had affected his business practices:

> We have a policy to get the best workers and pay them well [the average wage is 150% of the area average]. They do a special kind of job with high technology. We've never had a strike for economic [internal] reasons [only solidarity strikes].

After the interview was over I headed to the center of town, to meet friends at a bar. They told me that this firm is known for making low-interest loans to employees on the occasions of their weddings or when they want to buy cars or apartments. These workers are later pressured into repaying the loans by working overtime and weekends, something that their contract prohibits. In this firm, no members of syndicates had been elected to the Workers' Council, and only five of a total of eighty-three employees were affiliated with syndicates.

Neither of these firms was suitable for my comparison, because of their unusual records of labor peace, but they point to the effect that the cooperatives had on the local business climate. These firms shifted my perspective on the cooperatives, since their labor practices fell between those of cooperatives and standard firms. I began to see co-ops not so much as a distinct business form but as part of a continuum of business styles. Moreover, the cooperative-like management practices of noncooperative firms indicate the effects of the Mondragón model on the town itself. Since the cooperative model has earned a reputation as the best way to do business, private owners experiment with and implement aspects of labor–management cooperation, and their efforts subverted independent syndicates.

Some local owners experience the cooperative model as a burden. One interviewee in his mid-thirties, the son of the owner of a private firm, brought up the comparison with the cooperatives before I had a chance to ask.

> The cooperatives have it much easier since they don't have syndicates always watching them. The Social Council is a real source of support. I have to give the syndicates financial reports that they can bring

somewhere else and scrutinize them. They look for anything they can have a confrontation about. Here it's all confrontation.

This man had taken over the family firm while his brothers went to work in the cooperatives. One is an engineer, the other a high-level manager. Both, he told me, are very "cooperativista" (procooperative, or supportive of cooperative ideology). What struck me about this interview was the resentment he expressed. He felt that cooperatives' labor relations gave them a business advantage, and he seemed to feel maligned by their example versus his firm's record of strikes and conflicts. I considered studying his firm further, but it was too small—he had just over one hundred employees—and had a more combative labor climate than most of Mondragón's firms.

I extended my search outside of Mondragón to neighboring Bergara. There I found Mayc, S.A., a top-loading washing machine manufacturer that was in the same domestic-appliances sector as many of the Fagor cooperatives. Like Clima, Mayc was mid-sized, with 612 employees. However, the fact of Mayc's location was problematic, given the different political histories of Mondragón and Bergara. In recent years, however, these distinctions have not been manifest in significant differences in election results. Furthermore, syndicate locals in Bergara have close ties with Mondragón, since the comarcal offices are located in Mondragón, where positions and tactics for the area are formulated. Syndicalists I talked to believed that Mayc was the best choice I could make.[5] Thus, I decided to compare Mayc with the cooperative Fagor Clima.

Fagor Clima

Fagor Clima (known as Clima) produces gas water heaters for domestic use. Originally it was a section of the Fagor refrigerator plant, but it became an independent enterprise in 1984 (and in 1991 reunited with other Fagor branches to form Fagor Electrodomésticos). It is located alongside the Deba River at the edge of town, in the same industrial complex as the Fagor refrigerator plant and the central offices for the Fagor Group.

When I first visited Clima in the spring of 1989, 250 people worked there (they would accept a group of fifty new members six months later). All but a handful were from Mondragón. Fifty were not members but hired laborers who worked on temporary contracts. About eighty were women, and the average age of the work force was forty-five. The average anticipio payment for a production worker was 128,000 pesetas a month; in addition, two bonuses of one month's earnings were paid in a year. A typical annual payment for Clima workers was 1,792,000 pesetas (US$17,568 at the 1990 exchange rate), which was equivalent to the wages of local workers in private

FIGURE 17

Entrance to Fagor factories and central offices; Fagor Clima to the right. Credit: Sharryn Kasmir.

FIGURE 18

Water heaters produced at Fagor Clima. Credit: Sharryn Kasmir.

firms and provided what was considered by local standards to be a comfortable lifestyle. A single earner in a family of four could afford a mortgage on an apartment (if it was purchased before the real estate boom of the late 1980s), car payments, and an annual vacation for the family, camping, perhaps, in a coastal town in the province of Galicia or in the Pyrenees mountains. On a more mundane level, this salary also bought after-work rounds in the bars, paid for school tuition or after-school lessons, and provided an allowance for teenage children who frequented bars on weekends with their friends.

A head of department with a rating of 2.8 earned 3,850,000 pesetas (US $37,745). These differences were very slim by regional standards, but they were important indicators of inequality to workers. Both also received a share of annual profits. One high-level manager showed me his bank book. "Look what I have after twenty years in the cooperatives." He had US$35,000 in earnings which would become his upon retirement. By showing me his bank book, he meant to convey that his financial rewards were modest, that he was not motivated by money. Since profits are paid in proportion to job rating, manual workers with the same seniority have smaller savings accounts. He lived differently from workers I knew, but the material differences were small. He had a nicer (but still modest) car, lived in a nicer home, and his son was a bit more expensively dressed than many of the teenagers I knew. While these differences were modest, they coincided with more significant social differences. I never ran into him in town bars, and only occasionally did I see his son in bars frequented by other people his age.

In Clima, there were 160 blue-collar workers in preassembly, putting together parts and components or operating presses and other heavy machinery to make the bodies of the heaters. The majority of the machinists were men. Much of the parts work was done by women in individual stations outfitted with new computer-assisted machine tools. The other half of the plant worked on the assembly lines. Since preassembly had recently been modernized, two shifts were introduced in order to amortize the investment. Some of the plant was on flex time, allowing workers to adjust their own schedules between the hours of 7:00 A.M. and 4:00 P.M.—this was very popular among workers. Clima was much like other Fagor cooperatives in its market considerations, production process, level of automation, and job skills, and Clima's workers were like other cooperators. They were neither more dissatisfied with their jobs nor more active than co-op workers elsewhere.

Mayc

Mayc was founded in 1941 by three families from Bergara. Over the years, they sold small amounts of stock but retained majority ownership of the

FIGURE. 19

Mayc, S.A. Credit: Sharryn Kasmir.

firm. When the owners experienced financial trouble in the recessionary year of 1981, the Fagor Group communicated its interest in buying the plant. The possibility of Mayc becoming a cooperative was discussed among workers. I interviewed members of the Trotskyist Liga Komunista Iraultza (LKI) about the proposed sale, and they told me that workers had voted against it because they believe that cooperativization was not in their best interest; they felt they would be better off in a private firm, protected by their syndicates. Members of the radical nationalist syndicate LAB remembered events differently. According to their version, the majority of workers favored the sale, "preferring to fall into the hands of the cooperatives than the hands of a multinational." According to LAB, the owners of Mayc and the directors of Fagor—not the workers— decided against the sale.

Whichever version of events one accepts, the fact is that a formal offer of purchase was never made by Fagor. The discrepancies in the stories are interesting, because they follow the lines of the 1970s splits in ETA that I discussed in chapter 4. LKI echoed the arguments of the leftist factions of ETA from which it evolved—that cooperatives subverted syndicates and class-based action. LAB, like the historic ETA, from which it evolved, favored cooperatives because Basque-owned capital was preferable to Spanish or foreign capital.

The fact that the sale had been discussed among workers was important for my comparison because it meant that they had collectively considered the pros and cons of a cooperative firm over a private firm.

In 1992, the local owners of Mayc sold 64 percent of the shares to the Italian multinational Candy. At the time of the sale, Mayc had eight percent of the Spanish washing-machine market, with sales of three hundred thousand.[6] In 1989, Mayc employed 612 people; by the end of 1992, 129 jobs had been eliminated. This was precisely the situation LAB warned about regarding foreign ownership. (These jobs may be regained in 1996 [see page 141].)

Mayc manufactured its top-loading washing machines under the brand name Ostein. It also produced under contract for a number of other companies including Fagor and Westinghouse, a common practice whereby companies put their own brand names on products manufactured by their competitors. In its early days of operation, Mayc produced small motors. Later it manufactured washing machines (using in-house motors) and hot-water heaters, using its foundry to make its own parts. By spring 1989, Mayc was producing its last water heaters. In 1985, the state's industrial conversion plan, prepared for Spain's full entry into the European Community, had concentrated water heaters in three firms throughout Spain. Fagor Clima was one of three firms to receive credits and loans to modernize its water heater plant. The Fagor Group as a whole consolidated its status in the household-appliance sector. Consequently, Clima was able to offer full cooperative membership to fifty new people in 1991, while other factories in the area, including Mayc, reduced their work forces.

The 1985 plan allowed Mayc to apply for government credits of two billion pesetas to modernize its washing-machine plant, on the condition that it cease production of other products. Mayc received the credits and began its reorganization in 1987. Most of the money was spent on automated machinery and on a plan to reduce the size of assembly lines; both were requirements for receiving state assistance. In 1989, Mayc had five short assembly lines and two long ones, one of which had two hundred workers and operated on two shifts. The second shift became the object of a labor–management conflict discussed below.

The only production done at Mayc after the summer of 1989 was assembly of washing machines. This is a common trajectory for heavy manufacturing both in Euskadi and in other industrial centers. Once, the hallmark of mass production was vertical integration, whereby a single factory made a product from start to finish. But vertical integration was largely defunct by the 1980s. It was replaced with a system of subcontracting smaller firms to produce pieces and do preassembly work. This subcontracting system is a key feature of flexible accumulation and is at the heart of the economic boom in central and northern Italy, because it shifts costlier, labor-intensive phases of production to shops which are often non-unionized and which pay lower wages (often to female workers) and rely on family labor (Blim 1990; Enloe 1989). Subcontracting similarly contributes substantially to Toyota's success (Keeney and Florida 1988).

At Mayc, 498 of the employees were manual workers; 114 were clerical staff, engineers, and managers. The personnel managers of Clima counted ninety nonmanual workers (nearly one-third of the work force), a fact that reveals the middle-heavy profile of the cooperatives, where there are considerably more low- and mid-level managers than in private firms in the area. The average age of Mayc employees was forty-two. One hundred twenty-eight women were employed, only 21 percent of the labor force as compared with 32 percent in Clima. Ninety-eight women worked on the shop floor and most of the remaining thirty in clerical jobs. Only one woman was a manager. In the co-ops, most women employees also work in low-skilled production jobs, but a handful hold engineering or managerial positions. This reflects the greater, though still unequal, opportunities for employment and advancement for women in the cooperatives (see Hacker and Elcorobairutia 1987; Hacker 1989).

The average salary for manual workers at Mayc was 130,000 pesetas per month with two yearly bonuses of 130,000 each, for a yearly wage of 1,820,000 (US$17,843 at the 1990 exchange rate) slightly higher than the average earnings for Clima workers. This was a typical wage for the area and provided workers with a standard of living similar to Clima workers. Sixty-five to eighty workers were on short-term contracts—as much as 13 percent of the total labor force worked without the promise of permanent employment. The cooperatives, too, hired contract workers.

Often the children of long-time Mayc employees, temporary workers earned monthly salaries that were comparable to those of permanent workers, but the contracts were for short periods of time. Six months was common and one year was the maximum. Contract workers cannot therefore afford the lifestyle of permanent employees. Many manage to buy a car, are able to spend freely in bars and restaurants, and take vacations considered by permanent workers to be extravagant (for example, to New York or South America). However, they cannot buy an apartment (there are few rentals) and begin an independent life outside of their parents' homes. This division between temporary and permanent workers manifested itself as a generational difference. Unlike their parents, working-class people in their twenties do not create stable homes for themselves. Rather, for the most part, they spent their incomes on consumer goods and services.

With this introduction to each firm, I turn my attention to labor relations and to addressing these questions: How effective is the Social Council in representing cooperative workers? How does it compare to the Workers' Council in a private firm?

A Normative View of the Social Council and the Workers' Council

In chapter 1, I outlined the committees that plan and manage production, sales, and personnel in individual cooperative factories: the Governing Council is an elected body that functions like a board of directors; the manager is appointed by the Governing Council to oversee daily operations; the Management Council oversees and advises the manager; and the General Assembly is constituted by the entire membership of the cooperative and convenes once a year to ratify business plans and policy. All of these organs draw cooperators into decision making and management as co-owners of the cooperative. The Social Council is the only body that convenes cooperators as workers (Greenwood and González et al. 1989, 68; Whyte and Whyte 1988, 213). Social Council members, like Workers' Council members, are elected. Typically, one representative is elected for each section of the plant, including the engineering and management offices; thus, the Social Council represents the interests of both production workers and managers. This is also the case in private firms, where low- and mid-level managers are represented by the Workers' Council.

The Social Council was introduced in Ulgor in 1957. It was modeled on the Factory Councils (*jurados de empresas*) that were introduced by the Franco regime. The 1947 decree that constituted the Factory Councils charged them with helping management to improve production, reduce waste, and increase efficiency; ensuring that management complied with all social legislation; advising on issues of physical, moral, cultural, and social betterment of workers, including professional training; being informed on production figures, supplies, and deliveries; and keeping abreast of bonuses, piecework, and contracts (Larrañaga 1986, 11–13).

The fascist-designed Factory Councils had a dual character. On the one hand, they were intended to protect workers, even if their scope was limited to pay and safety. On the other hand, they were to assist management in running the factory. The cooperative Social Council, founded while Factory Councils still operated in standard firms, mimicked this dual character. After Franco's death, independent syndicates were legalized and Workers' Councils were introduced; Workers' Councils took on a confrontational form, but the cooperative Social Council retained its twin mission. The Social Council is both the workers' voice of opposition to management and an extension of management's voice on the shop floor. Today, the powers and responsibilities of the Social Council include the following:

• improving decision making by integrating, or at least taking into consideration, different points of view regarding business objectives and plans;
• examining business plans and contributing proposals;

- analyzing and proposing changes in cooperative rules and norms;
- participating in studies and proposing alternatives regarding the organization of work and labor relations;
- preventing accidents and monitoring health and safety;
- monitoring social security and health benefits;
- participating in annual evaluations of pay rates;
- keeping workers informed of management projects and decisions of a daily nature as well as annual business plans, proposals for new products, and the economic condition of the cooperative;
- informing workers regarding the activities of the Social Council and disseminating information on the mechanisms for participation;
- maintaining an open dialogue with all members so that they can raise questions, proposals, and inquietudes, and facilitating the flow of this information back to management;
- analyzing the objectives and methods for improving labor relations;
- evaluating the system of information flow from managers to workers and vice versa;
- deciding to submit to a vote of the General Assembly whether or not workers will participate in solidarity strikes;
- establishing subcommittees and study committees, and developing a list of candidates for the Management Council. (Larrañaga 1986, 19–25)

Like the Social Council, the Workers' Council in a private firm is elected to represent workers to management, yet its nature and scope is different. Spanish labor legislation drafted in 1988 gives the Workers' Council the rights and responsibilities to:

- receive information trimesterly on production figures, sales, production plans, and future employment projections;
- be informed of the firm's finances, including accounts and shareholders;
- inform workers of any plans that the company has regarding restructuring the plant, layoffs, training programs, changes in work organization, new quality control systems, time-motion studies, productivity-linked bonuses, or job ratings;
- transmit information on any change in ownership of the firm that might affect employment;
- be familiar with labor contracts;
- be informed of the penalties and sanctions applied to workers who break rules;
- know the rate and causes of absenteeism, accidents, work-related illnesses and be familiar with studies regarding work environments;

- actively ensure that the company abides by all regulations concerning social security, unemployment, and health and safety and take legal action when necessary;
- participate in the management of social projects for the benefit of workers and their families;
- collaborate with management to maintain and increase productivity, in accordance with the agreement made in the annual contract. (*Estatuto de los Trabajadores* 1988, 64–66)

Clearly, the Workers' Council is conceived as a body that challenges management. In an environment where labor and management are seen as adversaries, the Workers' Council is prevented from participating in decision making, which is management's prerogative. Conversely, the cooperative Social Council is designed for an environment in which workers and managers are assumed to share many of the same interests. In the event that something goes wrong, the Social Council is supposed to defend workers, but the normative situation is one of collaboration on planning, communication, and decision making rather than conflict over managerial decisions. Which is a better strategy for representing workers?

This question goes to the heart of current trends in labor–management relations in Western Europe, the United States, and Japan. Advocates of labor–management cooperation schemes suggest that workers, along with owners, benefit when unions adopt less confrontational tactics or when firms are not unionized at all. Similarly, proponents of the Mondragón model suppose that since workers have broad rights to participate in the management of their firms, they have better working conditions, are less alienated, and are generally more satisfied with their work lives. To evaluate these arguments, it is necessary to look beyond their respective rights and to examine the actual functioning and the real powers of the Social and Workers' Councils (cf. Greenwood and González et al. 1989, 86).

Rights versus Powers

The Social Council has considerable and comprehensive democratic rights that the Workers' Council does not, but in my interviews with Social Council members, I learned that there were several obstacles in their path. An important difference between the Social and Workers' Councils is the compensation time allotted to representatives. Spanish labor legislation establishes the number of paid hours delegates receive for council work. In a private firm with fewer than 100 workers, the Workers' Council members are given fifteen hours per month; twenty hours in a firm with 100–250 workers; thirty hours for 251–500; thirty-five for 501–750; and forty hours for larger firms (*Estatuto de los Trabajadores* 1988, 62–69). Cooperative Social Council members do not get nearly this much time. Cooperative bylaws provide that they have two meetings a month, and are given about one paid hour per month to report to their sections on what transpired at those meetings. Beyond this, they have little time to study plans and prepare responses.

I interviewed members of Social Councils in several Fagor cooperatives, and they all felt that they did not have enough time to do their jobs adequately (something Workers' Council members never said). Antxon, a line worker and Social Council representative at a Fagor cooperative, explained how lack of time limited participation in the Social Council:

Each Social Council representative gets only three-quarters of an hour each month to report to his twenty-five constituents what occurred in the monthly meetings, one on a social theme, the other on an economic. This is not enough time, especially if you want a certain level of participation.

We are not given a room to talk. We have to talk right in the factory, and there is a lot of noise. We're not given any tools, like an overhead projector to display figures.

Furthermore, Antxon said, the amount of time they were allowed to do their work was unclear to them. Carmen, a Social Council member, told me:

Each time you have a concrete problem you want to deal with, you have to ask for free time. If you ask for time for a concrete thing, you will usually get four to five hours. In an average year, we get less than twenty hours to do our Social Council work. Everything we do is on our own time.

Antxon said:

Management is paid to develop plans, and when they present them to us, they look very "bonito" [nice, pretty]. We are supposed to present an alternative to these plans, but it is all we can do to criticize them. After work we have to spend our own time reading and analyzing the plan. We are in no position to actually prepare alternative plans.

Once, I spent forty hours preparing a document that was to decide whether or not there would be a vote to censure management. Not to do anything, just to decide if we would take it to a vote. The vote was 211 to 167 in favor of calling the vote. But we were stopped from doing more because we didn't really have viable plans outlined.

> They [the other Social Council members] have this same problem. They don't get free time during work to prepare position papers, do economic studies or prepare any kind of viable alternative. They get a few hours per month to do their work. I take more, but the others are not as forceful.

The flexible nature of time for Social Council work depended too much on the individual council member; individuals who were less comfortable asserting their rights got less time. Moreover, the time they were allotted was inadequate.

Antxon raised another concern about the Social Council; not only are members hampered by time limitations, but they do not have the professional expertise they need in order to exercise democracy. While syndicates have staff lawyers, economists, and engineers who help Workers' Councils with the challenges of evaluating management proposals, Antxon explained, "We are not free to use a lawyer or an economist from outside the co-op to help us prepare any documents. If we were to do so, we'd get expelled." It is against co-op regulations to seek external professional help. Instead, the Social Council is supposed to rely on co-op staff, but this is often impractical, as these staff people prepared the plans in the first place. Council members do not always trust them to revise their own projects. Antxon believes that lack of access to outside professionals impeded workers' ability to exercise their democratic rights to manage their firms (see also Whyte and Whyte 1988, 216).

Greenwood and González et al. (1989, 95–150) conducted a study of co-operators' opinions and perceptions of their system of participation. The authors are themselves a team of Fagor members (unfortunately, overwhelmingly from the ranks of management [168–69]) who designed and carried out their own research with the assistance of anthropologist Davydd Greenwood. They first distributed a questionnaire to a sample of Fagor members, then followed up the questionnaires with interviews and, later, round-table discussions in which people from all job categories participated. During the discussions, an interesting contradiction emerged. Cooperators felt that they were inundated with technical information about accounts, business plans, and production, but they also believed that key information was being kept from them (145–49). Antxon also talked about this:

> They [management] give the members a lot of things to read. Rather than reading it all, members look to someone who they agree with politically and ask him what he thinks. Then they have the same opinion as he does.

A good deal of the frustration that workers feel about information (which may be expressed in their contradictory statements) can be attributed to their inability to make effective use of it. It is not the case that in private firms, where less information is shared, workers master all of it themselves. They also look to someone they trust inside the plant to interpret information, but this falls well within the expectations. Similarly, members of the Workers' Councils are not expected to interpret the material themselves but to seek the assistance of labor lawyers, engineers, and economists who are hired by the syndicates to interpret data and plans and to analyze effects on the work force. All members of the cooperative are given a great deal of information, which they simply cannot get through. Social Council members who make the effort to synthesize the material often find they need help interpreting information, but they are restricted to seeking the advice of cooperative personnel, who produced the information in the first place and are often seen as being unlikely to have manual workers' best interests at heart.[7]

Workers' apathy is another reason commonly given for the ineffectiveness of the Social Council. Greenwood and González et al. (1989, 114) found that, on questionnaires, many cooperators expressed distance from or disillusionment with the cooperative, but when asked to explain during interviews, responses were more contradictory. Nonetheless, apathy was a theme in my after-work conversations with workers and interviews with managers and Social Council members. Usually individuals are blamed. The Social Council requires a lot of commitment, people explain, and the strength of the council depends on its members. Unfortunately, workers are often apathetic, and they are uninterested in serving on the Social Council. Rather than voting for the person who they feel is most likely to fight for them, as is customary in private firms, they "vote for the new guy, the jerk who doesn't know any better and can't get out of it," as one cooperator told me. This apathy limits effective use of the democratic rights of the Social Council—that is, of turning rights into power.

There may be ideological obstacles as well. In 1981, the central offices of the Fagor Group authorized a study of the Social Councils in individual factories. In Ederlan, a foundry located three kilometers from Mondragón in the town of Aretxabaleta, a team of Social Council representatives found that the Social Council did not function as it was supposed to. Representatives did not attend meetings, and even when they did, they were disinterested. The 1981 Ederlan report sparked a controversy because it charged that the causes of apathy were not personal but structural.[8] It argued that cooperative ideology was meant to convince workers that their workplaces were free from labor–management conflict; thus, workers became apathetic and willingly ceded power to technicians and managers. Although the report did not specify the relationship between ideology, apathy, and surrendering of power, it proposed that a relationship did exist. The report further claimed that while business plans were supposed to be discussed annually by the General Assembly, in reality, workers simply rubber-stamped management plans without engaging in critical dialogue. The document concluded that the structures of democracy had to be changed in order for workers to truly participate in their firm.

The Ederlan team developed a plan for restructuring the Social Council, and designed several new positions, including a social delegate (who would be concerned with health and safety, work organization, calendars, and criticizing management business plans), and a factory council (which would keep workers informed about production issues).[9] These recommendations were never carried out by the Management Council. This suggests that disarticulating the Social Council's dual mission and clarifying its ideological character was not acceptable to management. Furthermore, the opportunity to examine possible connections among cooperative ideology, worker apathy, and passivity vis-à-vis management were lost.

Rights versus Powers: An Example from Fagor Clima

These same issues surfaced in the spring of 1989 in Fagor Clima. Members of Clima's Social Council wanted to change the process by which lower-level jobs were reassigned among workers in the plant. They wanted available jobs to be posted on the factory bulletin board, and they wanted the selection process standardized, procedures that would be followed in any union shop in the United States or in local private firms. Maite, a member of the Clima Social Council, explained the Social Coun-cil's position:

For the lowest jobs, with the lowest ratings of 1.0 to 1.3, when a position opens up, they don't bother to put it on the board so that people can apply. The supervisor or the department of personnel decides who to give it to. We wanted it to be fair. We wanted a formula. Ten points for basic familiarity with the job (which more or less everyone has). Ten points for seniority. Ten points for speaking Euskera if it requires relations with others. . . . Ten points that the supervisor can give you at his/her discretion. . . . In this way, they can't just decide themselves.

Management rejected the proposal, and Social Council members looked for a way to communicate their message. Maite described their strategy:

We searched for a cooperative bylaw which would allow us to disband [the Social Council]. It took us a long time, but we found a bylaw that required the Social Council to step down if the majority of workers signed a petition requesting their resignation. This bylaw was written to be a check on a Social Council that was not functioning properly. It was never

conceived as a tool of protest for the Social Council itself. The Social
Council dissolved itself in protest of our limited powers to be involved in
management decisions.

Maite had also been a leader of the 1974 strike in Ulgor and was, at the time of
our interview, a member of Kooperatibisten Taldea, a small group of co-op
workers, many of whom had been affiliated with leftist factions of ETA in the
1970s (see pp. 114-18). She told me that, just like in 1974, managers told her
fellow workers that she was a "troublemaker," "españolista" (she is ethnically
Basque). This time, her co-workers, many of whom voted to fire her in 1974,
were not persuaded by this manipulation of Basqueness. They told her so and
signed the petition. Maite told me that Social Council members collected signatures from an overwhelming majority, but no managers signed. "The Social
Council members who represented their sections of the plant [the main offices,
engineering department, maintenance] didn't get involved, so they were reluctant to sign." The Social Council disbanded and the Management Council took
over its work. This was historic for the cooperatives; never before had the Social Council resigned en masse in protest. The Social Council reconvened a few
months later, as Maite said, "feeling the responsibility to do our job in representing the workers."

Rights versus Powers in Mayc's Workers' Council

A few months after the Social Council in Clima disbanded over their inability to affect the procedure for making job assignments, the Workers' Council in the privately held Mayc struggled to extend its rights to be involved in
managerial decisions. As in many other firms in this competitive sector, Mayc
managers were seeking ways to increase output. Mayc already produced
230,000 washing machines a year, but production plans called for an increase
of 5,000. Consultants from the cooperative Fagor Sistemas (which assists
firms with production flows and designs and advises on automation) were
brought in to study the plant. They determined that a lack of space on one of
the assembly lines made it impossible to meet the necessary quotas. The consultants concluded that they would have to add a second shift, affecting the
schedules of about two hundred workers and creating jobs for temporary
workers. As required by Spanish labor law, Mayc management sent an official
dispatch to the Workers' Council, informing them of the proposed changes in
work hours.

In Spain, the Workers' Council is not permitted a voice in planning production and cannot make recommendations to change the design of the plant.
Manuel, the head of Mayc's Workers' Council, explained to me how they
nonetheless got involved in the design of the assembly line:

We are allowed to respond to proposed changes in shifts. And what they proposed was an added shift. [Using that argument] we asked syndicate engineers to design a plan that would increase output without adding a shift. Our plan increased the space available for production by adding tables alongside one section of the assembly line.

Though they were not permitted to be involved in managerial planning, the Workers' Council representatives argued before the labor court that their intent was not to plan production but to protect work schedules, which was their domain.

When I left Mondragón in 1990, the two plans were still being considered by the labor court in Donosti, the provincial capital. I did not expect the Workers' Council to win. Indeed, in the short run, they lost. The second shift was introduced, with some compensations (bonuses and break time), but in 1992–1993, the Workers' Council plan was implemented. More assembly lines were added, and everyone was back to work on a regular shift. Moreover, there are plans to increase production again in 1996, and the goal is to increase the number of workers rather than add a shift. Even if they had not won, the fact that the Workers' Council gathered legal and engineering experts and did work that was considered a managerial prerogative is an important commentary on workplace democracy. This example of Workers' Council activism shows that sometimes syndicates are as involved in management as Social Councils (and sometimes more so) despite the fact that the Social Council is charged with participating in management and the Workers' Council is formally prohibited from doing so. This involvement can make a syndicalized workplace de facto democratic.

However, just as the strength of the Social Council depends in part on the commitment of its members, it takes an activist Workers' Council to do what the Mayc Workers' Council did. And, as in the case of the Social Council, both individual and structural factors matter. Syndicates do not stand up to management equally; ideology, political affiliation, under-the-table deals, and Spanish statewide accords all affect the character of local syndicates.

Perhaps the most important factor influencing the local labor movement is the Pacto de Moncloa, signed between the major syndicates and the central Spanish government in 1978. Leading syndicates and the parties with which they were affiliated—in particular, UGT and PSOE, and CCOO and the Spanish Communist Party (PCE)—were welcomed into the post-Franco parliamentary democracy. In return, the syndicates committed themselves to accepting changes in labor law. Ironically, these new laws offered fewer protections to workers than did rigid labor law under Franco, which made it difficult to lay off workers or cut back work schedules even in times of economic crisis. In 1984, legislation permitting temporary contracts was introduced in Spain.

142   *The Myth of Mondragón*

TABLE 5.1

Workers' Council Elections, Alto Deba Comarca, 1986 and 1990

Syndicate	Party	Percentage of Vote, 1986	Percentage of Vote, 1990
ELA-STV	PNV	44.18	41.51
CCOO	EMK/LKI	22.09	20.56
UGT	PSOE	16.86	14.53
LAB	HB	12.2	21.1
Independents/ Others		4.64	2.26

Source: CCOO and LAB

This followed six years of increasingly flexible uses of labor after the Mon-cloa accord (Albarracín 1987, 39–69). Thus, at the state level, UGT and CCOO cooperated in instituting a more virulent form of capitalism in Spain (Albarracín 1987, 39–69).

In Euskadi, PNV has recently combined its forces with PSOE to consti-tute a governing majority in the Basque parliament. Thus, ELA (tied to PNV) often behaves like UGT. Both syndicates often approve annual contracts with-out a fight and oppose the activism of other syndicates in factories. For ex-ample, both opposed the efforts of Mayc's Workers' Council to redesign the assembly line. It was CCOO and LAB which led that fight in Mayc, against management and against UGT and ELA.

In towns like Mondragón, where leftist factions of ETA were strong, Maoists (EMK) and especially Trotskyists (LKI), rather than PCE, took over the leadership of CCOO after ETA turned its political energies to creating LAB. Both CCOO and LAB, therefore, remain combative vis-à-vis management. They are both strong in the Alto Deba, making for a rather forceful syndical presence in local factories like Mayc. The strength of each syndicate in the co-marca is reflected in election results for Worker Councils in all factories, small shops, and services (table 5.1). Though only about 15 percent of workers are affiliated with syndicates, most workers still vote for a syndical rather than an independent slate. And while LAB and CCOO do not hold a majority of Work-ers' Council seats, their combativeness is an important influence in many fac-tories, including Mayc.

Conclusions

The struggle in Mayc over the second shift held great significance for me. While Social Council members in Clima took decisive action to disband on a matter of significance to the work force, in my eighteen months of fieldwork, I had never seen the Clima Social Council (or any other Social Council) so decidedly roll up its sleeves, design a production plan, or consult lawyers, economists, or engineers. This comparison led me to believe that there is an important distinction between rights and powers; normatively the Social Council extends considerably more rights to cooperative workers, while these rights to participate and plan are protected managerial prerogative in private firms. In practice, however, the individual characteristics of Social Council members and structural factors (not having enough time, receiving too much complex information, not being able to seek the help of outside professionals, and having a dual role of the council as both a managerial and a workers' voice) can limit its effectiveness. The same is true in a private firm, where, if members of the Workers' Council (or their syndicates) are inactive or the conflict between syndicates is too great, the exercise of rights is compromised. Yet an activist Workers' Council such as Mayc's can be effective.

After comparing the actual functioning of the Social Council and Workers' Council, I concluded that concepts of participation and democracy needed to be revisited: Is participation what syndicates do in the course of labor–management conflict? Is the interaction between syndicates and owners—where each party is considered to represent different interests—also a form of democracy? Perhaps genuine participation and democracy occur when both sides summon their respective powers to promote their own interests. Similarly, I wondered about the issues of activism and passivity in relationship to democracy. Could cooperativism be termed participatory or democratic if, as the 1981 Ederlan report charged, it generated passivity among workers? In the next chapter, I take a closer look at workers' experience inside Fagor Clima and Mayc, in an effort to deepen my comparison of the cooperative and private business forms.

6

Fagor Clima and Mayc, S. A.

When I left Mondragón in 1990, it appeared that Unión Cerrajera would soon close. It was terrible to imagine the disappearance of the firm that had shaped the town for more than half a century, and to think of the economic and emotional impact of the loss of several hundred jobs. Facing an uncertain future, a Unión Cerrajera production worker, who was an active syndicalist, got an idea to turn the oldest of the factory buildings into an industrial museum. While it was tragic to plan for the company's closing, he was committed to commemorating workers' history. He contacted Maribel, a young woman from Mondragón who was pursuing a degree in museum studies, and asked her to develop a plan for a museum. She took on the assignment as the final project for her university degree.

When I returned to Mondragón in 1991 for a short visit, I met with Maribel and the Unión Cerrajera worker to talk about the project. We discussed critical theory of museum design, which Maribel was studying at the university; they wanted to make sure that the museum did not privilege technology over labor. During the meeting, we talked about the factory as an historical landmark and as a public place. Several months later, Maribel applied for and received a small grant from the Mondragón municipal government to complete her study. She asked townspeople to contribute photographs, old industrial products, and documents to the new museum. Recently, she organized an exposition of the artifacts in Monterrón, Mondragón's cultural center, and public enthusiasm for the project grew.

While the plans for the museum were being developed, Unión Cerrajera's Workers' Council was negotiating the sale of the ailing firm to the remaining employees. The syndicates lost the battle to convince owners to stay in Mondragón, but after protracted and difficult negotiation (including many disagreements between the syndicates), the owners sold the firm to its employees. Workers have purchased an aging, decapitalized firm, and the future looks bleak. Nevertheless, the simultaneous struggle for the firm and for the museum is meaningful. It was also exemplary of the activism I saw in Euskadi. This instance involved only one Unión Cerrajera worker and is particularly dramatic—a worker in Mondragón had never before taken on the design of a

FIGURE 20

Workers protesting at the gates of Unión Cerrajera. The banner reads "The Unión
Cerrajera Corporation and Lobo [a major stock holder] get rich, Unión Cerrajera [the
local factory] disappears." Credit: Arrasate Press.

museum—but it was not outside the scope of the *ekintza* (activism) that was
part of life in Basque towns (cf. Zulaika 1988, 67).

I did not see or hear of this kind of activism or creativity pertaining to
their workplaces among cooperative workers. There were conflicts, and workers found clever ways to solve problems, such as the dissolution of the Clima
Social Council, but these struggles did not go beyond conflict to become larger
projects. Cooperative managers, on the other hand, do develop projects; there
is a museum to Father Arizmendiarrieta in Ikasbide, and system managers recently designed and implemented the plan for sectoral groups and the overar-
ching Mondragón corporation.

In this chapter, I evaluate the extent and nature of the differences between
cooperative workers and managers. Further, I compare Fagor Clima and Mayc,
S.A., to explore differences between cooperative workers and workers in private firms. I draw on data from several interviews with the members of Mayc's
Workers' Council and representatives of Clima's Social Council. I toured Mayc
on one occasion, in the company of the head of the engineering department and

the head of the Workers' Council. I toured Clima several times, first with the personnel manager and during subsequent visits with two head engineers and the factory nurse. I also socialized with many of these same workers in local bars, and attended demonstrations and rallies with some of them. I knew workers, as well as managers, in several contexts, and had opportunities to talk with them in a variety of settings about their work lives and their perceptions and opinions of cooperativism. I also met with syndicalists who were concerned with particular conditions in each plant and the overall status of the comarcal labor movement.

After twelve months of formal and informal interviews, factory tours, library research in Ikasbide, and participant observation in town, I distributed a survey in each firm. I involved managers and workers in writing the questions, discussed the results of the survey with them, and incorporated their comments into a report I presented while I still lived in Mondragón. I present the results of this survey here. It is my intention to portray working conditions, to convey what workers themselves think and feel about their workplaces, and to describe some of the effects each firm has on the political experiences and consciousness of its work force.

Labor–Management Conflict at Mayc

When I arrived for my first meeting with Mayc's personnel manager, Gregorio Etxeberria, he asked me if I wanted coffee. I said Yes and he phoned his secretary, who entered his office several minutes later with two cups of coffee on a serving tray. I usually had coffee in the cooperatives I visited as well, but on those occasions, the personnel manager always fetched the coffee himself or herself, usually from a public vending machine. Later, when he wanted cigarettes, Sr. Etxeberria phoned his secretary again, and she brought him a pack. I had not seen such obvious indications of status inequalities in any of the cooperatives I visited. (Indeed, I write of him now using the title Señor because he did not encourage familiarity.) Sr. Etxeberria described himself to me as a "very cold" manager:

I came to Mayc after working in Germany at a General Motors/Opel plant where there were cooperative labor–management relations. The company had installed a 35,000-volume library for workers, which was never used. Eventually, the library was donated to the town. I think the General Motors/Opel policy was paternalistic. I believe that a worker should earn a decent wage and be left alone to live his or her life outside of the factory.

Mayc is run on the presumption that labor and management have different interests. I am often in the labor courts over a grievance.

My initial contact with Mayc was made through José María Larrañaga of Ikasbide. José María called Sr. Etxeberria and asked him to assist me. On my own, I met with members of Mayc's Workers' Council. After interviewing Sr. Etxeberria, the head engineer arrived to give me a tour of the plant. Sr. Etxeberria did not feel comfortable enough with the production process and the machinery to conduct the tour (an indication of a level of division of labor among managers I had not seen in the cooperatives). Within a few minutes, the president of the Workers' Council, Manuel López (from CCOO), found us. Unbeknownst to me, Manuel had arranged with Sr. Etxeberria to be present during the tour so that he could give me the "workers' perspective of the plant," as Manuel put it. He was supposed to have been notified when I was ready to see the factory, but this message was never conveyed by Sr. Etxeberria to the head engineer. Nobody went to get Manuel when we were ready to start our tour. Manuel was angry and began to yell at the engineer, and he took off in search of Sr. Etxeberria. The engineer and I stayed put. There was an argument between Manuel and Sr. Etxeberria; only after their argument did I tour the plant, with a rather annoyed engineer and Manuel.

After this incident, the management of Mayc was not anxious to continue to help me. While I could have continued my study with the assistance of only the Workers' Council, I waited to smooth things over. With the help of José María of Ikasbide and after six months had passed, Sr. Etxeberria reluctantly agreed to let me proceed with my survey.

My reception in the cooperatives was very different; there, personnel directors showed me the plants. During none of my cooperative tours was it considered that a Social Council member should accompany me, or that the workers might have a different way of seeing the plant that could alter my impressions. Even when I asked to interview cooperators who were known to be critical of the cooperative, managers offered to arrange interviews for me in the factory during work hours.

There are two ways to interpret the different receptions in the cooperatives and in Mayc. In keeping with cooperative ideology, it could be argued that since labor relations in the cooperatives are not combative, managers have nothing to hide. In the private firm, where labor–management relations are by definition conflictual, the question of perspective was contentious. Indeed, the incident could even be interpreted as a case of syndicate bureaucracy: I witnessed and was part of a typical labor–management dispute over (a rather minor point of) shop-floor control.

An alternative interpretation is that cooperative workers had less control in their factories, which they could not show to an outsider. Instead, cooperative workers were interpreted by personnel managers who spoke for them and who described their experiences; workers did not speak for themselves, nor did a representative of the Social Council speak for them. When I met with contentious workers, it was arranged by management and the meeting took place inside the factory. It could be argued that in this way, management was able to normalize discontent by portraying it as an acceptable part of the cooperative process. Even as serious a matter as the disbanding of the Social Council in Clima could be discussed inside the factory. Following this interpretation of power relations, management and syndicates in Mayc had separate arenas of power. While managers dictated the terms of production, the syndicates were ready to grieve any infraction of the contract or syndical prerogative (for example, my tour). It is also possible that in normalizing conflict in Clima, and by presenting it as a regular part of the cooperative business form, the independent activism of workers was claimed by managers and subsumed by the system. The cooperative form, including the ideology of participation and the norms, bylaws, and organs that enable dissent and term it "dialogue", may create the sense that the system, rather than the workers, is the creative and dynamic agent. A belief by workers that their efforts are subsumed in this way may lead to feelings of apathy or passivity.

Syndicates

Mayc's Workers' Council had seventeen members; six from ELA-STV; four from CCOO (including the president of the Workers' Council); four from LAB; and three from UGT. Workers' Council representatives are elected every four years and can run independently or on a syndicate slate. Syndicate representation in Mayc was typical for the comarca (see table 5.1) where ELA has a majority, but LAB and CCOO together comprise a powerful block. Syndicate membership is not public knowledge (each syndicate keeps their number of affiliates quiet), but members of CCOO and LAB gave me similar estimates of membership in Mayc (see table 6.1).

Conflict and divisions among syndicates make them less effective advocates of workers' rights. For example, in Mayc, ELA and UGT did not support the redesign of the plant discussed in chapter 5. Instead, they preferred the addition of a second shift, which LAB and CCOO opposed. One reason they favored the second shift was that it would create jobs for temporary workers. The majority of temporary workers in Mayc were affiliates of ELA or family members of affiliates. It was common to hear ELA accused of running a "mafia" to get its people temporary positions. Popular rumor and political accusation had it that ELA allowed management to turn jobs into temporary positions, and management in turn promised ELA those positions.[1] This won ELA affiliates among some young people who knew this was their best

TABLE 6.1

Syndicate Membership & Representation in Mayc

Syndicate	Number of affiliates (estimated)	Number of representatives on Workers' Council
ELA	150	6
CCOO	115	4 (including president)
LAB	60	4
UGT	50	3
Total	375	

Source: Syndicate Officials, Bergara

avenue for jobs (though they were not likely to be committed syndicalists), but it did not make ELA an effective syndicate. (Another reason for ELA's support of the second shift is that members of ELA represent lower and middle managers on the Workers' Council who bring a management perspective to that body.)

However, syndicate action is quite capable of promoting solidarity. Workers in Mayc had waged a strike in 1974. As in the cooperative Ulgor in the same year, Mayc workers struck over salaries. A worker recalled the strike:

During the strike, some workers were fired. We demanded their readmission. The strike was settled in a month. Those who were fired got their jobs back two weeks later. We won a salary increase and equal pay for women. During the strike, several people met [the people who would become] their husbands and wives. We spent a lot of time together and we got to know people in a different way. It was kind of romantic.

Other Mayc workers remembered the strike fondly, as a time "when we got to know our co-workers."

Cooperation at Fagor Clima

Whereas labor–management relations in Mayc are based on conflict, in Clima they are premised on solidarity between managers and workers. In Clima, as in all of the cooperatives I visited, I asked the personnel director: "How many workers and how many managers are there?" I was typically told, "*Somos todos obreros*" (we are all workers). Personnel managers repeatedly reminded me that cooperative ideology held that all cooperators, regardless of their jobs, are *obreros* (workers); cooperatives did not have social classes. The personnel directors' mental map of social groups were instead divided between *mano de obra indirecta* (indirect labor) and *mano de obra directa* (direct labor). The distinction was between those whose labor directly transformed the product (directa)—making parts, assembling, painting—and those whose labor was removed from the product (indirecta)—shipping, warehousing, bookkeeping, managing. Skill, pay, and status did not figure into this classification. For instance, a maintenance person who oils the presses or stocks the warehouse, the director of the marketing department, and the general manager are indirect laborers, despite the fact that the maintenance person works with machines, wears blue coveralls, and earns less than one-third of what the general manager earns.

Unlike managers, workers at Clima spoke of definite inequalities in their plant. They most often talked about "*los de arriba*" (those on the top) versus "*los de abajo*" (those on the bottom). Workers also spoke of themselves as "*curelas*" (working stiffs) and called managers "*jefes*" (bosses). "Jefes" was used interchangeably for managers and engineers as well as for the elected representatives to the Governing Council and the Management Council, suggesting that workers perceived them as management-controlled bodies rather than democratic organs that represented workers' interests. Often the two were referred to jointly as "they." "They" was also a flexible category. "They" always meant the general manager, the Management Council, Governing Council, departments heads, and high-level engineers (or any combination thereof); often it included mid-level managers and engineers, but only occasionally did it include low-level supervisors.

Two personnel managers at Fagor Garagartza, where front-loading washing machines and stoves are manufactured, were unusual in that they suggested that there were discernible inequalities in the cooperatives. They used the terms "mano de obra directa" and "indirecta," but overlaid these classifications with a second category of those who were "socially" engaged in direct or indirect labor, despite the technical aspect of their jobs. To them, these distinctions were bound up with status, suggesting that, contrary to official ideology, conventional social classes did indeed exist in Garagartza.

These class differences were not nearly as extreme as they were in Mayc. All cooperators receive anticipios, removing the distinction between hourly workers and salaried employees, and the difference in their earnings was slim. Moreover, the dress code in the cooperatives reflected a flexible notion of hierarchy; engineers commonly wore jeans and a button-down shirt, and high-level managers wore a jacket but no tie, compared to the more formal dress in private firms (including those that used labor–managers cooperation techniques). Nonetheless, the kind of job performed, the extent of control over that job, earnings, and office versus shop work mattered. It seemed clear to me that there were structural inequalities in Clima but that these inequalities were more meaningful to those on the bottom than to those on the top. Official ideologies about the value and meaning of labor seemed to be more significant for managers' perceptions of factory life than for workers, and managers were more inclined to defend those ideologies. Managers had a normative view of egalitarianism—we are all equal, regardless of differences—whereas workers often expressed frustration because the ideological pronouncements of managers denied their experiences. Comparing his situation to that of workers in a privately held firm, one Clima worker told me, "At least there they don't pretend that there is equality." Workers often made comments like this. They said they were tired of being told that, since they were all worker-owners, there were no classes in the cooperative.

Greenwood and González et al. (1989, 105–10, 132–36) collected similar data from interviews and discussions with members of Fagor, who continually referred to los de arriba and los de abajo. Similarly, their informants did not distinguish between managers and representatives of the Management and Governing Councils—all were los de arriba. Greenwood and González et al. report that when they probed further, informants could not draw a clear line between those on top and those on the bottom. They were, nonetheless, "vehement" in their claims of inequality:

No, of course, we are not all equal.

We are not different from other businesses in any way.

It doesn't matter how equal we are in theory, in practice we are not. (Greenwood and González et al. 1989, 134)

Perhaps the emotion with which these cooperative workers express themselves reflects their frustration with cooperative ideology, which denies the reality of their daily experience and denies them a language in which to speak about it. Greenwood and González et al. (1989, 112–14) describe this phenomenon as well. They quote one of their informants:

What good does it do me that they call me a collaborator when they treat me like a subordinate; in a private firm, they call you a subordinate but they recognize that this is what you are.(113)

A Clima worker remarked to me: "At least in a regular firm you can call the boss a son of a bitch."

The terms "arriba" and "abajo" are at odds with a formal analysis of property relations. Structurally, workers and managers have the same class posi-

TABLE 6.2

Stratification in Cooperatives, Workers' Point of View

Gerencia (Management)
Three people in Clima in this category. Above 2.60 job index.
Directores (Department Heads)
Four people. 2.30–2.60 job index.
Técnicos (Technicians)
Forty people. My informants distinguished between high-level and low-level technicians. Some low-level technicians were considered to be more like workers.
1.40–2.30 job index.
Jefes de área/Mandos (Area Chiefs/Supervisors)
Eight people. 1.40–2.00 index rating. There was not a great social distance between this group and the category of workers.
Mano de obra directa/Obreros (Workers)
Everyone else. 1.00–1.30 job index.

Source. Interviews with workers, Fagor Clima

tions, since they are co-owners of their firms. In one interview, I asked members of the Clima Social Council who worked on the assembly line to reproduce their mental map of social class in the cooperatives. They described a five-part scheme, which I then drew on paper for them to check and refine (table 6.2). I learned two things from this exercise. First, their concepts of inequality are not vague, and when they use their own language (despite official or structural notions that they might be "wrong") they are able to speak about inequalities with precision. Second, I learned the parameters of inequality from a workers' perspective. Their scheme indicated that control over work, job classification, ratings, and perceived social distance were significant markers of inequality, and these differences were more significant to workers than the legal fact of joint ownership and their's and manager's common formal class position of worker-owner.

Mobility

Talking about socioeconomic class in the cooperatives is complicated further by the nature and extent of job mobility. None of the high-level managers I met at Mayc were promoted from the shop floor. While most assembly workers at Clima will never move into managerial positions, I met a few managers who began their work lives as manual workers, including the head of the engineering department. Mobility is related to the cooperative education system. Only recently have young people from Mondragón gone away to university with any frequency. It is more common for young people to study at the Polytechnical and Professional School, beginning at age fourteen. Those who pursue the most basic course of education, the equivalent of a vocational degree, are prepared for manual labor at the age of eighteen. Those who stay on for college-level courses are trained for technical and engineering positions and often work in the cooperatives. Later, they can return for master's-level course work, and this continuing education is linked to promotion. A new cooperative school, housed in Oñati, where students can earn an administrative degree, offers accounting, bookkeeping, and some managerial course work.

Women Workers in Clima

The school for administration is also important because it may be a route for more women to become managers. Hacker (1989, 95–120) reports that, though few, there are still more women in management in the cooperatives that there are in private firms. In manual jobs, too, women fare better in the cooperatives than in local private firms. They make up 28 percent of the cooperative work force, compared with 25 percent in regular firms. In my experience, the issue of gender was debated and taken seriously in the cooperatives in a way that it was not in regular firms. Despite the fact that Mayc had a strike in 1974 which included demands for pay equity, a gendered view of the shop floor was not a topic of conversation among workers, nor was it an important aspect of the syndicate's struggle. It was, however, significant for the Clima Social Council.

In 1989, Clima produced 180,000 hot-water heaters; the aim was to produce 300,000 in 1990. Engineers determined that the second floor, where most of Clima's women members worked, would have to be overhauled if that goal was to be achieved. Previous attempts to reorganize production there had failed. Several years earlier, work teams were introduced among groups of women in an effort to improve production. According to managers as well as to the women themselves, the teams failed because the women preferred to work alone. One woman who was part of a team felt that

> competition undermined it. Group members were paid the same, despite individual differences in performance, and this led to quarreling. The team members didn't like being responsible for each others' work.

The experiment was abandoned and the women went back to their old jobs. Since then, women workers have been defined by themselves, by their male co-workers, and by managers, as something of a problem.

Data from other factories on the effects of the team concept on work life suggest that the problem lies elsewhere. Taylor (1988) studied team concept experiments in the Fagor cooperative Copreci, where both women and men comprised the groups. While Taylor observed that women were less comfortable expressing their opinions at team meetings (largely, he believed, because they had less experience talking in front of groups), he did not report a difference in men's and women's success in the teams. Tensions between workers are common in private firms when the team concept is introduced, regardless of the gender of the workers involved. (Parker and Slaughter [1988] argue that encouraging workers to manage and supervise each other, with consequent tensions, is one of the main goals of the team concept.)[2] Lamphere (1992) argued that women in a U.S. factory she studied were more likely to develop a collectivist work culture on their own and, thus, were more disposed to accepting the cooperative labor–management techniques being introduced by managers, including the team concept. These cases indicate that, in Clima, the reasons for women's lack of interest in the work groups was more complex than the management and shop-floor common sense that "women are just more difficult than men."

Women I interviewed told me that there was considerable petty competition among them, more so than among male workers, because "we don't have access to better jobs, like repairing machines." Women explained that since they were confined to jobs on the lower end of the pay scale (see Hacker 1989; 97–100), even the smallest differences in their job ratings took on great importance—that is, class and gender were intertwined. It was an attempt to remedy this situation that led women to be active in the drive to disband Clima's Social Council in protest over the assignment of low-level jobs. They reasoned that if job assignments were standardized and not the prerogative of management, they could address some of the gender inequity in the plant. Maite, who believed it was her job to bring gender issues to the Social Council said that

if a man and a woman have the same points, then give the job to the woman, since historically women don't have a chance. Men have always had better economic chances.

Women's dissatisfaction in their work, and their reported activism in the 1974 Ulgor strike and in the disbanding of Clima's Social Council, deserves further investigation. Are these events also interpretable as women's efforts to equalize job opportunities and pay rates in the cooperative system (see Morrison 1991, 149–50)? Tackling this question would constitute a significant contribution to the literature on Mondragón.

Control over Production

In Clima, women's dissatisfaction with the work teams left unresolved the problem of reorganizing the second floor of the plant. Some individual work stations were designed, but in 1989, the remainder of the work was done on one long assembly line. Managers considered the assembly line to be inefficient and believed it had to be reorganized to meet production goals. In August, when Clima was closed for its annual vacation, the assembly line was broken down into six short lines. Throughout the 1980s, small, flexible assembly lines have replaced larger lines in factories throughout the world.

An engineer at Clima took me on a tour of Clima that summer. With the plant quiet, he explained the design changes they were going to make. He showed me where the small assembly lines were to go and said that "there [will be] fewer people dependent upon the output, quality of work, attendance or lateness of any individual." He also told me that the cooperative had purchased numerical-control machine tools to automate production. Additionally, a system was to be introduced to mark pieces with an identification number "so that individual workers can be held accountable for the quality of their work. The work is going to be more controlled."

A year later, I met Maite in a quiet bar. She brought me up to date on some of the changes in the plant since I had last been there several months earlier. She was always passionate when she spoke with me, but on this occasion she spoke with even more urgency. A private consultant company (not Fagor Sistemas) had been brought in to do a study of efficiency in Clima:[3]

> They said they were coming to organize the factory. They said Clima would get seventy-five million pesetas more [a year] just by reorganizing. They said that, on average, people had to increase productivity by 18 percent. Some people had to increase 30 percent. They said they were not going to make us work faster, just cut out dead times.

> The consultants gave us sheets of paper to fill out. What do you do in an hour really? Then the consultants stood behind us when we were working. We had the experience of what happened in [two other Fagor cooperatives where consultants had completed efficiency studies in the last year].

> We met with the Management Council and the manager and we said that we were not going to cooperate. They said we had to because it is in the co-op statutes. So we called an assembly of the workers. We de-

cided to all fill out [on the sheets of paper] the productivity level that we were supposed to have, and when they came to watch us, we wouldn't produce any more or less than that.

The sheets didn't help the consultants at all. So now the manager has threatened us with a time-motion study. This might be better for us because they have to give you a sheet with all the different movements and times, and if you don't agree you can dispute it. With the consultants you couldn't dispute it because nothing was written down.

Despite the fact that they had democratic rights to participate in planning production, the response of Clima workers when faced with a more stressful work pace was to protest. They relied on conflict rather than designing an alternative strategy for increasing production. Although they had the technical right to do so, workers did not exercise managerial rights to ameliorate the situation.

Temporary Workers

Another important aspect of cooperative life is the prevalent use of temporary labor. In 1989, fifty people worked in Clima on temporary contracts. Government incentives made it especially attractive for businesses to use contract workers. Since the state gave subsidies to firms that hired people from the unemployment rolls, it was possible for a company to extend a six-month contract to a production worker at virtually no cost to the firm. After six months, the worker was let go. He or she would apply for unemployment and, when that ran out, seek another contract. By 1990, these credits to firms had been cut, making it less advantageous to hire temporary laborers; in 1992, unemployment benefits were restricted, as workers received fewer months of unemployment and had to work more months in order to qualify.

In 1989, however, the system was going strong, and, as a friend who worked in Mondragón's unemployment office told me, it was used particularly effectively by the cooperatives. Fagor Garagartza had four hundred contract workers in May 1989, a full third of the total labor force, and 20 percent of the work force in Clima was temporary. Nash (1989, 312) described similar practices in General Electric in Pittsfield, Massachusetts, where she called contract workers "industrial Kelly Girls." The cooperatives behaved like other firms in the changing international environment.

Inside the factories of Fagor, there were two kinds of workers: worker-owners, who were members and had rights to participate in management and shared in yearly profits, and hired laborers, who could not vote in the General Assembly and did not participate in the decision making. Many of my friends were contract laborers in the cooperative. They felt doubly exploited in their jobs, by managers and by permanent co-op members, whom they felt acted like *jefecitos* (little bosses). One friend told me that "they are always watching, criticizing our work, and complaining when we smoke a cigarette or take a coffee break." Another temporary worker told me that she went to the Social Council to complain about these "problems of *compañerismo* [collegiality], for an excess of bossing between workers of the same level." Many co-op members believed that contract workers were lazy and careless. This ill will was not part of the workplace relations in Mayc, where temporary workers felt part of the firm and accepted by their co-workers.

In Clima, temporary workers were assigned the most routinized and unpleasant jobs in the factory; some worked extra hard, in the hopes of being offered permanent employment, and often they were bitter when they were not. Others were disaffected and made an effort to work as little as possible. The practice of hiring temporary labor in greater percentages than in private firms, where at least some syndicates fought against abuses of the system, created divisions and conflicts on the shop floors of cooperatives such as Clima that did not exist in private firms. One private owner told me:

> Temporary workers have more rights here [in his firm] than in a cooperative. We leave them alone because of the syndicates. But not in a co-op. They have shifts, so they give the temporary contract workers the worst shifts. I would like to use more temporary workers but the syndicates won't let me. The co-ops use a lot more.

The cooperative system's practice of hiring temporary labor transformed life outside of the factories as well. In the late 1980s, the town's young people worked in the cooperative factories on short contracts, often during school vacations, while their peers elsewhere were unemployed. These young people, mostly in their twenties, had considerable disposable income, especially since they did not earn enough to move out of their parents' homes and therefore had few monthly living expenses. The result was a temporary and minor consumer boom in Mondragón relative to other towns. When state grants to firms were cut back in the 1990s, however, this relative affluence faded, and more young people were unemployed.

Workers' Feelings, Opinions, and Attitudes

How do these divisions between managers and workers compare with management–syndicate and intersyndicate conflict in Mayc? What do workers

TABLE 6.3

Respondents to Survey in Mayc, S.A., and Fagor Clima

Mayc		Clima	
Total:	36	Total:	58
Sex:		Sex:	
Male	26	Male	35
Female	10	Female	23
Job:[a]		Job:	
Manual	24	Manual	27
Nonmanual	6	Nonmanual	22
No answer	6	No answer	9
Low-level technician	2	Low-level technician	6
Mid-level technician	1	Mid-level technician	5
Administration	1	Mid-management	6
Secretary	2	High-level technician	1
		High-level management	4
Contract: Permanent	30	Contract: Member	57
Temporary	6	Temporary	1

[a]Manual and nonmanual job categories are the same as the categories mano de obra directa and indirecta, except that I included stock and maintenance positions in the category of manual jobs. I categorized levels of technical and managerial workers by job category and (for the cooperative) job index. For example, someone who reported that he was a supervisor (and had a 1.6 job rating) was categorized as a low-level manager. Those who reported being managers or working in personnel (with a 2.8 index) were classified as high-level managers.

think and feel about their respective workplaces? How do cooperative managers and workers differently experience their workplaces? In order to assess feelings and attitudes of workers and managers, I distributed a survey in both firms. The surveys were not given to a preselected sample. Rather, I delivered one hundred copies of the survey to each firm. In Mayc, the members of the Workers' Council distributed them for me; in Clima, the factory nurse did so. Of the one hundred copies I left at Mayc, only thirty-six (or 6 percent of the plant) were returned. In Clima, fifty-eight (19 percent) were returned. Respondents from Clima were more likely to skip questions and returned more incomplete surveys, but they also sometimes wrote comments on the survey to clarify their points or critique my question (perhaps an indication of what Greenwood and González et al. [1989] call a "culture of dialogue" in the cooperatives).

In neither Mayc nor Clima did I get a representative sample. Age distributions were representative, but gender distributions were not. In Mayc, where women make up 21 percent of the work force, 28 percent of my respondents are women. In Clima, 31 percent of the plant is female, compared with 40 percent of my sample. The survey from Mayc is also overrepresented for syndicate affiliates (69 percent in my sample as compared with an estimated 63 percent in the firm).

Furthermore, I distributed the survey after fifty new people were hired in Clima (17 percent of the total work force), and they were thirteen (22 percent) of my respondents. The thirteen had worked in Clima for a year or less; two worked as temporary workers and had just been offered membership, but most had transferred in from other Fagor cooperatives that had an excess of members. I discussed the early results of my survey with Clima's personnel director, and he pointed out that short tenure probably unfairly weighed their opinions on several questions. Where relevant, I indicate how short tenure affected my results (something I did not do in the original paper I distributed in Mondragón). It is also important to keep in mind that, as transfers between cooperatives become increasingly common (and they are becoming common in the new, flexible group structure—something I discuss more in chapter 7), the composition of the work force in Clima is less anomalous and more the norm.

Finally, I must note that, since my sample size is small, I present survey results with the caution that I do not consider them definitive. Rather, in conjunction with interviews and observation, I use them to suggest the opinions and attitudes I saw in Mondragón as well as the effects of the different factory regimes on workers.

Identification with the Firm

Advocates of the Mondragón model assume that because cooperators are co-owners and because they participate in management, cooperators feel a closer identification with their firm than do workers in regular firms. Bradley and Gelb (1983) argue that this is responsible for increased productivity. Identification with the firm is also considered a measure of worker satisfaction and an indication of the success of participation and democracy. Whereas cooperative managers often told me "the cooperative belongs to everybody," I never heard a worker refer to a cooperative as "mine" or "ours." I wondered if the notion of ownership or being part of the firm was more an imposed ideology than something workers truly felt. I more often heard questions like "They say it's ours, but what does that mean?" as one assembly worker in Clima asked. I evaluated workers' sentiments and determined the nature of identification with the firms by asking the following questions, with these results:

In your job, do you feel that you are working as if the firm is yours?

Mayc			Clima		
	Number	Percent		Number	Percent
Total			Total		
Yes	10	28	Yes	23	40
No	25	69	No	33	57
No answer	1	3	No answer	2	3
Manual Workers			Manual Workers		
Yes	5	21	Yes	6	22
No	18	75	No	21	78
No answer	1	4	No answer	0	
Managers			Managers		
Yes	2	50	Yes	15	68
No	2	50	No	7	32
No answer	0		No answer	0	

Cooperators were more likely to feel that the firm was theirs (40 percent in Clima versus 28 percent in Mayc). Nonetheless, ten Mayc employees who held no stock in their firm also believed that the firm was theirs. However, when looked at by job classification, these differences diminished. Just five manual workers in Mayc and six in Clima (21 percent in each) considered the firm theirs, despite the fact that cooperative workers are legally owners. If there is a strong sense of ownership in the cooperative, it seems to be among technicians and managers. Fifteen considered the firm theirs (68 percent); in Mayc two managers considered the firm theirs, and two others did not. In Clima, eleven of seventeen low- and mid-level technicians and managers (65 percent) considered the firm theirs, compared with four of five high-level engineers and managers (80 percent). One high-level manager who felt the firm was his spoke more generally; he added the comment, "Not mine in particular, but everyone's in general." However, most assembly workers did not agree with him.

In Clima, gender is also an important factor. Five of twenty-three women cooperators (21 percent) felt the firm was theirs, compared with eighteen of thirty-four men (52 percent). Short tenure in the cooperative also influenced identification with the firm. Only four of those who worked one year or less felt the firm was theirs (21 percent), compared with nineteen (nearly half) who worked at Clima longer than a year. However, gender, shortness of tenure, and being an assembly worker overlap; seven of the thirteen new workers who returned my survey were women, and all were assembly workers. This overlap and my small sample size make it impossible for me to determine which of these factors weighs more heavily and how they are related, but this relationship merits further study.

While a feeling of ownership grows somewhat over time, the cooperative does not seem to transmit a strong sense of ownership except to those in high positions. If feelings of ownership do not contribute to identification with the firm, perhaps Clima workers feel they "are part of the firm" (parte de la empresa), a phrasing that people in Mondragón advised me would meaningfully capture a sense of personal identification with the firm.

Do you feel that you are part of the firm?

	Mayc				Clima	
	Number	Percent			Number	Percent
Total				Total		
Yes	23	64		Yes	34	59
No	13	36		No	21	36
No answer	0			No answer	3	5
Manual workers				Manual workers		
Yes	16	67		Yes	13	46
No	8	33		No	14	50
No answer	0			No answer	1	4
Managers				Managers		
Yes	2	50		Yes	17	77
No	2	50		No	4	18
No answer	0			No answer	1	5

The cooperative appears to generate less of a feeling of being part of the firm than the private firm (59 percent versus 64 percent). The difference is even more striking when discussed in terms of job classification. Sixteen (67 percent) manual workers in Mayc felt they were part of the firm, compared to thirteen (46 percent) in Clima. One worker wrote that he did not feel part of the firm, "because your opinion on whatever topic is being debated between the shop floor and management generally doesn't matter." Again, cooperative managers felt most identified with their firm; twelve low- and mid-level managers and all high-level managers (seventeen total) felt part of the firm. Gender was also relevant in Clima; fifteen women felt part of the firm and six did not, while eighteen men felt part of the firm and seventeen did not. (This is a curious reversal of the gender split that characterized feelings that the firm is theirs; a more thorough analysis of women in the co-ops could grapple with the ways in which gender impacts identification with the firm.) These gender differences did not appear in Mayc. Length of tenure also mattered. Forty-six percent of new workers (men and women equally) did not feel part of the firm, compared

with one-third of the older workers. Conversely, in Mayc all of the six temporary workers felt part of the firm. This result raises an important question about
the increasingly common practice of transferring workers between cooperatives: Are transfers creating a strata of workers who are less tied to their firms?

The suggestion that cooperative workers feel less part of the firm than do
private workers challenges the presumption that cooperatives create a sense of
participation. Belonging seems to be a stratified feeling in the cooperatives.
Managers, especially those in the highest positions, are strongly tied to their
firm, whereas workers' ties are weaker. These results also raise questions about
the nature of workers' feelings of ownership and identification with their firm.
One worker I interviewed said, "I am the owner of my job. The only property
I have is my job." I often heard similar statements from other cooperative workers. This concept of owning their jobs is understandable, given regional labor
conditions—the unemployment rate in Euskadi was nearly 25 percent during
the time of my study—but it is hardly an indication of a strong sense of participation or activism.

Solidarity

While advocates of cooperativism often assume that working in a co-op makes
people feel part of a collective or revives communitarianism, my interviews
with Mayc workers suggest that labor conflicts also create close bonds between
workers. In Basque workplaces, a common form of association is to purchase
lottery tickets with a group of co-workers. In Mayc, 56 percent of respondents
(20) reported playing the lottery with co-workers frequently, compared to 36
percent (21) in Clima. The primary form of association in Basque towns is the
after-work round of the bars. This is a ritual for the childhood-formed friendship group, or cuadrilla; co-workers are less likely to share this time, on a regular basis, but they sometimes do. The occasional after-work txikiteo is more
common in Clima, where 76 percent (44) of respondents reported drinking with
co-workers, compared with 69 percent (25) in Mayc. (These percentages held
across gender, length of tenure, and job category.)

Clima workers also reported feeling solidarity with their co-workers. Of
the cooperators, 97 percent felt solidarity with their fellow workers, compared
with 86 percent of workers in Mayc. It appears that rifts from the Ulgor strike
are either forgotten or not relevant for daily life. Maite attributed these feelings
of solidarity to the recent activism of Clima's Social Council; she felt that relations among workers were deepening as they engaged in struggle.

Cooperators also expressed solidarity with workers and politics outside
of the cooperatives. Twenty Mayc employees (56 percent, including two
managers), compared with thirty-one in Clima (53 percent, including fourteen managers of all levels), had participated in a solidarity strike. Age was a
factor in cooperators' experiences. Fewer Clima members who were under
thirty-five years of age (and therefore likely to have missed out on much of

activism of the Franco years) had participated in solidarity strikes than did their contemporaries in Mayc (11 of 28 in Clima, 8 of 16 in Mayc.) The sense that cooperators are less solidaric with the rest of the working class and less active in this form of politics may hold true for younger members, but there may be a disjuncture between community perceptions of cooperators' inactivism (chapter 4) and older cooperators' self-reported participation. This possible disjuncture merits further study.

Competition

Feelings of solidarity do not mitigate the strong sense of competition in Clima. Seventy-two percent of cooperators said they believed there was competition over salaries in Mayc. Of the cooperators, 79 percent said there was competition over jobs, compared to 56 percent in Mayc. Along with the data from participant observation and interviews, it seems clear that competition is a genuine problem in the cooperatives. One Clima worker wrote on his survey that "here no one supports anyone, everyone does their own thing." Significantly, women cooperators were no more likely to feel that there was competition than were men.

Is there any competition over salaries/job indexes?

| | Mayc | | | Clima | |
	Number	Percent		Number	Percent*
Yes	20	56	Yes	42	72
No	16	44	No	14	24
No answer	0		No answer	2	3

Is there competition for jobs?

| | Mayc | | | Clima | |
	Number	Percent		Number	Percent*
Yes	20	56	Yes	46	79
No	16	44	No	10	17
No answer	0		No answer	2	3

*Rounded off to the nearest percentage point; totals do not equal 100%.

The Social and Workers' Councils

To determine whether cooperators felt better represented than workers in regular firms, I asked: Do you think that the Workers'/Social Council has real power to improve conditions? Eight manual workers in Mayc said that they felt that the Worker's Council had real power. Seven manual workers in Clima said that the Social Council had real power. (Being new did not decrease faith in the Social Council; in fact, it seemed to decrease over time. Five out of thirteen of the new workers said they believed that the Social Council had real power to improve conditions.)

Neither Clima nor Mayc workers expressed strong confidence in the organs that represented them. While this is what advocates of labor–management cooperation would predict for a private firm, it is contrary to presumptions about the Mondragón model—cooperative workers do not seem to feel better represented by cooperative labor-management strategies. Cooperative managers, however, do believe in the Social Council. In Clima, fourteen managers of all levels (64 percent) thought that the Social Council had real power to improve conditions.

Syndicates' Role in the Cooperatives

If cooperative workers did not believe that the Social Council was effective, did they believe that the syndicates should play a role in the cooperatives? (I did not ask if they should play a "large role," as did Bradley and Gelb 1983.) Thirteen manual workers said Yes; eleven said No. Only four managers said Yes. Clarifying what that role might be, I asked: Do workers in Clima need the support of syndicates? Do they need the right to ask syndicate lawyers, economists, and engineers for help with developing alternative production and business plans? Fifteen manual workers answered Yes to both questions. Only three managers believed that workers needed the support of syndicates, and only two believed they needed professional and technical assistance. One high-level manager, who saw no need for syndicate involvement, wrote: "Internal conflicts can be discussed in the General Assembly among all members." Significantly, he wrote elsewhere on his survey, "We are all workers." A mid-level manager thought syndicates were unnecessary because "there are specific cooperative organs. There is no reason. It's possible to fire even the highest-level managers." He also believed that the Social Council had real power in the cooperative; workers disagree.

Though one-half of the manual workers may have wanted some involvement of syndicates in the cooperatives, this feeling did not motivate them to affiliate with syndicates, something that co-op bylaws permitted individuals to do even if syndical activity inside the factories was barred. In 1990, local syndicates reported that only a handful of cooperators were members.

Significantly, favoring syndicate involvement did not mean that cooperators would prefer to work in a private firm. Only six said they would. In Mayc, where many workers had participated in discussions in 1981 about joining the Fagor Group, seven said they would prefer to work in a cooperative. Though critical of the cooperative, cooperators did not want to see their firms privatized. One cooperator wrote that she wouldn't prefer to work in a private firm, "but I would like it if things changed a lot in the cooperatives." Another worker explained his preference for a cooperative: "because in theory we are worker-owners and the decisions are made by the manager as well as the guy who sweeps the floor."

Class Identification

In order to determine if the cooperatives had affected cooperators' sense of class consciousness, I asked: "What social class are you?" In Mayc, eleven workers (46 percent) said they were working class, while six (25 percent) identified as middle class. In Clima, nineteen manual workers (70 percent) said they were middle class, and eight (30 percent) identified as working class. One high-level manager wrote in response to my question the rhetorical question "What is social class?" Another high-level manager wrote that cooperators "are all middle class." All but one manager self-identified as middle class.

In chapter 3, I argued that the tendency for cooperative workers to identify as middle class was evident in the cooperative movement from its beginnings, rooted in the social vision of Father Arizmendiarrieta and the political project of PNV's nationalism. However, the process of middle-class formation among cooperators does not appear to be seamless, since workers in Clima also perceived class differences within their factory. They may see themselves as middle class compared to workers in regular firms, but they do not consider themselves to be like cooperative managers.

Conclusions

An article appearing in the *Harvard Business Review* (Hoerr 1991) concluded that employee participation and ownership programs work best when unions are involved. Even when social councils are formed in firms with employee participation, they usually have little efficacy if they are not backed by a union that has access to institutional forms of power outside the company (see also Mishel and Voos 1992). My study of Fagor Clima corroborates the conclusions of that article. In Mondragón, where workplace democracy and participatory management are highly developed, there is still no guarantee that in all areas workers will fare better in a cooperative than in a standard firm.

My comparison of the cooperative Fagor Clima and the privately held Mayc showed that market competition places similar demands and stresses on both groups of workers: both plants have been automated; both have temporary workers; and both have similar struggles over control of the work process. In

Clima, the Social Council was often unable to adequately represent workers. In Mayc, the Workers' Council was able to successfully resolve an important conflict with management, and, in so doing, it participated in planning the production process. There was more competition between workers in Clima than there was in Mayc, and co-op workers reported feeling less identified with their firm, and, perhaps, more alienated.

Cooperative managers had a very different experience; they consistently reported believing more firmly in cooperativism than did shop-floor workers. Based on my comparison of Mayc and Clima, it seems that the cooperative structure successfully ties managers to their firm, and cooperative managers believe more in their business form than do managers in private firms. In short, the cooperatives promote identification and participation for cooperative managers, and most especially for high-level managers. In this marked difference between workers and managers may lie part of the explanation for workers' apathy or inactivism. It is possible that the participatory structures and ideology effectively nurture and cultivate managers' initiatives and activism but not those of workers.

These differences between managers' and workers' experiences indicate that scholarship that focuses only on managers portrays an overly positive evaluation of cooperativism. This selective representation of the cooperative experience is at the heart of the myth of Mondragón, and in creating the myth, researchers have missed important insights. While standard labor management conflict does not adequately represent workers in Euskadi—there is inter-syndicate conflict; individual workers defer to the Workers' Council rather than developing a command of the issues; gender issues are not sufficiently tackled—it does appear to give workers a greater sense of power and identification with firms that some even consider to be theirs.[4]

Cooperative workers and managers also disagreed about the meaning and extent of equality. Managers were convinced that equality existed, while workers insisted that inequality was real and meaningful. Their disagreement over the interpretation of equality parallels historic debates about Basque egalitarianism. As I discussed in chapter 3, the myth that Basque society was traditionally egalitarian has appealed to different classes at different economic and political moments. Like the egalitarian myth, the ideology of cooperative equality changed over time. It was originally articulated by the PNV-nationalist founders of the cooperatives in the hope of promoting a social project that would generate ethnic rather than class alliances. The language of equality became part of the management style of the cooperative factories. By the 1970s, however, workers perceived that class differences were real. Workers' frustration with official cooperativism is evident throughout this chapter; during interviews and in their responses to my surveys, workers wanted to express that there was inequality in the cooperatives, that social classes did exist, and that they felt controlled by a language and ideology that denied these facts.

But the struggles between workers and managers over work pace and shop-floor control that occurred in Clima portended a larger trend in the cooperatives that would transform the argument about equality. Toward the end of 1990, co-op managers were beginning to reject the ideology they had previously promoted. They argued that the cooperative was never meant to create equality but something more flexible such as "equilibrium" or "solidarity." Managers increasingly used words that were a part of a global language about industry, including "efficiency," "crisis," and "competition," to convince workers of the urgency of business and production plans that called for increased production and lower earnings (see Taylor 1994). "Efficiency, "crisis," and "competition" began to replace "we are all workers" and prior ways of speaking to and motivating workers, such as "we are all in this together." The monograph by Greenwood and González et al. (1989) exemplifies this shift; in many regards, the book is a self-reflective effort on the part of cooperative managers to think out and understand this transition in their language and according to their ideology.

Once having formulated the ideology of equality, however, managers could not fully control its use. Workers who were previously cynical about equality began to demand it, and many began to turn to syndicates. This is the subject of the next chapter.

7

Cooperatives, Politics, and Working-Class Life

Every year in Mondragón, as in other Gipuzkoan towns, there is a strike over the provincewide labor contract for the metal sector. The first of these strikes took place in 1962, when the Franco regime first empowered the vertical syndicates to bargain with employers, and there was a twenty-day strike in Unión Cerrajera (see chapter 4). In a zone where the metal contract affects the material lives of so many people, the annual strike is a central event. Hundreds, sometimes thousands, of workers and their supporters take part. Just as the 1962 strike ushered in the remaking of Mondragón's working class after the Spanish Civil War, the annual conflict over the contract affirms that remaking. During negotiations between the business owners' association and the syndicates over wages, conditions, schedules, and vacations, metal workers from town factories walk off the job to demonstrate their collective strength. They do so even in years when the talks are going well. Sometimes, the two sides simply go through the motions so that the structure of the contest does not break down. Thus, the strike is not always a genuine struggle between labor and owners but a ritual of class solidarity.

Yearly, the strike stops production in most shops for several hours. In February 1990, however, workers did not act out their parts as they had for nearly three decades. A walk-out was called for the morning, but in some factories, workers did not assemble before their shifts to vote to join the action and remained at work. In other factories, the customary assembly was held, but workers voted to stay on the job. A demonstration was planned for the afternoon, but only sixty people showed up, myself included.

Like other kinds of rituals in which people act out the contours of their cultures, Basque demonstrations have a recognizable structure. First, everyone present gathers in an assembly; this transforms the loosely knit group into a more cohesive body for the duration of the demonstration. A spokesperson then addresses the assembly:

Three people from Mondragón were arrested yesterday . . .

Today is international women's day . . .

> This year profits are up, but the owners say they can only afford to
> give us . . .

After the spokesperson talks for about five minutes, others speak, contradict-
ing the spokesperson, articulating the political argument of another party (often another party on the left), adding information, or contributing a personal
account. The spokesperson then proposes that the group march through town.
If the route differs from the one usually taken, the change is noted, and if anyone disagrees with the route, he or she speaks up.

The importance of choice of route and the attention given to this decision reveals that Basque demonstrations are simultaneously about specific issues and a more general contest for territoriality. Valle (1988) makes this
connection in her analysis of the biannual *Korrika,* a race to raise money for
the ikastolas (Basque-language schools) associated with the radical nationalist
movement. When the runners move through all the towns and cities of Euskadi (both in France and Spain), they claim and validate the territoriality of
the Basque nation as they promote Euskera education. Local demonstrations
are likewise choreographed to command territory, not for the purpose of trac-
ing the outlines of the nation but to claim space for a political ideology within
a given town.

On the day of the metal sector strike, the assembly listened to the
spokesperson propose a route. Someone from the syndicate UGT suggested that
there were too few people to march. He thought the group should stay gathered
in assembly and simply discuss the contract; he was concerned that the poor
showing would make a bad impression. Two members of CCOO argued that the
group should march. They wanted to make an ambitious circuit, through the
town center and the working-class neighborhoods of Musakola and San Andrés.
The assembly decided to march, but instead of going through the neighborhoods, it took a shorter route and walked only through the center. The group's
presence there symbolized working-class claims to the streets in the center of
Mondragón, but it chose to forgo symbolic claims to other districts. The march
was short. The entire event was over in half an hour and was disappointing for
all who participated.

Notably, not a single cooperator was in attendance. Although the provincial contract does not determine salaries in the cooperatives, where pay is
linked to profits, it does indirectly influence co-op pay. In principle, the co-ops
pay anticipios at a percentage that equals the wage level in the area, and low-
end salaries are pegged to the local labor market. When the provincial contract
increases base pay by 5 percent, for example, anticipios are generally increased
by 5 percent. Thus, the metal contract does have an impact on cooperative
workers, and cooperators have always made some showing in the past. As one
syndicalist told me, "No one expects the cooperators to call the strike to a vote
in their workplaces" (since the relationship of the contract to co-op wages

makes it ambiguous whether or not this would be an internal strike and thus an infringement of cooperative bylaws). Nor did syndicalists blame the failure of the demonstration on cooperators; they never counted on cooperators' attendance in any significant numbers. Syndicalists were disappointed, nonetheless, that not one cooperator showed up for the afternoon demonstration. "Surely someone on the late shift could have come before going to work," one demonstrator commented.

The poor turnout indicated that labor's strength had dwindled in Euskadi. It also signaled that there was a more local problem in the radical nationalist movement in Mondragón. While workers were expected to show up for a variety of events organized by radical nationalists—demonstrations organized by Herri Batasuna or Koordinadora Abertzale Sozialista (KAS) for independence for Euskadi, environmentalist campaigns, vigils for ETA prisoners held by the amnesty organization—these same groups did not mobilize their members for the metal strike. Townspeople I knew who worked in cooperative factories, small stores, and bars, who regularly participated in radical nationalist activities did not come to the demonstration. As I marched through the town center with the demonstrators, I passed the radical bars where I often spent time. The bars were open, and I saw several of my friends inside; during other demonstrations, these bars were closed, and my friends were in the street.

This image of my friends inside the radical milieu of the bars made a deep impression on me. I understood that it reflected a political shift in Mondragón, that the once dense interaction between labor and nationalist struggles had been undone. During the march I walked beside Patxi, a leader of the radical Basque nationalist syndicate LAB. He was worried by the lack of participation. "Mondragón," he said "should be like Hernani," a heavily industrialized town near Donosti known for its working-class militancy and its radical nationalist movement. "Mondragón used to be like Hernani, but the cooperatives have changed it." In the year that I had known Patxi, this was the first time he criticized the impact of the cooperatives on Mondragón. Indeed, the radical nationalist movement, of which his syndicate is a part, has publicly maintained its support of the cooperative system for over thirty years.

Patxi's comment marked a significant juncture in my research; it suggested to me the impact of the cooperatives on the political life of Mondragón. His comment also evidenced an important change in the radical nationalist relationship to the cooperatives. This chapter is about this shift in the radical nationalist position and the transformations inside the cooperatives that impelled it.

Radical Basque Nationalism and the Mondragón Cooperatives

An indication that LAB's public stance on the cooperatives was changing came in September 1989, when an article criticizing Fagor was published in *Egin,*[1] the daily newspaper associated with the radical nationalist movement. *Egin* ran a full-page story claiming that the Fagor Group planned to cut its work force by 1,038 through early retirements. The article charged that the cooperatives had come to behave just like private firms.

Companies in Euskadi and throughout industrialized economies use early retirement plans to reduce their work forces. Sometimes, handsome sums are offered to older employees who are close to retirement age. Early retirements are not nearly as devastating for individuals as are lay-offs; indeed, they may be welcomed by some workers. Early retirements are, however, devastating for industrialized regions, since jobs vacated by retirees are not made available for younger, permanent employees. Instead, companies use the opportunity to eliminate permanent positions, filling them with temporary workers, if they fill the jobs at all. Early retirement allows firms to rid themselves of full-time and permanent contracts and to increase their pool of temporary, part-time, or seasonal workers. By employing casual laborers, companies save the cost of benefits, paid vacations, and regular raises. Hence, early retirement is an important strategy for the current phase of flexible accumulation.

The *Egin* article drew a connection between global changes in labor relations and local conditions in the cooperatives. A representative of LAB was quoted as charging the cooperatives with

> becoming like any private firm, from the point of view of daily work, the cooperative member is as exploited in his/her job as any worker in a capitalist firm by increased production, mobility, schedule changes, etc.
>
> We don't understand why the managers don't present a proposal to lower the age of retirement in the cooperatives. . . .Instead, they opted, just like owners of private firms, to achieve profitability by the same methods as capitalist firms: lay-offs, increasing productivity, temporary contracts, etc.

The day after the article appeared, Fagor management denied that it had any plan for early retirements and accused LAB of stirring up trouble, but LAB stood by its charge. If such a plan existed, it was never implemented. The compelling question for my research was this: Why did LAB, which had never before issued a public criticism of the cooperatives, choose this time to level such a serious charge? In answering this question, the complex relationships between Basque nationalism and class politics that had made the Ulgor strike so divisive surfaced once more. The cooperatives were again a stage upon which the major political and ideological dilemmas of Basque nationalism were being acted out.

Changing Relations between Nationalists

In chapters 3 and 4, I showed that the cooperatives shared with the Partido Nacionalista Vasco (PNV) the social and political project of eliminating class conflict and heading off socialism by generating ethnic solidarity and developing Basque nationalism. The radical nationalism created by ETA in the 1960s reconfigured the relationship between class and national politics. ETA was more firmly based in class politics and sought alliances between the Basque working class and petty bourgeoisie. In the 1970s the radical nationalist movement developed beyond ETA. Herri Batasuna was founded to articulate this vision in electoral politics, LAB in the syndical arena, and KAS as the coalition for the many organizations affiliated with the movement for national liberation (MLNV). The projects of conservative and radical nationalists diverged in many spheres of social and political life but often overlapped in the cooperatives.

Despite their different approaches to class politics and their different conceptions of Basqueness, radical nationalists largely accepted PNV's control in the cooperatives. This was partly because, like PNV, radical nationalists conceptualized the cooperatives as Basque institutions that owed an allegiance to Euskadi. During one of my interviews with Patxi, he explained why LAB supported the cooperative purchase of the private firm Fabrelec

before it fell into the hands of foreign capital. LAB sees the cooperatives as valuable national resources, capital that is tied to Euskadi. Since the cooperators are owners, they have to vote to approve the movement of capital out of Euskadi. That would be a vote to lose their own jobs, to create unemployment. They wouldn't do it.

Iban, a member of LAB, who worked in a cooperative for twelve years, told me that the cooperative bank "will invest in Euskadi. The Caja will stay here even if we vote tomorrow to separate from Spain." This was different from PNV's opinion of Basque capitalists earlier in the century; radical nationalists did not believe that local capitalists were less exploitative of workers inside their factories, they simply believed that capital tied to Euskadi advanced the economic base of nationalism.

Moreover, the cooperatives offered political opportunities for both conservative and radical nationalists. In the political arena, PNV benefited from its control of the cooperatives. José Antonio Ardanza, the president of the Basque autonomous government, previously held a managerial position in the cooperative bank. Others in the Basque government, as well as some in leadership positions within PNV, have been managers in the cooperatives. Conversely, the cooperatives benefit from their governmental ties: The Basque autonomous government in Gasteiz is a major funder of the Ikerlan cooperative research and development institute, and gives grants to assist startups of new cooperative enterprises (Whyte and Whyte 1988, 65, 79). The Mondragón group also benefited from the 1993 Cooperative Law of Euskadi. It is this law, rather than standard labor law, that regulates labor–management relations in the cooperatives. Amendments made in 1993 increase the permissible percent of non-member contract employees from twenty to thirty percent, a change that responded to the needs of Mondragón's cooperative factories.[2]

Radical-nationalist organizations also benefited, though to a lesser extent, from the experience their members gained in the cooperatives. Xabier Zubizarreta, the Herri Batasuna mayor of Mondragón since 1987, is an engineer in one of the Fagor factories; he has a reputation as a good administrator and is well liked even by townspeople who do not support HB. Likewise, the mayor of the neighboring Gatzaga is the head of Fagor Clima's engineering department; though he ran as an independent, he is active in HB and LAB. Txomin Iturbe, a leader of ETA until his death in 1987, was a founding member of a Fagor cooperative. Furthermore, my research in Mayc and Clima suggests that HB has more support in the cooperatives than in private firms, something that townspeople suspect but are unable to quantify. In Clima, 36 percent of respondents to my survey sympathized with or were militants in HB, compared with 22 percent in Mayc. Significantly, it was low- and mid-level managers who were responsible for the higher percent of HB supporters in the cooperative.[3]

Patxi told me that LAB's goal was to place its affiliates and win sympathizers among the middle rungs of management:

> LAB is interested in having qualified people in the cooperatives. This is because LAB is part of the larger movement of MLNV and KAS and wants independence for Euskadi. We can't allow political power and government positions to pass us by because our people are not qualified. There, our people have access to promotions, to getting an education, although I know this is mostly theoretical because people don't really move up through the cooperative system. But there is the possibility, and this is crucial.

In a 1985 booklet entitled "Ponencia sobre cooperativismo y posición de LAB ante la S.A.L." (Report on cooperativism and LAB's position on employee ownership), LAB also noted its potential base of support among shop-floor workers and low- and mid-level managers. "The directors of the cooperative group identify with 'moderate nationalist' positions, but among ordinary members we find very widespread radical-nationalist sentiment" (14). "Ponencia sobre cooperativismo" also acknowledged the importance of the

FIGURE 21

José Antonio Ardanza (right) with two founders of the Mondragón Cooperatives (first two men on left. Credit: Arrasate Press.

cooperatives' role in promoting technological development in Euskadi. Ikerlan made important strides in machine-tool automation and design, making the region less dependent on foreign inventions and patents. The cooperatives created a local technocratic class, and that class was more likely than engineers and managers in private firms to support HB's version of nationalism.

Nonetheless, the cooperatives did not fit seamlessly into the radical-nationalist world, and the contradictions were especially acute for LAB, the radical nationalist organization charged with carrying out class politics and representing workers. Rather, the radical nationalists' acceptance of the cooperatives was both complicated and politically determined. LAB's 1985 booklet on cooperatives indicated this compromise. Restating ETA's position from 1963, (p. 94), LAB criticized cooperativism in general, arguing that cooperatives were incapable of transforming the economy within a capitalist mode of production. In the Mondragón cooperatives in particular, there was

> fake internal democracy, a division of labor, economism, tecnocratism, education subordinated to production. . . . consumerism. . . . production of socially unnecessary goods [which all] continue to reproduce the defects of the capitalist system. (LAB 1985, 12)

Meanwhile, *Egin* published a multipage tribute to the cooperatives.[4] During my discussions with Patxi and Iban, they cautiously negotiated between the potential political and economic benefits of the cooperatives for Euskadi and the ways in which the cooperatives failed shop-floor workers, from increasing work pace and stress levels to the inability of the Social Council and General Assembly to ensure democracy (problems I had seen in Clima). But their criticisms remained rhetorical. It was not until relations between moderate and radical nationalists in the wider political arena became acrimonious that LAB's compromise with the cooperatives broke down, and their criticisms turned to action.

The Ajuria Enea Pact

PNV and HB and the political groups in their respective camps competed for votes, influence in social life and worldview, and power, but they also joined forces when basic aspects of nationalist politics, such as autonomy for the Basque provinces vis-à-vis Madrid, were at stake. However, relations between the two nationalist camps deteriorated, and their sometime alliance shattered in 1988 with the Pacto de Ajuria Enea. The pact, signed by all the major political parties in Euskadi except HB, united the signatories in a condemnation of the political violence of ETA.

PNV would not have signed this pact a few years earlier, since ETA members were considered patriots, even national heroes, by a large segment of the

Basque population, including many who voted for PNV. In the political arena, PNV laid historic claim to ETA, periodically reminding the electorate that ETA was originally (if briefly) linked to PNV. This won PNV votes (Clark 1990, 2–3). But ETA's popularity had declined in the late 1980s, paralleling the decline in popular support for leftist movements in Europe, especially after the fall of communist governments in Eastern Europe, but it was due also to particular circumstances in Euskadi. In 1987, ETA bombed a French-owned supermarket in Barcelona to symbolize the boycott of French goods that was called by radical nationalists to protest the French government's extradition of ETA members to Spain. While ETA reportedly warned the manager to vacate the premises, the supermarket remained open and eighteen people were killed. ETA had never before chosen so civilian a target, and the Basque public began to turn away from ETA. PNV also distanced itself from ETA, and waged a political and ideological war against HB. HB was branded "anti-democratic" by the other political parties for its refusal to condemn ETA and for its connections to the armed organization (Cueva 1988).

In this context, radical nationalists began to see PNV as the political enemy. When I was in Euskadi in 1989, a new slogan peppered radical nationalist demonstrations: "PNV, traitor!" During one demonstration in Mondragón, several young people removed the Basque flag from the PNV social club, making the point that PNV members did not deserve to identify themselves as Basque.

In the wake of the pact, PNV took on HB in local settings. In 1990, PNV developed a campaign to curb the public display of political posters. PNV mayors in several towns, including Oñati, banned the use of paste for putting up posters (typically wallpaper paste was used). Postering with paste became an offense for which activists could be arrested. Tape was to be used instead, to make removal easier and cleaner, thus making posters a less permanent part of the town's decor. Further, postering was to be limited to designated areas, leaving the facades of buildings free of political debate. Given that radical nationalists had quite effectively commanded public space through graffiti and posters, PNV saw that it was to their advantage to control this form of communication. Radical nationalists interpreted the new regulations as an attempt to impose a new aesthetic, one they considered to be more middle class and European than what they believed was the working-class and Basque tenor of their towns.

In Mondragón, the battle between PNV and HB came to a head after the 1991 municipal elections, when the mayorship was to be decided. In Spain's parliamentary democracy, municipal council seats are distributed in proportion to percentage of votes. The elected council members (Mondragón has twenty-one) cast their vote for mayor. With 24.4 percent of the vote in Mondragón, HB was the largest single party, with a slight margin over PSOE (with 24.1 percent). Still, HB did not have a majority, and its control of the mayorship was vulnerable. At the regional level, PSOE and PNV had a plan to defeat HB in key towns. PSOE and PNV crafted an agreement whereby PNV instructed its council members in various towns and cities to give their votes to the PSOE candidate. This goes against standard practice whereby each party votes for its own candidate. Mondragón was singled out, since it was the largest and most important town where HB held the mayorship; together PSOE and PNV had 45 percent of the vote and could have won. In other places, the pact had success-fully defeated HB.

For days before the mayorship was to be decided, rumors abounded about what the PNV councils-elect were going to do. I was back in Mondragón for a visit during this time. On the day of the vote, I joined hundreds of angry and unruly observers, mostly HB supporters, congregated in the town hall. The PSOE choice for mayor was Nekane Iglesias. Nekane is a Basque name, but every time a vote was cast for her, the audience yelled "Loli," a Spanish name. Their point was that since she was involved in an effort to take away the may-orship from HB, she was not Basque. After the third time that this happened, the person who was reading the ballots (who was brought in from out of town) called her "Loli." When someone from PSOE told him "Nekane," he said, "But the people call her Loli," and he kept reading "Loli." (I initially interpreted this as a rather innocent attempt by an out-of-towner to side with the crowd, but I later learned he was an affiliate of HB). The HB choice was Xabier Zubizarreta, the current mayor. When the ballot reader called his name, no one from PSOE attempted to undermine his claim to Basqueness. In a dramatic and tense finale, two of the four PNV councils-elect refused to give their votes to Nekane Igle-sias. The HB candidate won the mayorship, and the hall filled with shouts and cheers from the townspeople who had crowded in to witness the proceedings (see Kasmir 1992b).

Despite the stand taken by individual PNV council members, the party as a whole allied with PSOE to defeat HB, which contributed to the atmosphere of animosity between PNV and HB. Amidst the Basque/anti-Basque dichotomy that characterizes life in Euskadi (cf. Heiberg 1980, 1989), this placed PNV in the anti-Basque, pro-Spanish camp with PSOE. It was in this political climate in which LAB reversed its long-standing, conciliatory position toward the co-operatives. This shift coincided with a restructuring of the cooperative system and the deterioration of shop-floor conditions, which resulted from strategies to cope with worldwide economic crisis.

Crisis and Change in the Mondragón Cooperatives

With its industrial economy based largely in steel, Euskadi suffered the effects of worldwide crisis much like the historic industrial centers in the north-east United States or the "rust belt" in the Midwest. Bluestone and Harrison (1982) described the effect of economic crisis on the United States:

By the beginning of the 1980s, every newscast seemed to contain a story about a plant shutting down, another thousand jobs disappearing from a community, or the frustrations of workers unable to find full-time jobs utilizing their skills and providing enough income to support their families.(4)

From 1973 to 1975, advanced industrial regions across the globe saw a fall in production, a decline in the rate of profit, and an increase in the cost of living (see Howard and King 1990; Mandel 1978, 1–46). Euskadi was partly sheltered by Spain's relatively closed market under the Franco regime, but after Franco's death (1975) and the opening of the Spanish market, Spain was exposed to the full impact of crisis. The ramifications for the relatively noncompetitive Spanish economy were acute (Albarracín 1987, 38–48).

Euskadi experienced decapitalization of factories, factory closings, and massive job loss. The port city of Bilbo was severely affected. As the ship-building and steel sectors were restructured, entire working-class neighborhoods that had depended on these industries became depressed. There was a violent strike in 1977 to prevent the closing of the ship-building firm Euskalduna (CAT 1985). This dramatic and violent strike made the Basque public aware of the impact of the crisis on Euskadi, which was to be long-term. It is estimated that between 1976 and 1991, almost 113,200 industrial jobs and 60,000 jobs in fishing and agriculture were lost.[5] This meant loss of membership for the syndicates. Simultaneous with the crisis, the syndicates signed the Pact of Moncloa (1978), in which they accepted more flexible labor laws, thereby providing the legal framework for restructuring the labor market. These trends were exacerbated by Spain's efforts to comply with European regulations against price and market protections in order to become a full member of the European Community by 1993.

In the Alto Deba there were more than four thousand jobless workers in each of the years from 1986 to 1989, bringing the unemployment rate to approximately 20 percent, a proportion that made the comarca typical in Gipuzkoa. But unlike surrounding firms, the Mondragón cooperatives thrived throughout the 1970s. By the early 1980s, however, crisis hit. Cooperative managers and Governing Councils proposed amendments to the cooperative structure in hopes of preserving profitability and promoting growth. Previously independent cooperatives were organized into geographic and sectoral groups. New democratic and management organs were created at the group level: the Central Social Council served as the workers' representative for all the cooperatives in the group; a Central General Assembly gathered representatives from the individual cooperatives; and groupwide Governing and Management Councils were established. This centralization necessarily transferred some aspects of decision making from the shop floors and offices of individual factories to the group's central offices (Greenwood and González et al. 1989, 76–78; Whyte and Whyte 1988, 131–49).

Policies to channel more money into capital reserves were also introduced. Members were asked to make additional contributions to their individual capital accounts in the co-op bank in order to increase funds available for investment. The proposals were approved by the cooperative membership, which, on the whole, was willing to sacrifice disposable income for the long-term survival of the firms (Whyte and Whyte 1988, 131–49). There were a few dissenting voices, but most cooperators dug in their heels and waited for times to get better. By the late 1980s, shop-floor workers in cooperatives brought home slightly less pay than their fellow workers in private firms (as was the case in Clima relative to Mayc [see chapter 5]). They also invested more money in their cooperatives, increased their levels of production, and worked extra hours. When these sacrifices were followed by qualitative changes in cooperative structure and working conditions, workers began to rebel.

Structural Change: The Cooperative Congress and the Mondragón Cooperative Corporation

As I noted in chapter 1, the Cooperative Congress was established in 1987. This biannual Congress transformed the loose affiliation among individual cooperatives into a more formal vehicle for planning and decision making. The Congress serves as an advisory body to the cooperatives and is constituted by some three hundred representatives from the more than one hundred fifty Mondragón cooperatives. It is governed by a Permanent Commission, made up of all the heads of the cooperative groups, and a Governing Council, which includes the president and other officers as well as representatives from the Congress. The Second Congress (1989) streamlined the geographic and sectoral groups of the early 1980s into tightly knit sectoral groups and created the Fund for Education and Intercooperative Development to move capital between cooperatives more easily (Whyte and Whyte 1991, 201–4). These structural changes drafted by the Congress were later ratified by the General Assemblies of individual co-ops. The Third Congress (1991) went furthest in redesigning the cooperative system; it proposed a new corporate structure, the Mondragón Cooperative Corporation (MCC). The choice of the word "corporation" (never before used to name a cooperative body) was significant; it promoted a businesslike and powerful image. The organization of MCC reflects "the need to achieve maximum business efficiency in the new competitive context of Europe" (statement released by MCC, quoted in *El Diario Vasco,* 21 December 1991, 35). Similarly, the cooperative bank later changed its name from Caja Laboral Popular (working people's bank) to Caja Laboral, presumably hoping to cast a less populist image.[7]

MCC encompasses the Cooperative Congress and all of the cooperative enterprises. (Its governing structures and relationship to the Cooperative Congress will no doubt evolve over the next several years.) MCC is incorporated as a holding company and is comprised of three groups: financial (Caja Laboral and the social security cooperative Lagun Aro), retail (led by the consumer cooperative Eroski), and industrial (comprised of ninety factories). The three groups are in turn divided into nine divisions and twenty-five sectoral groups. The Third Congress proposed the creation of another new business entity, MCC Inversiones S.A., an investment firm made up of Caja Laboral and Lagun Aro, and two new Lagun Aro financial and insurance firms. The denomination S.A. (*sociedad anónima*) indicates that this is a standard private firm instead of a cooperative. Its legal status opens channels for private investment, but the only investors to date are cooperatives. Moreover, MCC Inversiones can invest in the co-ops through the holding company, and since its noncooperative structure admits private capital, private investors now have a pathway into the individual cooperatives. MCC Inversiones can also offer public stock in the future. This would dramatically change the nature of the cooperative venture, in which, until recently, only members shared ownership and capital was tied to labor.[8]

MCC Inversiones was also structured to facilitate future purchases of private firms, allowing for more acquisitions like that of Fabrelec in 1989 and Luzuriaga in 1990. In the past, private firms have been converted into cooperatives, but the purchases of Fabrelec and Luzuriaga were different. They were the first purchases for the purposes of controlling a company that remained private. MCC now owns two private firms and employs their more than two thousand workers, who are not co-op members, do not have a vote in a General Assembly, do not share profits, and who are represented by a syndicate rather than a Social Council.

These structural changes were ratified by the General Assemblies of the member cooperatives in 1992, but from the perspective of the shop floor, the cooperative system began to look more like a sophisticated multinational corporation than a local, Basque enterprise. Furthermore, both the Cooperative Congress and MCC lack a basic component of cooperative democracy—a Social Council that would, at least formally, represent cooperators in their capacity as workers to these larger corporate bodies.[9]

Productivity and Stress on the Shop Floor

Simultaneous with these structural changes, some of the larger cooperatives reorganized production, and shifts were introduced to amortize investments in new machinery. Two and three shifts were scheduled to keep machines running twenty-four hours a day, seven days a week. Managers argued that this was the only way to remain competitive, especially as they looked toward full

integration into the European market in 1993. Workers objected: Shifts inter-
rupted their home lives, and since their schedule changed weekly, their sleep-
ing patterns were disrupted.

Shift work also interfered with social life. A friend of mine worked at
Fagor Garagartza, where his shift changed monthly. When he worked during
the day, he spent time in the bars after work and was active in radical politics.
When he worked at night, he was not around for weeks, a pattern that made him
peripheral to social life. With hundreds of cooperators working different shifts,
the previously collective schedule of social life was individualized, thus jeop-
ardizing the ritual poteo. Shifts were thus an assault on Basque culture and identity. After-work activities, such as making rounds of bars, eating with friends in
social clubs, going to the mountains, and taking language classes, make community life rich in Basque towns. Participating in these activities is part of being Basque. Many people, especially those involved in radical nationalist
politics, who pioneered an associative Basque identity in the 1960s and 1970s
believe that their high degree of association is their best defense against what
they call the "Europeanization" of their society. They imagine and have seen
Europe as a place where, as a friend of mine, Amaia, said,

> People are in their homes by nine o'clock in the evening. They may in-
> vite a small group of friends over or just watch television or a video with
> their husbands or wives. There is no one in the street. You can't even find
> an open bar after nine.

Amaia described this scene in a monotone that conveyed the soullessness which
she believed characterized this kind of a privatized existence. In contrast, the
streets of Basque cities and towns are crowded until eleven o'clock at night
during the work week and until the early morning hours during the weekend.

The collectivity that is constructed in public bars has a political dimension as well. Politics are discussed among friends and with bartenders. Bartenders take on an important role in communicating information and shaping
political ideas; the bar is an locus for generating ekintza (Kasmir 1992a,
1992b). Shift work in the cooperatives diminished the role of the bar as a gath-
ering place, and, like PNV's campaign to rid the streets of political posters, it
was a threat to Basque politics and identity.

The issue of shift work and collective social forms is, however, complicated by the simple fact that without both the stable employment and temporary contracts created by the cooperatives, people in Mondragón would not
have the money to frequent bars. Although a txikiteo is economical (in 1990,
the small glass of wine cost about twenty-five cents), the frequency and duration of the ritual means that afternoons and evenings out can get expensive. Pro-
longed unemployment can make it difficult to participate in bar life, and in

towns were the unemployment rate is high, bar culture is significantly affected. Eibar is such a town; its bars and streets are dreary compared to Mondragón's. Paradoxically, the cooperatives are responsible for the continuation of bar culture in Mondragón, while shift work in the cooperatives threatens bars' ability to bring people together on a dependable and collective schedule.

In addition to shift work, there were other changes in the shop floors of the cooperatives. As in Clima, consultants were brought into Fagor Garagartza to redesign production. A Garagartza worker, Kris, described her experience of being evaluated by a consultant:

> I was very nervous. It was very stressful. I didn't know what to do. He stood behind me while I was working, watching me. I was afraid that I wasn't working right. He just watched. I wanted to say to him, "You do the work if you are so expert at how to do it most efficiently."

Kris was a temporary worker, and, as much as she disliked her job preassembling washing machine parts, she wanted to be a co-op member. She was twenty-five and lived with her parents. Her family needed her income and the financial security of membership, and she wanted to buy her own apartment and begin an independent life. A few months later, she was made a member of Garagartza, for which she was grateful; but as a result of the consultants' study, Kris was now told how to coordinate the movements involved in her preassembly task, and she was expected to do her work faster. I met her after work one day, and she told me that she was nervous all the time. Her hand shook as she lit her cigarette.

After the jobs had been redesigned, Garagartza introduced just-in-time production. Just-in-time production sets work schedules according to incoming orders, requiring workers to stay late some days while they are sent home early other days, without prior notice. Just-in-time production does away with the regular work schedule. Since Garagartza produces refrigerators and stoves, which sell well in the summer, managers proposed that workers' August vacations be cut from one month to two weeks, making the most of summertime demand. The remaining two weeks' vacation could be scheduled individually later in the year. Like many European towns, Mondragón virtually shuts down in August, when families and friends vacation together. Changing the schedules of hundreds of workers at Garagartza would disrupt these patterns of leisure and family time. When management brought the proposal to change vacation schedules to a vote of the Garagartza annual General Assembly, it was soundly defeated. In the days following the vote, there was a lot of talk in town about this major and historic defeat of management. The attempt to change the vacation schedule took on importance partly because it represented another case of management's valuation of profitability over social life. Partly, it was just the last straw; after a decade of loss of pay, increased investment, harder work, and extra hours in the name of efficiency, crisis, and economic survival, workers felt they had been pushed far enough.

Furthermore, managers' credibility was waning as they talked more and more about efficiency and less about equality, democracy, and other principles upon which cooperativism was supposed to be based (cf. Taylor 1994). Workers noted the change in language and managerial style. They blamed it on a new, younger generation of managers who were less likely to have worked their way up from the shop floor but went directly into office jobs after earning degrees at the cooperative Polytechnic and Professional School or at university. Unlike the first generation of managers who founded Ulgor, these younger managers were not even committed to the nationalist policies of PNV. They were perceived by radical nationalists and by many shop-floor workers as "yuppies," whose interests lay outside of the community in European values and lifestyles, and who would sacrifice the daily and annual cycles of the community for profit. One worker explained:

> The cooperatives are going through a transitional phase, when the business is more important than the person. There is a great dis-ideologization. It coincides with the retirements of the top leaders, the founders, who at least believed in cooperativist ideologies.

Shop-floor workers also blamed this new economism on inherent flaws in cooperativism. As economic competition intensified, it became clear that cooperatives were never an alternative to capitalism. As one worker said, "Cooperatives are no different from capitalist firms. If anything, they are more sophisticated at capitalism because the workers have no protections." Lacking syndical representation, not bound by the metal-sector contract, able to transfer workers between factories, and permitted to have 30 percent of the work force on temporary contracts (as of 1993), the cooperatives had perhaps the most flexible labor force in the region.

Protest in the Cooperatives

Garagartza workers' rejection of management's vacation proposal attracted attention outside the factory in the town, because it represented a change in labor–management relations inside the cooperatives. Workers *organized* to build a consensus against the proposal before the meeting of the General Assembly. This "No"-vote campaign was spear-headed by a small opposition group of cooperative workers called Kooperatibisten Taldea (Cooperative Group), or KT. KT had been in existence since 1982, when perhaps a dozen workers began publication of the monthly magazine *Kooperatibisten Taldeak*

FIGURE 22

Worker in Fagor refrigeration plant. Credit: Sharryn Kasmir.

(though actual publication was spotty), in which they detailed their many crit-icisms of the cooperatives. Essays, satirical articles, cartoons, and letters ob-jected to reserved parking places for co-op executives; discussed the alienation of co-op workers; analyzed the negative effects of sectoral groups on the au-tonomy of individual firms; argued that participation and democracy were weak; and detailed instances of crisis-induced cuts in pay and increases in work pace and overtime. The first edition in March 1982 contained an article entitled "Overcome the Crisis by Increasing the Pace of Production," which claimed that managers ignored "the inhuman working conditions in which large sectors of cooperative workers live." It also ran the first chapter of a "Political Tri-bunal" on the history and future of the Mondragón Cooperative Movement; the cooperatives were judged harshly. Later editions became even more sarcastic and biting.

By their own estimates, KT claimed no more than fifteen active members in early 1989 and only twice as many sympathizers. Each time I visited a co-operative and interviewed the personnel manager, I asked what he or she thought of KT. Invariably, I was told that in that co-op there were one or two members and few, if any, sympathizers, and that their effect was minimal.

KT was not affiliated with any party, but some of the activists were mem-bers of the once-Maoist EMK or the Trotskyist LKI. Several had been involved in the 1974 strike in Ulgor, and many townspeople still associated them with the leftist factions of ETA that supported that strike. Most were in their late thir-ties, had worked in the cooperatives all of their adult lives, and had low-level jobs on the shop floor. They believed, as they did in the 1970s, that the Social Council did not effectively represent them as workers and that, without the right to strike, the Social Council had no leverage against management. I met with KT as a group on three occasions. While their analysis was often not far from the sentiments of cooperative workers, as my study of Fagor Clima indicated (see chapters 5 and 6), their critical style earned them the reputation of being too hardline. Just as the leftist factions of ETA remained isolated from the main-stream of cooperative workers in the 1970s, KT failed to gain broad support in the 1980s. Toward the end of 1989, however, KT's popularity began to grow, and this enabled the group to successfully organize workers to defeat the pro-posal to cut August vacations in Garagartza.

KT owed its newfound acceptance to a campaign it launched with the syndicate CCOO several months earlier against Método de Medición de Tiem-pos (MMT). MMT is a method for measuring workers' productivity that was newly introduced into the cooperative Copreci, which manufactures fittings for copper tubing. Copreci had recorded losses the previous year, and in order to boost production, it hired a Belgian consulting firm to reorganize the plant. These consultants were consistently called the "Americans" by shop-floor workers I talked to. When I reminded them that the consultants were from Belgium, they remarked, "Whatever" or "It's all the same," and continued to speak about "the Americans." For co-op workers, Americans symbolized unbridled and unwanted industrial progress, just as Europeans symbolized a threat to Basque identity and popular culture.

The consultants videotaped Copreci workers performing their jobs; every part of their bodies was filmed so that the whole body could be mobilized for production. The specialists also analyzed the videos to determine the smallest components of each motion required for all jobs. Jobs were then redefined to cut out what were considered to be inefficient movements (it was determined that there were twelve essential movements in production and that all other movements were unnecessary) and to eliminate what were determined to be unnecessary rests. Workers were expected to perform their jobs in this way throughout the day. The normal rhythms of work—fast in the morning, a slump in the afternoon—were discarded as inefficient. Mondragón's CCOO issued the following statement in criticism of MMT:

> This system doesn't take into consideration the person, it doesn't take into consideration personal characteristics (if the person is old, prior work habits). . . . MMT rationalizes jobs to the most basic, necessary movements, so that the jobs lack any content. They could be performed by a robot.[10]

With the new standard, output increased by 25 percent, but workers complained that the rate was exhausting and stressful. CCOO had evidence from a General Motors plant in Zaragoza, Spain that workers suffered from stress-related psychological and physical problems when MMT was used. A KT member told me that in Copreci,

> Ten to fourteen have fallen ill with hysteria, depression, nerves, vomiting. They are treating us like chickens in a coop. We stand totally still with all the parts at our sides. They said that there were dead times, that they didn't increase the work, just took out the dead times in between movements. And, they took out the time when we made a bad piece. They said there shouldn't be any bad pieces, so that time wasn't calculated in.[11]

CCOO and KT argued that the system went beyond simply rationalizing jobs. MMT was an even more brutal process than the efficiency studies used in Clima and Garagartza, since it was designed to evaluate workers who operate numerically controlled (computerized) machinery. Linked to computer-controlled work stations, MMT allows managers to take continuous readings of output and to calculate the precise amount of labor power needed at any moment. This gave Copreci the capability of making constant minute adjustments in the work force. After instituting MMT, Copreci determined that it had excess workers, who they then transferred to other cooperatives, including Clima.[12] MMT also allowed for a monitoring of output that could facilitate a shift to a system of just-in-time production and, thus, more flexible work schedules.

KT and CCOO distributed leaflets in cooperative work places, put up posters in the portalón (the main entrance to the town center where political news is announced), and organized a forum on MMT in Mondragón's cultural center, the Palace of Monterrón. The forum was attended by approximately eighty people, considered to be a good turnout; most were low-level workers in the cooperatives. The guest speaker was a CCOO affiliate who had worked in the Zaragoza plant, and he told of how MMT caused physical and emotional stress among his workmates. Someone from the audience asked him to talk about the difference in workers' reaction to MMT in the cooperatives and in private firms. He answered:

> I don't know, but I know the issues are more clear in a private firm, where there is an owner and a worker. The issue is clear, that it challenges the fundamental rights of human beings. A human being should have more rights than a machine.

A man from the audience yelled:

> In the co-ops, we should have more rights; it is written that we should have more human rights!

The discussion turned to a more philosophical consideration of the meaning of cooperativism. A member of KT asked rhetorically:

> What are the co-ops? What are the objectives of the co-ops? The cooperatives, where are they headed? If they once talked about what it was to be human, now they talk only about profits.

Someone else responded to his comment:

> The cooperatives have created a culture in Mondragón of working more and more hours, of living more for yourself. The cooperative spirit we had is lost and only a few people in the vanguard do any syndical work. They [management] know that they are not going to encounter any struggle against MMT. We have to coordinate forces.

After the forum, KT members told me that they considered MMT to be the "most serious labor problem facing local workers," and they hoped LAB would get involved. They saw LAB, with a more moderate image and more support among radical nationalists in the cooperatives, as having legitimacy and support that they did not. I asked Patxi, a local leader of LAB, about his syndicate's position on MMT. Patxi told me he was concerned because "the cooperatives are the business leaders in the area, and if they implement this, other firms will follow." It was in the next several months that LAB's public position on the cooperatives shifted. In August 1989, there was a small article in *Egin*,[13] which termed the imposition of MMT "anti-democratic," since the Social Council and the workers were opposed. LAB accused co-op "technocrats" of undermining the democratic and humanist principles of cooperativism. These views were echoed in the larger and more controversial article on early retirements, which appeared less than a month later. Together, these articles placed LAB in a confrontational relationship with the cooperatives, and it was just five months later that Patxi shared with me his frustration over the disappointing turnout for the metal-sector strike and the effects of the cooperatives on Mondragón's working class.

LAB's position was more measured than KT's; it called for a return to the values of cooperativism, especially equality. LAB used cooperative ideology itself to rally workers. Toward the end of my fieldwork in 1990, cooperative workers were discussing equality differently. Rather than seeing equality as a cynical managerial ideology, (the way Begoña had over our dinner in 1987 [see page 122], when I first sensed that workers felt manipulated by cooperativism), they began to talk about it as an important cooperative value. More significantly, they began to embrace it as *their* value, which *they* had to defend against managers, who were willing to forgo equality for the sake of efficiency. Even those who had been the most vocal critics of cooperativism began to use the words "cooperative" and "equality" as weapons, and embraced egalitarianism as a working-class philosophy.

One of the most popular dimensions of cooperation was pay equity. In 1990 and 1991, proposals were made at the yearly General Assembly of the social security cooperative and in a meeting of the Fagor Group to widen the pay ratio to 1:9 or 1:10. On both occasions, the proposals were soundly defeated (at Fagor, workers spoke so vociferously against the proposal that it never even came up for a vote.) Co-op workers refused to allow the principle of pay equity to be violated, and LAB followed suit, publicly arguing that this showed that workers were more cooperativist than managers. Even HB, which had until then left criticism of the cooperatives to LAB, warned of the dissolution of cooperative principles.[14]

In 1992, LAB formed its own group in the cooperatives called Talde Cooperativista. Like KT, it is an opinion group; but, whereas KT is independent of political parties and syndicates, Talde Cooperativista is linked to a syndicate. Articles authored by Talde Cooperativista criticizing the co-ops appeared periodically in *Egin,*[15] a departure from the laudatory tone of *Egin's* pre-1989 reportage. LAB also expressed its support for syndical intervention:

> The absence of syndicates in the cooperatives has negative repercussions for workers. Workers lack an organizational form, and the directors of the cooperatives take advantage of this fact by making substantial changes in working conditions (increasing work pace, changing schedules, abusing temporary contracts, etc.) which would not so easily be accepted by workers in private firms.[16]

In 1992, the votes to ratify the recommendations of the Third Cooperative Congress were held in the General Assemblies of all the member cooperatives. While the sweeping changes regarding corporate restructuring and the establishment of MCC were approved, two salary proposals were defeated. The first was the proposal to allow for a widening of the salary ratio, in the short run to 1:7 or 1:8 and with larger spreads in the future. The second was over the anticipo payment. The Congress recommended paying profits at a percentage that left workers' pay below that stipulated for private workers by the metal contract for Gipuzkoa. Cooperators demanded that their pay levels be increased to equal those of the sector. Both proposals were voted down in most Fagor co-ops by overwhelming majorities; 68 to 84 percent of the members voted against them.

While the structural changes that were approved are no doubt just as significant for cooperators' futures, perhaps these two votes on salaries—more concrete, more clearly linked to concepts of equality—were accessible fights for cooperative workers who have not organized on their own behalf in nearly four decades.

Syndicalization of the Mondragón Cooperatives?

In 1990, the cooperatives sponsored a locally broadcast television program on syndicalization, and the official magazine of the cooperative, *Lankinde,* has featured articles on the topic.[17] Toward the end of my fieldwork, managers who told me eighteen months earlier that syndicates had no place in the cooperatives began to respond more moderately to my questions. They said that it might be appropriate for syndicates to operate in a limited way. ELA and UGT have also publicly called for the syndicalization of the cooperatives, though they have yet to form any organizations within the co-op factories.[18]

In 1994, KT joined with CCOO and the small independent syndicate ESK-CUIS to form the quasi-syndical coalition Lankideak (Fellow Workers). Currently Lankideak, KT, and Talde Cooperativista are each discussing the best

FIGURE 23

Members of Lankideak preparing for a meeting in Mondragón's town hall.
Credit: Arrasate Press.

strategy for intervening in the cooperatives: Should they fight to change the by-laws that prevent syndicates from operating in the cooperatives? Should they first work to increase the number of members in their respective groups? Should syndicates be allowed to run slates for Social Council and Governing Council, as they would for the Workers' Council in a private firm, or should they concentrate on getting individual members elected to important positions in the co-ops? Are these quasi-syndical opinion groups more appropriate than formal syndicates for the cooperatives?

All of the syndicates see in the cooperatives a work force of more than twenty thousand potential members who could do a lot to boost affiliation rates in the labor movement, which is losing membership as deindustrialization advances. For Basque syndicates, tackling the difficult problem of organizing workers who are also owners mirrors the complex problems facing syndicates and unions elsewhere, whose potential constituencies work part-time or on temporary contracts, or are unemployed. This crossroads for the cooperative system raises important questions for those who cast Mondragón as a prime example of industrial restructuring. If workers in the Mondragón cooperatives, who work in an environment that is widely considered to be the leading alternative to standard labor–management conflict, are considering syndicalization, what does this mean for the status of the Mondragón model? More generally, what does it mean for the ideology of labor–management cooperation internationally?

Conclusions

In January 1994, there was a general strike in Spain to protest the central government's labor law reforms. The reforms would make it easier to lay off workers, make it legal to schedule workers twelve hours a day and sixty hours a week, allow the month-long vacation to be broken into two two-week periods (something the cooperatives had already done), legalize two full weeks of work without a day off, and eliminate overtime pay for night shifts. A friend wrote me a letter about the strike:

> In Mondragón, the strike was total. Even though in some of the cooperatives, the vote was not a full two-thirds majority, and they stayed at work. Still, some of the cooperatives went out, and the strike was successful.

Dramatically different from the 1990 metal-sector strike, the general strike of 1994 would seem to indicate a new phase for the cooperatives, in which internal organization may lead to activism and solidarity with the rest of the labor movement. Perhaps cooperative workers (once disillusioned and apathetic) will begin to utilize the democratic organs within the cooperatives to exercise meaningful control and ownership over their firms. In so doing, perhaps they will transform the structure of those institutions to make them more democratic. Perhaps, too, co-op workers will determine that they need syndicates to press their claims and, in the process, maybe they will build a new kind of model in Mondragón.

Conclusions

Myths are a source of popular memory and identity, and they often provide emotional and ideological inspiration for activism. They survive, are transformed, and are retold because they are useful. Often, their utility is related to class interests and political projects. In Mondragón, the legend of the dragon, as it was told to and by townspeople, created a historical picture of an artisan town. Contemporarily, this tale empowers workers to claim the town as theirs, which they do during demonstrations, as they turn the streets and bars into arenas for identity formation and political discussion, and as they conceptualize town architecture, monuments, and museums. Similarly, the myth of Basque egalitarianism provides a cultural and economic argument for Euskadi's claim to independence and socialism. These stories are perhaps no more "true" than the myth of the Mondragón cooperatives, yet I have treated them more kindly. Workers in Mondragón, and radical nationalists throughout Euskadi, retell their allegories of the dragon and an egalitarian past in a political contest over the class character of their town and the legitimacy of their nation. In contrast, the tellers of the myth of the cooperatives (academics, journalists, business consultants) claim that theirs is a nonideological story, yet it is not.

Researchers have listened to the accounts of personnel managers, presidents of cooperatives, heads of cooperative groups, and public relations staff at Ikasbide or the Caja Laboral. Without interviewing cooperative workers, local syndicalists, or political activists, they have crafted a model of the cooperative system. In their model, there is no class conflict, democracy serves the interests of all, and ownership motivates workers and gives them a sense of identity with their firm. Workers, however, tell a different story. I decided to write about the cooperatives from a working-class perspective in order to correct this imbalance and because, like many people, I was first attracted to the case of Mondragón because I believed it made industrial work more meaningful and industrial society more just. I therefore judged the cooperative myth by its impact on workers, in Mondragón and elsewhere.

The Mondragón cooperatives were packaged as an international model for industrial restructuring at a time of worldwide economic crisis. Understanding this economic context is a necessary step in determining the implications of the model for working classes. The global discourse about work began to shift dramatically in the mid-1970s. Fordism, with its commitment to localism, stable work, and family wage (a reality for a segment of the working class but only a promise for the rest) was the dominant organizing principle of industrial capitalism in the post–World War II period (Aglietta 1978; Gordon, Edwards, and Reich 1982; Harvey 1989). Flexibility is now the axiom of industrial organization (Harvey 1989). Permanent and unionized jobs are being replaced with contract and part-time positions, and workplaces are being redesigned with "de-bureaucratized" managerial strategies (Grenier 1988), such as the team concept, quality circles, and employee ownership. A correlate of these strategies is the claim that unions and labor–management conflict are less effective in representing workers' interests than is cooperation. Cooperation is a new ideology for the current phase of flexible accumulation, and Mondragón is the most developed example of this non-unionized, cooperative workplace. It may also be the most flexible (cf. Greenwood 1992).

In situating the Mondragón cooperatives within the global economy, the first lesson of Mondragón becomes clear. Worker-owners are not shielded from the forces of the world market: Just-in-time production was introduced in Fagor Garagartza; consultants conducted efficiency studies in Fagor Clima, Copreci, and Garagartza, and managers in these plants increased the pace of production; temporary workers were hired on six-month to one-year contracts to do jobs that might otherwise be performed by members; and cooperative members were transferred between plants, allowing regular adjustments of the work force. These local developments in Mondragón parallel trends in the world economy. In the cooperatives, managers had more leeway to hire temporary workers and transfer workers than did owners of local private firms. My comparison of Fagor Clima (a cooperative) and Mayc. S.A. (a local private firm), in chapters 5 and 6, reveals that workers in both firms confront the same strains of industrial production: shift work, the assembly line, routinization of tasks, and ever-increasing productivity. Workplace democracy or worker ownership does not ameliorate these daily pressures.

Some advocates of Mondragón will argue that efficiency and the increasing sophistication of the cooperative system is the best way to preserve cooperativism. High-level managers in Mondragón argue that the meanings of equality and democracy must remain fluid. They explain that specific co-op principles were always in flux and that there is no essential connection between cooperativism and equality or democracy (cf. Greenwood and González et al. 1992). Others who follow Mondragón may consider that developments such as the new system for measuring worker efficiency (MMT), the investment branch of the Mondragón Cooperative Corporation, or managers' repeated efforts to widen the pay ratio indicate the disintegration of cooperative ideals, a phenomenon that is common in cooperatives that are economically successful (cf. Cornforth et al. 1988, 10–17; Nash, Dandler, and Hopkins 1976, 17). In retrospect, it appears that the 1974 Ulgor strike was a harbinger of a growing conflict between managers and workers that may have come to a head in 1992, when workers rejected the recommendations of the Cooperative Congress to widen the salary differential between the lowest- and highest-paid members (chapter 7). It may be that the Ulgor strike was an early sign of how worldwide economic crisis would undermine cooperative principles.[1] However, my analysis of the history of the town of Mondragón and the development of the cooperatives (chapters 2 and 3) points to another interpretation, one that does not represent the cooperatives as having broken with their past but sees these recent changes as being consonant with the original political vision of the cooperative founders. Cooperativism was founded as an entrepreneurial alternative to working-class activism and socialism. From their inception, the cooperatives were intimately tied to PNV's anti-socialist political project for Basque society and were conceptualized by Father Arizmendiarrieta as a means of overcoming class conflict by creating Basque-owned businesses. Following this argument, the cooperatives have not devolved, rather they appear as the reformist project they originally were, with significant benefits for the Basque economy and drawbacks for working-class activism.

The second dimension of the myth of Mondragón is the assertion that the cooperatives are apolitical institutions. As we have seen throughout this book, this claim misrepresents the character of the cooperatives and ignores the scope of political activity and the significance of activism in Mondragón. Ekintza, the Basque concept of taking action, is a core cultural value in Euskadi (cf. Zulaika 1988, 67). Basque towns are centers of political activity. In Mondragón, political discussion takes place in bars, demonstrations are frequent, and town walls are covered with posters, murals, and graffiti, making them dynamic arenas for political debate. Far from generating ekintza among workers, however, cooperativism appears to engender apathy. The cooperative Social Council in Fagor Clima was not as proactive an organ as the Workers' Council in the private firm Mayc. Moreover, survey results indicate that cooperative workers felt less a part of their firm. Instead, it was Clima's managers who most identified with the cooperative and were most convinced that the democratic organs were effective (chapters 5 and 6). These findings should raise basic questions for those who believe that Mondragón-style cooperatives will generate broader community or social commitments among workers.

The cooperative business form does, however, seem to generate commitment and activism among managers. Managers of all levels are more tied to their firm and have more faith in the efficacy of democratic structures. High-level managers move into political positions, design and implement sophisticated business plans, and interact with international visitors to imagine a model system. Meanwhile, workers do not make effective use of the democratic and participatory structures available to them. This may suggest that a global implication of the Mondragón model, and more broadly of labor–management cooperation, is passivity among workers. These schemes (contrary to their public claims) may empower managers at the expense of workers.

It is possible that cooperative workers' relative inactivity is related to structural deficiencies of the cooperative Social Council—too few free hours, lack of external support from syndicates, and the dual role of the Social Council as a representative of workers to managers and of managers to workers. Inactivity among workers is also related to ideology, specifically, the notion that any conflict can be subsumed by the cooperative system. In chapter 5, I discussed how personnel managers in the cooperatives normalize conflict, even allowing me to meet with discontented workers during work hours. Similarly, those who have written about the cooperatives normalize conflict as part of the cooperative process. In both the literature and managers' framing of conflict, the business form, rather than class actors, emerges as the agent of social change. The cooperative *system,* complete with its seemingly innate ability to solve problems, is the model for social change, and the cooperative *structure* is replicated, not the qualities of activism of a particular group or class of people. (Hence local politics are irrelevant.) According to this conception of social change, workers are insignificant. This insight may provide a second lesson to those of us who became interested in Mondragón because we thought cooperatives provided a better alternative for workers: to be skeptical of models that make business forms rather than people the agents of social change.

A related lesson is that cooperatives can be social projects for the reform of working classes (cf. Foster 1974, 220–24). In Mondragón, this effort at reform was multifaceted. Father Arizmendiarrieta, the founder of the cooperative system, reorganized local education because he believed that education was a better way to serve one's people than was activism. The consumer cooperative Eroski introduced notions of "appropriate" consumption and pioneered consumer identity, which had been unfamiliar concepts in Mondragón. And, one of the most important forms of working-class association—the daily round of the bars—is jeopardized by shift work in the co-ops. The ways in which this reform has been effective and the ways in which it has failed are instructive.

The cooperatives have reshaped the local population by reforming class identity. More cooperative workers in Clima say they see themselves as middle class than do workers in Mayc. The production of a middle-class identity among workers may well be a global lesson of worker-ownership plans. In the United States, for example, as the disparity in wealth increases, worker ownership may be a new mechanism for creating consent and middle-class identity. Worker ownership may facilitate flexible accumulation in the way that Gramsci (1971) suggested that home ownership, family form, and other factors made Fordism successful. The effect of ownership on cooperators' class consciousness is, however, complex. Co-op workers envision themselves as middle class in relation to noncooperative workers but not in relation to cooperative managers. Rather, they see their experiences and interests inside the factories as being class determined, and (as I showed in chapter 6) they can draw clear class maps of cooperative social relations.

Moreover, cooperative workers do not link their class position to property ownership. They do not consider the firms *theirs* in any meaningful way (indeed, they reported feeling less this way than assembly-line workers in Mayc). This empirical data on the absence of a property consciousness is significant, for it contradicts the assumptions of politicians and policymakers who believe that ownership gives workers a greater stake in their nation. Ronald Reagan made exactly this supposition is his letter of support for populist (and renowned proponent of employee ownership) Senator Russell Long's campaign for re-election:

> Our duty is to foster a strong, vibrant, wealth-producing economy which operates in such a way that new additions to wealth accrue in greater measure to those who presently have little or no ownership stake in their country. (Quoted in Rosen 1981, 67)

Reagan saw an intimate connection between employee ownership, nationalism, and an identification with capitalism, but worker-ownership does not in fact seem to generate these kinds of ideological commitments among workers (see Kasmir 1991).

If one were choosing a laboratory for testing the relationship between small property ownership and nationalism, one could not choose a better site than Euskadi, where peasants have historically owned their land, small business has flourished, and nationalist sentiment is strong. Yet, in Mondragón, property ownership is not important to cooperators. I found a similar situation among women workers I studied in Fall River, Massachusetts. These women bought their textile firm and, with the help of the Industrial Cooperatives Association, formed a cooperative based on the Mondragón model. Contrary to the ideology of worker ownership, they continued to identify as working class. They did not, for example, envision their stake in their firm as something that would affect their children's lives. To the contrary, after buying their firms, they became more committed union members than they were before the buyout (Kasmir 1991). It seems, therefore, that property itself does not transform workers, though ideologies of worker ownership and cooperation do remake working classes in other ways.

The Mondragón cooperatives have transformed the nature of local working-class leadership, having failed to generate the kind of leaders that have emerged in private firms. For example, the comarcal director of LAB told me that he became a syndical leader during a months-long strike to prevent the closing of the factory where he worked. The strike was unsuccessful, but the experience transformed him from a class-conscious worker into a leader. As Lembcke (1991–1992) notes, the experience of big strikes can change a locality by creating what he calls a "political generation," people who have shared and been transformed by a common experience. The 1974 Ulgor walk-out might have been a moment in which working-class leadership was consolidated and a political generation formed, but the divisive way in which it was handled turned it into an involuted event. It remains to be seen whether the new phase of activism that began in 1990 with KT's campaign against changing vacation schedules, LAB's criticisms of the cooperatives, and workers' rejection of managers' proposals to increase the pay differential (chapter 7) will generate new leaders.

A central finding of this book is that cooperatives can divide working classes. As I showed in chapter 4, when the Basque working class reconstituted itself in the 1960s and 1970s, cooperators stood outside that process. Documents produced at that time, by sources as diverse as leftist factions of ETA and the Catholic Church, indicate that there was local concern about cooperators' distance from the rest of the working class. Cooperators were largely absent from solidarity strikes with workers from nearby private factories. The particular dynamism of working-class and Basque nationalist struggles that characterized Mondragón since the early 1900s was undermined as the cooperatives transformed the consciousness of a large segment of the working population. This fact was evident during the 1990 strike for the metal-sector contract, when not a single cooperator turned out to show solidarity with his or her fellow workers.

Working classes within nations have always been divided—craft, skill, gender, race, and ethnicity have been the most significant cleavages (cf. Gordon, Edwards, and Reich 1982). Worker ownership represents a novel division, as does participation, which engages some workers as "team members" or as part of a quality circle. There are new schisms in working classes between those who are expected to share a common interest with management and those who are not. As cooperative working arrangements become more common, these factory regimes will have an increasingly important impact on working-class life. More case studies will allow us to answer important questions: How do worker-owners interact with other workers in their communities? What are the effects of worker buyouts on local unions? How does labor–management cooperation affect relationships among co-workers?

This case study of Mondragón also calls upon us to rethink the concept of democracy. Despite formal democratic rights of the Clima Social Council and General Assembly to participate in management, these bodies were not more successful in representing workers than was the Workers' Council in Mayc. In contrast, there are examples in this book of democracy that come from daily politics (e.g., the opening assembly of political demonstrations). This democracy tends to be linked to activism. If workplace democracy is to be genuine, it seems that it must be premised on activism (cf. Grenier 1988, 125–26).

Throughout this book, we have also seen the manipulation of the concept of Basqueness and Basque egalitarianism over time and by various political groups. The way these ideologies were and are used is instructive for how we understand the current transformations of working classes elsewhere. Basqueness was used by cooperative managers to claim loyalty among workers during the Ulgor strike; Basqueness was contrasted with the class consciousness and internationalism of the strikers who were rhetorically constructed by managers as outsiders or españolista. Elsewhere, businesses use a variety of ideologies to mobilize labor. For example, in the shoe industry of Taiwan, familism and kinship are used to exploit the labor of female workers who are also relatives (Skoggard 1993). In central Italy, the ideology of family has been key in the success of small firms; workers find themselves tied to their jobs by family loyalty and often lack basic union protections (Blim 1990).

In the Mondragón cooperatives, the ideologies of equality and Basqueness have been mobilized against workers. In 1990, however, workers began to charge that the cooperative managers were more interested in global investment strategies than in Basque concerns, and they mobilized claims of localism and Basque identity to discredit management. Similarly, cooperators turned the notion of equality, which has been frustrating and burdensome, on its head in order to preserve pay equity. In this effort to reclaim cooperative equality they can make reference to the long history of Basque egalitarianism, and they can cast themselves as defending what is Basque and what is primordial.

Perhaps workers in other flexibly organized firms can also manipulate ideologies to their own advantage. Indeed, this is what Nash (1989) observed in Pittsfield, Massachusetts, where workers embraced the paternalistic attitudes of General Electric just as the company was divesting itself of any responsibility to the community so that it could pursue higher profits elsewhere. These developments suggest that in the current, flexible phase of capitalism, which draws on new and numerous ideologies for creating industrial organization, workers and unions have to consider new approaches and strategies if they are to survive. The strategy that syndicates formulate in Euskadi, such as LAB's strategy of reclaiming cooperativism, may turn out to be the most important lesson of the Mondragón cooperatives. It may foreshadow and inform the responses of unions to new working environments and new kinds of workers in other parts of the world.

Another lesson to be learned from the case of Mondragón is that of the importance of politics, the necessary role of organization, and the continuing value of syndicates and unions for transforming the workplace. It is clear that syndicates and unions have to respond to the growing criticism that they are "outmoded." Union structures have to be transformed to accommodate new work forces (which in many cases will require legal change), and they have to make room for part-time and temporary workers as well as worker owners. Perhaps the new syndical forms and strategies developed in Mondragón can provide examples of how to organize and represent these increasingly diverse working classes. Moreover, as unions struggle with the effects of the management ideologies of cooperation and participation on working classes, they will have to confront their own lack of internal democracy and the inactivism of their members; unions must promote rank-and-file participation in governance (something democratic union reform movements in the United States are trying to do).

In conclusion, I return to the issue of pragmatism that I raised in chapter 1. Over the past decade, it has become increasingly common to hear that we should forget about ideology and politics and find pragmatic solutions to our social and economic problems. The Mondragón cooperatives are considered a paragon of this pragmatism. Just as "efficiency" is evoked by co-op managers who are exacting give backs from workers and recasting cooperative ideology, "pragmatism" is a word that doubles as a weapon. Many of us feel that we cannot consider solutions that are not immediately attainable and for which we cannot spell out concrete means to the desired ends. Ironically, this yearning for pragmatism robs us of valuable tools. We are burdened with a practicality that often stops short our thinking and cuts off our imaginations. If there is any ultimate point to my writing this book it is to show that the Mondragón cooperatives are not purely pragmatic institutions but political and ideological constructs. In evaluating the cooperative system, we should, therefore, think in ideological terms, including imagining what it would be like if workers were active in larger political movements and if, in this age of flexible accumulation, we could build organizations that truly transferred power to workers and genuinely created more just workplaces.

Appendix: Basque Syndicates, Political Organizations, and Parties

ANV, Acción Nacionalista Vasca (Basque Nationalist Action). First socialist and Basque nationalist party in Euskadi. Founded before the Spanish Civil War but was shortlived. Did particularly well in Mondragón's municipal elections in 1931.

CCOO, Comisiones Obreras (Workers Commissions). Syndicate clandestinely organized from the late-1950s throughout Spain as an alternative to the fascist-controlled vertical syndicate. Affiliated with PCE in Spain, but in Euskadi, spearheaded early on by ETA. In Mondragón, is currently taking an active role in organizing in the cooperatives and is a member of Lankideak.

EA, Eusko Alkartasuna (Basque Solidarity). Political party founded in 1986 as a result of a split within PNV. Similar to PNV but firmer on the question of Basque independence.

EE, Euskadiko Ezkerra (Basque Left). Political party formed in 1977. Evolved from ETA(pm). Originally leftist, but became more moderate over time. Sometimes derogatorily referred to by radical nationalists as the "yuppie" party or as "Europeanizers."

Egin. Daily newspaper associated with the radical nationalist movement. Published its first critical article on the cooperatives in 1989.

ELA-STV, Eusko Langileen Alkartasuna-Solidaridad de Trabajadores Vascos (called ELA for short, Solidarity of Basque Workers). A Catholic syndicate tied to PNV. Evolved from the Asociación Obrera (workers' association). Founded as a syndicate in 1911, under the name Solidaridad de Obreros Vascos (SOV). Appeared in Mondragón after 1915 strike. Currently considered by CCOO and LAB to be too moderate on labor issues.

ESB, Euskal Sozialista Biltzarrea (Basque Socialist Convergence). Shortlived party that evolved in the 1970s from a faction of ETA. Attempted to bring together both socialist and nationalist concerns. Did poorly in Euskadi but relatively well in Mondragón, where it is reported to have garnered a good deal of support from cooperative managers. In some regards it is a precursor to HB.

ETA, Euskadi ta Askatasuna (Basque Homeland and Freedom). Founded in 1959. Began to use armed violence against the Spanish State in 1961. Calls for both socialism and independence for the Basque nation. Underwent various splits in the 1960s and 1970s, many of them over the relative emphasis on working-class versus nationalist struggles. First ETA arrest in Mondragón was in 1961.

ETA-berri (New ETA). Faction of ETA that split from the organization in 1967. Believed that class issues were more important than nationalism. Merged with MCE in 1971. Authored several criticisms of Mondragón cooperatives in the 1970s.

ETA-V. Faction of ETA that was responsible for the killing of Carrero Blanco in 1974. Along with ETA(m), considered the "historic" ETA, the direct predecessor of today's ETA. Never issued a criticism of the Mondragón cooperatives.

ETA-VI. Faction of ETA founded at the Sixth Assembly in 1968. Favored class over nationalist politics and was Trotskyist in political orientation. Joined LCR in 1973. Authored critiques of the cooperatives in the 1960s and 1970s.

ETA(m), ETA militar (Military ETA). Faction remaining after ETA(pm) left the organization in 1974. Along with ETA-V, outlived the other factions of ETA, and makes up the present-day organization.

ETA(pm), ETA político-militar (Political-Military ETA). Faction of ETA that split in 1974. Did not survive long as an armed organization, and soon became the legal political party EE. Authored critiques of the cooperatives in the 1970s.

HB, Herri Batasuna (Popular Unity). Radical nationalist electoral coalition, founded in 1978, that advocates socialism and independence for Euskadi. United with other radical nationalist organizations under the umbrella of KAS, and is a member of MLNV. Won the mayorship of Mondragón in the municipal elections of 1987 and 1991. Did not criticize the cooperatives until 1990s.

KAS, Koordinadora Abertzale Sozialista (Basque Socialist Coordinating Committee). Coalition of radical nationalist groups including LAB, HB, a feminist organization, an environmental group, and a group dedicated to international solidarity.

KT, Kooperatibisten Taldea (Cooperative Group). Opinion group critical of the cooperatives. Formed in 1982. Produced a magazine by the same name. In the 1980s it was a small and relatively inconsequential group. Has grown in the 1990s and has become active in organizing in the cooperatives. A founding member of Lankideak.

LAB, Langile Abertzaleen Batzordea (Basque Workers' Council). Labor syndicate that has origins in ETA's workers' front. Tied to HB and the umbrella groups MLNV and KAS. Until 1989, avoided public criticism of the Mondragón cooperatives.

Lankideak (Fellow Workers). A coalition of KT, CCOO, ESK-CUIS (a small independent syndicate in Mondragón), and individual members. Formed in 1994. Critical of the cooperatives and actively organizing on the issues of salaries, work pace, schedules, and internal democracy.

Las Cabras. Named for the founder of the group "el cabra". Originally a cell of ETA comprised of young people from Oñati and Mondragón. Broke with ETA and became autonomous in 1966, but lasted only until 1968.

LCR, Liga Comunista Revolucionaria (Communist Revolutionary League). Trotskyist Party, statewide in Spain. Member of the Fourth International. ETA-VI joined this party in 1973, signaling its concern for class questions over nationalism.

> *LKI, Liga Komunista Iraultza* (the Basque name for LCR). The shift to Basque-language name in the 1980s indicated the party's recognition of the importance of national identity in Euskadi. In the 1990s, joined with EMK to form the party Zutik.

MCE, Movimiento Comunista de España (Communist Movement of Spain). Maoist statewide party that was known for class-based critiques of Basque nationalism.

> *EMK, Euskadiko Mugimendo Komunista* (Communist Movement of Euskadi). Basque-language name of MCE. The use of Euskera reflects its reappraisal of nationalism in the 1980s. In the 1990s, joined with LKI to form Zutik.

MLNV, Movimiento de Liberación Nacional Vasco (Basque National Liberation Movement). Umbrella organization of radical nationalist groups, including HB and LAB.

PNV, Partido Nacionalista Vasco (Basque Nationalist Party). Founded in the late nineteenth century by Sabino Arana. Christian Democratic Party with moderate (and sometimes conservative) views on political and social issues. Currently heads the Basque autonomous government in Gasteiz. Associated with the ideology of the Mondragón cooperative movement.

PSOE, Partido Socialista Obrero Español (Spanish Socialist Workers Party). Founded in 1879. Currently Spain's ruling party. The Basque branch of the party is part of a coalition with PNV in the Basque autonomous government. Strong in Mondragón before the Civil War. Currently considered by radical nationalists to be anti-Basque and a symbol of the domination of the Spanish State over Euskadi.

TC, Talde Cooperativista (Cooperative Group). A group of cooperative workers formed by LAB in 1992. Has authored editorials in the newspaper *Egin*. Not part of Lankideak.

UGT, Unión General de Trabajadores (General Union of Workers). Labor syndicate associated with PSOE. Founded in 1882. First local formed in Mondragón after 1915 strike. Currently considered by Mondragón's CCOO and LAB to be a weak advocate of workers' interests. In 1992, along with ELA and CCOO, petitioned the Basque Government to legalize syndicalization of cooperatives.

Zutik (Stand up). (1) Name of ETA's clandestinely produced journal. Used to communicate strategy, analysis, and explanation of armed actions to the Basque public. (2) Leftist political party, composed of the former EMK and LKI. Zutik's magazine *Hika* often prints articles critical of the cooperatives. Members of this party are active in Lankideak.

Notes

Introduction

1. Whyte (1982) reports that the video was played on the White House system; Whyte does not indicate who showed it (or why) or who watched it.

2. It was British sociologist Robert Oakeshott's "Mondragón: Spain's Oasis of Democracy" (1975 [1973]) that first brought the Mondragón cooperatives to the attention of an international audience.

3. Gordon, Edwards, and Reich (1982) also explain cyclical capitalist crisis using long wave theory. They see the current economic crisis as parallel to other episodes of crisis. Each downturn is followed by a reorganization of economic, social, and political institutions that they call the "structures of accumulation." During crisis periods, there is a flurry of experimentation and innovation as states, businesses, and trade unions look for ways to promote recovery. The social, political, and economic structures that shape an epoch are realigned. New markets, energy sources, modes of transportation and communication, and economic policies are sought, and methods for organizing industry are formulated and implemented. The complete cycle of boom and bust constitutes a long, (approximately) fifty-year wave (see also Gordon 1978).

Nash (1985) criticizes Gordon, Edwards, and Reich for positing a nearly direct line of causation between structural economic change and workers' consciousness; this, she argues, limits the utility of their scheme for anthropological studies of community. Furthermore, Gordon, Edwards, and Reich's emphasis on structural causality ignores the effect of workers' and union activism on social change. Mandel (1975) also criticizes these kinds of structurally heavy-handed variants of long wave theory and argues instead that it is the agency of workers and unions that impels crises and recoveries. He believes that workers' struggles for such gains as higher wages, the eight-hour day, social welfare, and union recognition cause the declines in profitability and the rate of growth that trigger downturns.

Aglietta (1979) is another theorist of the post-1973 period. He, too, considers it a new capitalist epoch, characterized by the transformation of the material conditions of home and leisure that result from the dismantling of the consumer-based unionism of Fordism. Unfortunately, Aglietta's focus on well-paid union members tends to overlook the experiences of women, immigrant, and minority workers who were less often represented by unions and less likely to partake in the postwar boom. I use Harvey's concept of flexibility because I believe it sensitizes us to the range of workers' experiences and strikes a better balance between structural schemes, workers' agency, and social change.

4. Hogler and Grenier (1992) note that in 1968 U.S. and European workers were at their most active. They also were most able to bounce back from lay off, quit their jobs at will, find new jobs, and make monetary demands. Significantly, in that year, workers also demanded quality-of-work-life programs and participation in management (a social movement that is the subject of much of Andre Gorz's work.) Hogler and Grenier show, however, that the participation programs that were introduced in the 1970s did not respond to the demands of the workers' movement. Rather, they were management-initiated plans developed in the interest of profit and control.

5. It is often assumed that high productivity in Japanese industry is due to its motivated work force. Empirical studies, however, fail to show that Japanese workers are more motivated than other workers (Briggs 1988, 61).

6. Michael Moore's 1990 film, *Roger and Me,* chronicled the devastating effects of the closing of a General Motors plant on the working class of Flint, Michigan. In the face of massive layoffs, bank foreclosures on mortgages, and forced evictions, the suggestion that auto workers freely chose to leave Detroit for Tennessee is implausible.

7. I thank Jacqueline Urla for suggesting that I explore more thoroughly the significance of this concept. Valle (1988) analyzes the relationship of ekintza to Basque identity.

Chapter 1

1. This version of these events appears in a booklet entitled "Arrasateko herriak Euskadi osoari: 1.978-go azaroaren 15ean."
Readers may want to know my opinions about political violence in the Basque country. First, it is important for me to note that I never felt personally at risk of attack, nor did anyone I knew. It is uncommon for ETA to choose civilian targets (though a tragic exception is discussed in chapter 7). More common is the fear of police repression. Political violence is a tragic reality in the Basque Country. My sincere hope is that political negotiations between ETA and the Spanish government can bring about lasting peace as well as the degree of national self-determination desired by the majority of Basque people.

2. One of the earliest criticisms of cooperativism was made by the Fabian socialists Beatrice Potter and Sidney Webb in 1920. The object of their criticism was the Rochdale consumer cooperative which began to sell shares to nonmembers after it became economically successful. This led them to argue that cooperatives either fail or degenerate into capitalist firms. The Fabians withdrew their support for cooperatives based on Potter's and Webb's criticisms (Cornforth et al. 1988, 10–17). Gide made a similar observation about cooperatives in 1930 (see Nash, Dandler, and Hopkins 1976, 17), arguing that the more economically successful cooperatives become, the more likely they are to fail socially. Vanek (1977) has suggested ways to control for this kind of degeneration and has offered a framework for evaluating worker-owned firms which is a widely used resource for measuring both business functioning and workers' control.

3. Menzies's (1992) study of a fishing cooperative in western Canada re-counts a similar history. The co-op was founded in 1939 as a marketing concern, and, despite small conflicts, worked well with the fishers' union until the 1960s, when it expanded its operations to include processing. After this, their strategies diverged to such an extent that the two became incompatible. The unions emphasized the work-ing-class character of fishers while the co-op stressed their character as business people. During an important strike in 1967, the cooperators refused to honor the strike and continued to work, thereby solidifying hostilities between the union and the cooperative.

4. One could argue that the street is a central symbol in Basque culture, of the type of dominant symbol defined by Victor Turner (1967). Like other cultural poles of reference, the street has layered meanings that change over time and with con-text. At the turn of the century, during a period of rapid industrialization, "the street" referred to the urban street. It implied proletarianization, and alluded to socialist politics (Heiberg 1989, 95). From the perspective of a farmer, the most important attribute of the street is that it exists in opposition to the farmstead, and it is a cul-tural space where the farmer feels out of place and devalued (Zulaika 1988, 128–29). From the point of view of an older housewife, the street stands in opposition to the home. It is a space where her daughters may feel comfortable but she may not (for a discussion of the gendered division of space in Euskadi, see Aretxaga 1988; Valle et al. 1985). For young people, the street is the alternative to social and political passiv-ity. It is the major arena of participation and the place where they solidify their identi-ties as Basques.

5. See Hansen (1983) and Leonard (1991) for discussions of bars as locations for ethnographic research.

6. A *comarca* is a geographic/economic zone encompassing several towns. Hansen (1977) discusses the importance of the comarca in the economic life of Spain and its salience as a unit of study. Mondragón is in the comarca of the Alto Deba, along with the towns along the upper portion of the Deba River, including Bergara, Aretxa-baleta, Eskoriatza, and Gatzaga.

Schneider, Schneider, and Hansen (1972) make a similar case for the importance of the region as a unit of analysis in anthropology. Paying attention to this insight, my units of analysis are varyingly the town of Mondragón, the Alto Deba comarca, and the region of Euskadi.

7. The buy-outs of private firms were reported in *Egin* (17 May 1989, 24; 12 September 1989, 24; 20 June 1990, 27). The creation of the holding company was reported in *Diario Vasco* (17 March 1990, 30), *Egin* (20 June 1990, 27), and *Expansión* (19 November 1990, 12). Finally, the incorporation of the holding company as a sociedad anónima was reported in *El Correo Español* (17 November 1991, 43).

8. *Egin* (14 February 1990, 30).

Chapter 2

1. This and most other names of my informants are pseudonyms that I use to preserve their anonymity. I use actual names only when the individual is a public figure or when I think the individual would welcome recognition of his or her contribution to my work.

2. I thank Jane Schneider for pointing out this similarity.

3. Anthropological studies of the evolution of class-based society are helpful in sorting out Basque history. Kirchoff (1959) analyzed the intensification of lineage inequalities in clan-based societies and showed that when inequalities between patrilineages became extreme, these patrilineages were unrecognizable as kin and manifested themselves as classes. Leach's (1954) account of the cyclical movement between feudal and egalitarian social organization in highland Burma can also serve as a model for what might have been the class profile of Basque society. In Burma, patrilineages unevenly accumulated wealth, and wealthy patrilineages evolved into aristocratic-like classes. At some high point in interlineage differentiation, commoner lineages revolted, leveling the aristocracy and restoring what Leach considered an egalitarian clan-based social order.

A comparison of Basque social organization with that of the Scottish Highlanders, who also had clans amidst a feudal environment, is similarly instructive (Fox 1976; Withers 1988, 72–79). Withers encourages us to see the difference between highland clans and lowland feudal classes as fluid (1988; 72–79). Finally, Wolf (1982, 403) suggests that kin-ordered and feudal societies should be conceived of not as categorized types but as transformations of one another. These cases remind us that the historiographic uncertainty of classifying rural Basque society as either clan based or feudal probably falls well within what were actual ambiguities in daily life in the Middle Ages.

4. Urtiaga was a member of ETA. In his article on property forms (1962), he expressed the early ideological position of radical nationalists that Basque society was naturally communal. Urtiaga further argued that future socialist institutions could be built upon past egalitarian forms. (See chapter 4 for further discussion of ETA's conception of Basque egalitarianism.)

5. As Monreal (1980) notes, characterizing the relationship between Castile and Gipuzkoan towns is both historiographically and politically problematic. Whether one portrays the relationship as Castilian imposition or as willing collaboration on the part of Basques seeking help in the face of band wars carries political connotations for modern-day nationalist politics and the relationship of Euskadi (currently "plagued" by the political violence of ETA) to the Spanish state.

I was struck by this fact during interviews I had with members of Euskadiko Ezskerra (EE). Originally a pro-independence and leftist party, EE in the last decade has moved toward the center and toward Spain. I was told by EE affiliates that the heart of the Basque problem was that Basques were unable to get along with each other. One person pointed to the band wars as a prime example and explained that it took the Castilian king to pacify Euskadi. The implication for contemporary politics is that the "Basque problem" is becoming less an issue of confrontation with the Spanish state and more a conflict among Basque's. EE, along with PNV, blame Herri Batasuna for this internal fighting.

6. Zapirain and Mora (1993) detail complex seventeenth-century legal dramas in Mondragón. Many applicants who sought the right to vote and hold town office were sent away if they lacked proof of a family history in town and proof of pure Basque heritage, critical elements of hidalguía status. This further suggests that egalitarianism was not equally distributed.

7. See Gilmore (1977) for a detailed account of this disentailment process in an Andalucian town.

8. Rodríguez de Coro (1980, 206–16) provides a useful account of the competition in Mondragón between liberals and Carlists in the period from 1869 to 1876.

9. I thank Aitor Alberdi, who helped me compile the census data I use in this chapter. Thanks also to Kiki Arriola who double-checked census data for me.

10. Eibar, about thirty kilometers north of Mondragón on the lower part of the Deba River, is also exceptional. As is commonly noted, it was the Socialist center of the Basque Country since the turn of the century. Strikingly, Eibar also lacked a powerful seigniorial class (Azark 1988; Celaya 1970).

11. Work hours had been 6:00 A.M. to noon, with a half hour for breakfast at 8:00, and after lunch from 1:30 to 6:30, with a fifteen-minute break at 4:00 for a sandwich. Management unilaterally changed the hours to 7:30 A.M. to noon, with no break, and from 1:30 to 6:30, with no break. The series of documents pertaining to the strike collected by Oktubre Taldea (1987, 35–44) shows that management was concerned about the growing influence of the syndicates. Workers protested the change because of its effect on their eating schedule. They wrote to management that if they were supposed to come to work at 7:30 A.M., already having eaten breakfast, that would mean that the shopping would have to be done at 6:30; this, they argued, "would greatly disturb our wives and mothers and the widows."

12. The category of Spanish immigrants glosses over the cultural diversity among the immigrants themselves who came from regions as different as Asturias and Andalucía. "Spanish" is, instead, used in both popular and scholarly parlance to refer to all those who came from non-Basque provinces. Basque anthropologists have not yet studied the diversity of experience of Spanish immigrants based on their regions of origin; such a study will be an important addition to the literature.

While I do not have immigration data for 1900–1930, the compiled data for 1900–1950 (Mancomunidad del Alto Deba 1982, 68–70) is sufficient to make this case. Of the 1,273 immigrants who came to town in these fifty years, the majority were from other Basque towns; only 368 were from Spain. Moreover, many of them came after the war during the industrial expansion that was sparked by World War II.

13. See Heiberg (1989, 70–73) for a more thorough description of the social institutions that the Basque Nationalist Party maintained in each town.

Chapter 3

1. Barandiaran died in 1991 at the age of 102. The occasion of his one hundredth birthday in 1989 was celebrated with much popular fanfare, as he is held in high esteem as a folk hero by many segments of the Basque population.

2. For a detailed history of the cooperative Polytechnical and Professional School see Ornelas (1980).

The Escuela Politécnica is not the only example of a Basque cooperative school. Euskadi has a tradition, begun in the time of Franco, of creating non-state-financed civil institutions as a form of resistance to the fascist state. These institutions are public insomuch as they belonged to the town, but they were organized independently of the state and funded privately; the cooperative legal form was often favored. Basque-language grade schools, *ikastolas,* were founded (and financed) by parents and teachers who often ran the schools as cooperatives. The Escuela Politécnica was especially important because it was the first institution of what would later become the Mondragón cooperative system.

3. Indeed, my informant told me of a meeting that took place in the 1960s in which Arizmendiarrieta and one of these priests had an angry argument over the issue of class. I was unable to document this meeting, but other people I talked to had heard rumors about it.

4. In personal communication, Davydd Greenwood suggested to me that the enigma is at least partially due to our own misunderstanding of the nature of authoritarian regimes. The implication is that we need to look more closely at these regimes and to write about them in nonparametric ways.

5. The census figures differ from the SIADECO figures. (Throughout this work, I consistently use figures from the census or the census data compiled by the Mancommunidad del Alto Deba (1982).

6. In Euskadi, one's place of birth (or that of one's parents) and self-identification as Basque are separate issues. If these estimates reflect cooperators' self-reported Basqueness, it is fair to assume that the number of immigrants is actually higher, since many likely identify as Basque, despite being born outside of the region. This difference between ethnicity and Basque identity is discussed in the next chapter.

7. *Eroskide* (July–August 1989) features an article that considers "health as the right of the consumer" (p. 7). A second article is an interview with Eroski's representative to the European Community's working group on consumer education.

8. See Eroski's *Memoria Txostena* (1988); see also Eroski's 1989–1990 course guide "La educación del consumidor en la escuela" (supplemento no. 134, November 1989).

19. ETA (1981) vol. 17: 4.

20. ETA-V's analysis was published in *Zutik* (August 1975, 20–21). This was the same magazine that rejected the first criticism of the cooperatives in 1965. Only when ETA was controlled by the Trotskyist ETA-VI, did *Zutik* published an attack on the cooperatives (March 1973, 41–45).

Chapter 5

1. The first upscale hotel in Mondragón opened in 1992. Before that there was only one small hotel and a pensión. Perhaps the central location of this new hotel will encourage people to get to know the town beyond the cooperatives.

2. The tour is provided by the cooperative system, which devotes staff and resources without the hope of monetary return. Instead, they graciously extend themselves to meet the demand that international fame has placed upon them. I, too, depended upon their generosity, and I am very grateful to them.

3. Instead, they turn to their own observations in U.S. firms that have implemented employee participation and conclude that cooperative workers are more fully involved in management than are the U.S. employees. Firms in the United States are not, however, a fair comparison, since labor law and activism differ (for example, Basques can legally conduct solidarity strikes, which U.S. workers cannot). Rather, it is necessary to compare the cooperatives with local factories, where the strengths and weaknesses of the Basque labor movement are reflected in working conditions and workers' experiences.

4. My ease of access will surprise those who have conducted industrial-based studies elsewhere. Indeed, this access is part of the story of Mondragón. Since the cooperatives are so well studied, they are accustomed to accommodating researchers. Their openness has brought them many committed scholars whose research has contributed to the cooperative system. It has also created a tremendous amount of work for cooperative staff, sometimes for little gain (see Whyte and Whyte 1988, 293–95). However, some of my Basque friends interpreted my access in a cynical way, as part of the cooperative system's image-building. They interpret the entire range of courtesies—from tours to library facilities to arranging interviews at private firms—as a means of portraying a normative view of the cooperatives to the outside world. In this regard, public-relations personnel in Mondragón are part of the apparatus of myth making.

My visits to private firms were kindly arranged by José María Larrañaga of Ikasbide. Some private owners wanted to be part of the study; others, I suspect, accommodated me simply to maintain good relations with the cooperatives. One business owner told me quite directly that he agreed to meet me only because the cooperatives are such a powerful economic force in the area, and he was reluctant to say No to them.

214 *Notes*

5. Davydd Greenwood, who studied Fagor, conscientiously answered a letter in which I expressed doubt about the comparison, and he also felt it was the best choice I could make. I thank him for his advice.

6. *Egin,* 17 January 1992.

7. Nash wrote about a more extreme example of worker–management distrust in General Electric in Pittsfield, Massachusetts. In the 1970s, it was reported that PCBs were causing high rates of cancer in workers in the power-transforming division of the plant. The company's testing department investigated the problem and found that the reported PCB level was exaggerated. It also denied a link between PCBs and cancer. This did not inspire confidence among workers in the company experts (Nash 1989, 335–36).

8. March 1982, "Algunos elementos de una crisis," Ederlan, S. Coop.

9. October 1982 "Propuesta de los órganos sociales," Ederlan, S. Coop.

Chapter 6

1. LAB pamphlet, dated 5 July 1990.

2. The personnel manager of Mayc considered teams to be "top-down" and "paternalistic," and did not approve of them, just as he did not approve of factory libraries or other quality-of-work-life projects.

3. It is common to read and hear about consulting firms hired by companies to restructure the work process and work force. Since their recommendations come from outside the factory, and presumably have no relationship to either management or labor within the firm, they are considered to be removed from the arena of labor–management conflict, representing a neutral version of efficiency. The role of consultants in implementing corporate restructuring and flexible accumulation, and the way in which consultants are portrayed as impartial parties and experts deserves further study.

4. Perhaps these workers feel that their investment of their labor, rather than the legal and formal form of property available to co-op workers, conveys ownership (cf. Kasmir 1991).

Chapter 7

1. *Egin,* 7 September 1989, 3.

2. See *Egin* (22 June) 1993, 23) on the proposals for the new Cooperative Law of Euskadi. The relationship between the Basque autonomous government and the Mondragón cooperatives—individuals, legal arrangements, policy decisions, investments, and grants—is a complex one that deserves further study.

3. Before HB was founded in 1978, radical nationalism had an earlier incarnation in the political party Euskal Sozialista Biltzarrea (Basque Socialist Convergence, ESB). The party was shortlived, but its leadership and a good deal of its constituency was found among mid-level management in the Mondragón cooperatives. When ESB disbanded, some of its membership joined HB, including some who had campaigned against the Ulgor strikers. Others moved to more moderate nationalist parties (interview with ex-member of ESB).

4. *Egin,* 29 June 1986, 2–19. See also *Egin* "Monografias," 14 January 1978.

5. LAB pamphlet entitled, "172.600 lanpostu galdu dira."

6. CCOO del Alto Deba, 1 May 1989.

7. On the Third Cooperative Congress and MCC, see *El Diario Vasco,* 21 December 1991, 35; *El Correo Español,* 17 December 1991, 43; "III Congresso Cooperativo: proyecto organizativo de la M.C.C.," Fagor, 28 February 1993.

8. A colleague in Mondragón recently wrote me that a major Basque bank, the Banco Bilbao Vizcaya, has invested in the cooperative Consumer Division (Eroski). If this is indeed the case, this would be a significant development, indicating that the long-standing rule that only those who work in the cooperatives can be owners (or investors) had been broken.

9. I thank William Foote Whyte for pointing out to me the significance of this fact.

10. Leaflet entitled "El MTM es un sistema de explotación," CCOO, March 1989.

11. In Mazda and General Motors plants in the United States a similar time-motion study was implemented. At the Mazda factory, management offered ideas on how the entire body could be used in production. The training manual suggested that the number of hand movements could be reduced by using the feet—"not that you must constantly use your feet, but it is worthwhile to consider if you can freely use your feet" (quoted in Parker and Slaughter 1988, 3). The system was implemented along with just-in-time production and the team concept. While in theory the team concept encourages workers to participate in management and decision making, it was used in Mazda and General Motors to squelch conflict over the new pace of work (Parker and Slaughter 1988, 88–94).

12. Many of these ex-Copreci members were the new members who returned my survey in Clima and responded negatively to my questions about feeling part of the firm or feeling that the firm was theirs. I believe that their experience in Copreci, as much as their short tenure in Clima, left them feeling alienated from the cooperative system.

13. *Egin,* 12 August 1989, 12.

14. *Egin,* 21 July 1990, 23.

15. Other articles by Talde Cooperativista/LAB appeared in *Egin* on 10 July 1992 (10) and 14 August 1992 (9). The similarity of the names of LAB's Talde Cooperativista

and Kooperatibisten Taldea is noteworthy. So too is LAB's use of a Spanish-language name and the "ultra-leftist" choice of a Basque-language name, an ironic reversal of their 1970s roles.

16. Two-page leaflet, written by LAB. Not dated, but probably spring or summer 1991.

17. Mondragón has its own television station, *Arrasate Telebista,* which broadcasts in town. *Lankide* published an article entitled "Sindicalismo y cooperativismo, muchos puntos en común" (May 1989 [no. 325], 21–25).

18. ELA, UGT, and CCOO proposed an amendment to the Cooperative Law of Euskadi that would legalize the functioning of syndicates, allowing them to run electoral slates for the Social Council and other representative bodies and to represent workers as they would in a private firm (see *Egin,* 17 November 1992). No such amendment was included when the Basque government passed the new law in 1993.

Conclusions

1. Though empirical evidence is scant, it may be that from their founding in 1956 through the 1960s, cooperatives were significantly better workplaces than privately owned firms, even small, paternalistic, Basque firms. Perhaps the Ulgor strike was essentially about the growth of the system: not simply a failure to properly socialize new members as cooperators as Whyte and Whyte suggest (1988, 96–102) but a structural shift in the system itself, away from small-scale businesses toward more competitive enterprises, where, by definition, the level of exploitation was more like that in the world market. Further research on the relation of the Ulgor strike to the development of the cooperative system in the post-1973 period would be fruitful.

Works Cited

Newspapers, Magazines, and Archives Consulted

Newspapers

El Correo Español

El Diario Vasco

Egin

Expansión

Political Magazines

Berriak

Zer Egin

Zutik

(Collected documents of ETA were published as *Documentos,* 1981)

Archives (containing political, and labor leaflets and pamphlets)

CCOO archives, Mondragón

Ikasbide Library, Aretxabaleta

LAB archives, Mondragón

Censuses (held in the town halls or town archives of)

Bergara: 1900, 1930, 1950, 1960

Mondragón: 1900, 1930, 1950, 1960

Corporate Publication

Lankide, magazine published by the Mondragón Cooperative Group
(formerly *Trabajo y Unión*)

Articles and Books cited

Aceves, Joseph B., and William A. Douglass, eds. 1976. *The Changing Faces of Rural Spain.* Cambridge, MA: Schenkman.

Aglietta, Michel. 1979. *A Theory of Capitalist Regulation.* London: Verso.

Albarracín, Jesús. 1987. *La onda larga del capitalismo español.* Madrid: Economistas Libros.

Anderson, Perry. 1974. *Lineages of the Absolutist State.* London: Verso.

Aranegui, Pedro M. 1986. *Gatzaga, una aproximación a la vida de Salinas de Leniz a comienzos del siglo XX.* Caja de Guipúzcoa.

Aretxaga, Begoña. 1988. *Los funerales en el nacionalismo radical vasco. Ensayo antropológico.* Barcelona: Anthropos Editorial del Hombre.

Arizaga Bolumburu, Beatriz. 1990. *Urbanística medieval (Guipúzcoa).* San Sebastián: Kriselu.

Arocena, Ignacio. 1980. "Linajes, bandos y villas." In *Historia general del País Vasco,* 5: 7–124. San Sebastián: Haranburu.

Arrasateko Udala (Ayuntamiento de Mondragón), "Industria de Mondragón," n.d.

Azark, J. I. Paul. 1988. "Aproximación a las especificaciones del socialismo eibarese. Economía y conflictividad social (siglos XIX–XX)." In *Congreso de historia de euskal herria,* 5: 359–68. San Sebastián: Editorial Txertoa.

Azcona, Jesús. 1984. *Etnia y nacionalismo vasco: Una aproximación desde la antropología.* Barcelona: Antropos Editorial del Hombre.

Azurmendi, Joxe. 1984. *El hombre cooperativo. Pensamiento de Arizmendiarrieta.* Mondragón: Caja Laboral Popular.

Beltza (Emilio López). 1976. *Nacionalismo vasco y clases sociales.* San Sebastián: Editorial Txertoa.

———. 1978. *Del carlismo al nacionalismo vasco.* San Sebastián: Editorial Txertoa.

Blim, Michael. 1990. *Made in Italy: Small-Scale Industrialization and Its Consequences.* Westport, CT: Greenwood.

Bluestone, Barry, and Bennett Harrison. 1982. *The Deindustrialization of America. Plant Closings, Community Abandonment, and the Dismantling of Basic Industry.* New York: Basic Books.

Boggs, Carl. 1986. *Social Movements and Political Powers: Emerging Forms of Radicalism in the West.* Philadelphia: Temple University Press.

Bourdieu, Pierre. 1984. *Distinction: A Social Critique of the Judgement of Taste.* Cambridge: Harvard University Press.

Bradley, Keith, and Alan Gelb. 1982. "The Replicability and Sustainability of the Mondragón Experiment." *British Journal of Industrial Relations* 20(1): 20–34.

———. 1983. *Cooperation at Work: The Mondragón Experience.* London: Heinemann.

Brandes, Stanley. 1976. "The Impact of Emigration on a Castillian Mountain Village." In *The Changing Faces of Rural Spain,* ed. Joseph B. Aceves and William A. Douglass, 1–16. Cambridge, MA: Schenkman.

Briggs, Pamela. 1988. "The Japanese at Work: Illusions of the Ideal." In *Choosing Sides: Unions and the Team Concept,* eds. Mike Slaughter and Jane Parker, 60–65. Detroit: Labor Notes.

Bruni, Luigi. 1989. *E.T.A., historia de una lucha armada.* Tafalla: Txalaparta.

Butler, Judith. 1990. *Gender Trouble: Feminism and the Subversion of Identity.* New York: Routledge.

Caja Laboral Popular (CLP). 1983. *Pensamientos de Don José Arizmendiarrieta.* Mondragón: Caja Laboral Popular.

———. 1988. "Estudio comparativo trienal sobre niveles retributivos 1987." División Empresarial, Departamento de Estudios.

———. 1990. Annual Report.

Campbell, Alastair, et al. 1977. *Worker-Owners: The Mondragón Achievement.* London: Anglo-German Foundation for the study of Industrial Society.

Carbonella, August. 1992. "Historical Memory, Class Formation, and Power: A Central Maine Papermaking Community, 1920–1988," *Focaal* 19: 1001–23.

Caro Baroja, Julio. 1974. *Vasconiana.* San Sebastián: Txertoa.

———. 1972. *Los vascos y la historia a través de Garibay: Ensayo de biografía antropológica.* San Sebastián: Txertoa.

Carr, Raymond. 1966. *Spain, 1808–1939.* Oxford: Oxford University Press.

Casanova, José. 1983. "Modernization and Democratization: Reflections on Spain's Transition to Democracy." *Social Research* 50(4): 929–73.

Castells, Miguel Arteche. 1982. *Radiografía de un modelo represivo.* San Sebastián: Ediciones Vascas.

Celaya, Pedro Olabarri. 1970. *Eibar, síntesis de monografía histórica.* San Sebastián: Caja de Ahorros Municipal de San Sebastián.

Chaffe, Lyman. 1988. "Social Conflict and Alternative Mass Communications: Public Art and Politics in the Service of Spanish-Basque Nationalism." *European Journal of Political Research,* 16(5): 545–72.

Chilicote, Ronald. 1968. *Spain's Iron and Steel Industry.* Austin: Bureau of Business Research, University of Texas at Austin.

Chomsky, Ave, and Jon Aske. 1991. "The Basque Popular Movement." *Z Magazine* (February): 105–9.

Chrisleanschi, Rodolfo. 1989. "El imperio en el valle." *Geo* 34 (November): 108–22.

Clark, Robert P. 1979. *The Basques: The Franco Years and Beyond.* Reno: University of Nevada Press.

———. 1984. *The Basque Insurgents: ETA, 1952–1980.* Madison, WI: University of Wisconsin Press.

———. 1990. *Negotiating with ETA: Obstacles to Peace in the Basque Country, 1975–1988.* Reno: University of Nevada Press.

Cole, John. 1977. "Anthropology Comes Part Way Home: Community Studies in Europe." *Annual Reviews in Anthropology* 6: 349–78.

Colective Autónomo de Trabajadores de Euskalduna (CAT). 1985. *La batalla de Euskalduna. Ejemplo de resistencia obrera.* Madrid: Editorial Revolución.

Colectivo Unitario–LAB. 1989. *Obreros somos . . . 1969–1989. El movimiento obrero en la comarca de Tafalla. Tafalla:* Kultur Taldea.

Cooke, William N. 1990. *Labor–Management Cooperation: New Partnerships or Going in Circles?* Kalamazoo, MI: W. E. Upjohn Institute for Employment Research.

Coontz, Stephanie. 1992. *The Way We Never Were: American Families and the Nostalgia Trap.* New York: Basic Books.

Cornforth, Chris, et al. 1988. *Developing Successful Worker Co-operatives.* London: Sage.

Cueva, Justo de la. 1988. *La escisión del PNV. EA, HB, ETA y la deslegitimación del estado español en Euskadi sur.* Tafalla: Txalaparta Editorial.

Cumbler, John T. 1979. *Working-Class Community in Industrial America: Work, Leisure, and Struggle in Two Industrial Cities, 1880–1930.* Westport, CT: Greenwood.

Douglass, William. 1971. "Rural Exodus in Two Spanish Basque Villages: A Cultural Explanation." *American Anthropologist* 73: 1100–1114.

———. 1975. *Echelar and Murelaga: Opportunity and Exodus in Two Spanish Basque Villages.* New York: St. Martin's.

Earle, John. 1986. *The Italian Cooperative Movement: A Portrait of the Lega Nazionale de Cooperative e Mutue.* London: Allen & Unwin.

Eaton, Adrienne E., and Paula B. Voos. 1992. "Unions and Contemporary Innovation in Work Organization, Compensation, and Employee Participation." In *Unions and Economic Competitiveness,* eds. Lawrence Mishel and Paula B. Voos, 173–215. New York: M. E. Sharpe.

Ellerman, David P. 1984. "Entrepeneurship in the Mondragón Cooperatives." *Review of Social Economy* 42: 272–94.

Enciclopedia Histórica-Geográfica de Guipúzcoa. 1983. "Bergara." In *Enciclopedia Histórica-Geográfica de Guipúzcoa,* 4: 211–40. San Sebastián: Horanbu.

Enloe, Cynthia. 1989. "Blue Jeans and Bankers." In *Bananas, Beaches and Bases: Making Feminist Sense of International Politics,* 151–76. Berkeley: University of California Press.

Eroski. 1988. *Memoria Txostena.* Elorrio: Eroski.

————. 1989. "La educación del consumidor en la escuela," *Eroski* suplemento número 134.

Estatuto de los Trabajadores. 1988. Madrid: Editorial García Enciso.

ETA. 1981. *Documentos.* Donostia: Editorial Lur.

Etxezarreta, Miren. 1977. *El caserío vasco.* Bilbao: Fundación c. de Ituriaga y Mª de Dañobeita.

Fagor. 1986. *Estatutos sociales de Fagor Clima S. Coop.* 2 de junio de 1986.

Ferrer, Manuel Regales. 1966. "Iniciativa y promoción industriales en Guipúzcoa." In *Homenaje al Excmo. Sr. D. Amando Melón y Ruíz de Gordezuela,* 137–61. Zaragoza.

Flinn, M. W. 1955. "British Steel and Spanish Ore: 1871–1914." *Economic History Review* 8(1): 84–90.

Foster, John. 1974. *Class Struggle and the Industrial Revolution: Early Industrial Capitalism in Three English Towns.* London: Methuen.

Fox, Richard. 1976. "Lineage Cells and Regional Definition in Complex Societies." In *Regional Analysis,* ed. Carol A. Smith, 2: 95–121. New York: Academic Press.

Frankenberg, Ronald. 1990. *The Village on the Border: A Social Study in a North Wales Community.* [1957.] Prospect Heights, IL: Waveland Press.

Fusi, Juan Pablo. 1984. "El primer socialismo vasco 1885–1936." In *Nacionalismo y socialismo en Euskadi,* 87–107. Bilboa: IPES, Cuaderno de Formación N° 4.

General Motors, "Project Saturn," 1990 (public relations materials,

General Motors, Troy, Michigan.

Gilmore, David. 1977. "Land Reform and Rural Revolt in Nineteenth C. Andalucia." *Peasant Studies* 6: 142–46.

González, Manuel Portilla, and José María Garmendia. 1988. *La posguerra en el País Vasco: Política, acumulación, miseria.* Donostia: Krisleu.

Gordon, David. 1978. "Up and Down the Long Roller Coaster." In *U.S. Capitalism in Crisis,* ed. Union for Radical Political Economics, 22–35. New York: Union for Radical Political Economics.

Gordon, David M., Richard Edwards, and Michael Reich. 1982. *Segmented Work, Divided Workers: The Historical Transformation of Labor in the United States.* Cambridge: Cambridge University Press.

Gorroño, Iñaki. 1975. *Experiencia cooperativa en el País Vasco.* Durango: Leopoldo Zugaza.

Gramsci, Antonio. 1971. "Americanism and Fordism." In *Selections from the Prison Notebooks,* 277–321. New York: International Publishers.

Granja, José Luis. 1984. "La izquierda nacionalista vasca en la II República: A.N.V." In *Nacionalismo y socialismo en Euskadi,* 123–35. Bilbao: IPES, Cuaderno de Formación N° 4.

Greenwood, Davydd. 1976. *Unrewarding Wealth: The Commercialization and Collapse of Agriculture in a Spanish Basque Town.* Cambridge: Cambridge University Press.

———. 1977. "Culture by the Pound: An Anthropological Perspective on Tourism as Cultural Commodification." In *Hosts and Guests: The Anthropology of Tourism,* ed. Valene Smith, 129–39. Philadelphia: University of Pennyslvania Press.

———. 1986. "Labor-Managed Systems and the Second Industrial Divide: The Fagor Group of Mondragón." Paper delivered at the annual meeting of the American Anthropological Association, Philadelphia.

———. 1992. "Labor–Management Systems and Industrial Redevelopment: Lessons from the Fagor Cooperative Group of Mondragón." In *Anthropology and the Global Factory: Studies of the New Industrialization in the Late Twentieth Century,* ed. Frances A. Rothstein and Michael L. Blim, 177–90. New York: Bergin & Garvey.

Greenwood, Davydd, and José Luis González Santos et al. 1989. *Culturas de Fagor.* Donostia: Editorial Txertoa.

———. 1992. *Industrial Process as Democracy: Participatory Action Research in the Fagor Cooperative Group of Mondragón.* Maastricht: Van Gorcum.

Grenier, Guillermo. 1988. *Inhuman Relations: Quality Circles and Anti-Unionism in* ✓ *American Industry.* Philadelphia: Temple University Press.

Gui, Benedetto. 1982. *Basque versus Illyrian Labor-Managed Firms: The Problem of Property Rights.* Quaderno N° 24, Universita Degli Studi di Trieste, Istituto di Economia.

Gurruchaga, Ander. 1985. *El código nacionalista vasco durante el franquismo.* Barcelona: Antropos Editorial del Hombre.

Gutiérrez-Johnson, Ana, and William Foote Whyte. 1982. "The Mondragón System of Worker Cooperatives." In *Workplace Democracy and Social Change,* ed. Frank Lindenfeld and Joyce Rothschild-Whitt, 177–199. Porter Sargent.

Habermas, Jürgen. 1986. "The New Obscurity: The Crisis of the Welfare State and the Exhaustion of Utopian Energies." *Philosophy and Social Criticism* 11 2: 1–18.

Hacker, Sally. 1989. *Pleasure, Power and Technology: Some Tales of Gender Engineering, and the Cooperative Workplace.* Boston: Unwin Hyman.

Hacker, Sally, and Clara Elcorobairutia. 1987. "Women Workers in the Mondragón System of Industrial Cooperatives." *Gender and Society* 1(4): 358–79.

Hall, Stuart. 1988. *The Hard Road to Renewal: Thatcherism and the Crisis of the Left.* London: Verso.

Halle, David. 1984. *America's Working Man: Work, Home and Politics among Blue Collar Property Owners.* Chicago: University of Chicago Press.

Hansen, Edward C. 1977. *Rural Catalonia under the Franco Regime.* New York: Cambridge University Press.

———. 1983. "Drinking to Prosperity: The Role of Bar Culture and Coalition Formation in the Modernization of the Alto Panádes." In *Economic Transformation and Steady State Values: Essays in the Ethnography of Spain,* ed. J. C. Aceves, 42–51. Publications in Anthropology 2. Flushing, NY: Queens College.

Harvey, David. 1989. *The Condition of Postmodernity: An Enquiry into the Origins of Cultural Change.* Cambridge, MA: Basil Blackwell.

Heckscher, Charles C. 1988. *The New Unionism: Employee Involvement in the Changing Corporation.* New York: Basic Books.

Heiberg, Marianne. 1980. "Basques, Anti-Basques, and the Moral Community." In *"Nation" and "State" in Europe: Ethnic Minorites in Western Europe,* ed. R. D. Grillo, 45–61. New York: Praeger.

———. 1989. *The Making of the Basque Nation.* Cambridge: Cambridge University Press.

Hobsbawm, Eric J. 1962. *The Age of Revolution, 1789–1848.* New York: Mentor Books.

———. 1984. "The Making of the Working Class 1870–1914." In *Workers: Worlds of Labour,* 194–213. New York: Pantheon Books.

———. 1990. *Nations and Nationalism since 1780: Programme, Myth and Reality.* Cambridge: Canto Press.

Hoerr, John. 1991. "What Should Unions Do?" *Harvard Business Review,* May–June: 30–45.

Hogler, Raymond L., and Guillermo Grenier. 1992. *Employee Participation and Labor Law in the American Workplace.* New York: Quorum Books.

Howard, M. C., and John Edward King. 1990. "The 'Second Slump': Marxian Theories of Crisis after 1973." *Review of Political Economy* 2(3): 267–91.

Industrial Cooperatives Association, Inc. (ICA). 1985. "The Massachusetts Law for Worker Cooperatives: M. G. L. Chapter 157A." Sommerville, MA: ICA.

Industriegewerkschaft Metall für die Bundesrepublik Deutschland (IG Metall). 1984. *Action Program: Work and Technology.* *"People Must Stay!"* Frankfurt: IG Metall.

Judd, Karen, and Sandy Morales Pope. 1994. "The New Job Squeeze: Women Pushed into Part-Time Work." *Ms. Magazine* 4(6): 86–90.

Kamata, Satoshi. 1982. *Japan in the Passing Lane.* New York: Pantheon Books.

Kasmir, Sharryn. 1991. " 'Stickin' to the Union': Worker Ownership from a Working-Class Perspective." *Anthropology of Work Review* 12(1): 8–13.

———. 1992a. "Social Space and Political Culture: Radical Basque Nationalist Bars in Mondragón." Paper delivered at the annual meeting of the American Anthropological Association, San Francisco.

———. 1992b. "Making the Basque Working Class *Basque*: The Incorporation of Spanish Immigrants into the World of Basque Nationalism." Paper delivered at the annual meeting of the American Ethnological Society, Memphis.

Keeney, Martin, and Richard Florida. 1988. "Beyond Mass Production: Production and the Labor Process in Japan." *Politics and Society* 16(1): 121–58.

Kirchoff, Paul. 1959. "The Principles of Clanship in Human Society." In *Readings in Anthropology,* ed. Morton Fried, 2: 260–70. New York: Thomas Y. Crowell.

Kornblum, William. 1974. *Blue Collar Community.* Chicago: University of Chicago Press.

Lamphere, Louise. 1992. "The Gendered Nature of Workplace Culture: Comparing Male and Female Experience." *Anthropology of Work Review* 12(4) and 13(1): 21–22.

Lamphere, Louise, Alex Stepick, and Guillermo Grenier. 1994. *Newcomers in the Workplace: Immigrants and the Restructuring of the U.S. Economy.* Philadelphia: Temple University Press.

Lamphere, Louise, Patricia Zavella, Felipe Gonzales, eds., with Peter B. Evans. 1993. *Sunbelt Working Mothers: Reconciling Family and Factory.* Ithaca: Cornell University Press.

Langile Abertzaleen Batzordeak (LAB). 1985. Kooperatibismoari buruz txostena eta LAB-en jarrera S.A.L.-aren aurrean (Ponencia sobre cooperativismo y posición de LAB ante la S.A.L., (September).

Lannon, Frances. 1979. "A Basque Challenge to the Pre–Civil War Spanish Church." *European Studies Review* 9: 29–48.

Larrañaga, Jesús. 1981. *Don José María Arizmendi-Arrieta y la Experiencia Cooperativa de Mondragón.* Mondragón: Caja Laboral Popular.

Larrañaga, Juan. 1986. *El Consejo Social: pasado, presente y futuro.* Mondragón Caja Laboral Popular.

Leach, Edmund R. 1954. *Political Systems of Highland Burma: A Study of Kachin Social Structure.* Boston: Beacon Press.

Lembcke, Jerry. 1991–1992. "Why 50 Years? Working Class Formations and Long Cycles." *Science and Society,* 55(4): 417–46.

Leonard, D. Christopher. 1991. "After Class and after Work: Politics in a Northern Italian Region." *Socialism and Democracy* 13: 119–35.

Letona, José. 1975. *Mondragón sus calles.* San Sebastián: Ediciones de la Caja de Ahorros Provincial de Guipúzcoa.

———. 1987. "Algunos apuntes históricos e itinerario turístico monumental." Mondragón: Ayuntamiento de Mondragón.

Lindenfeld, Frank. 1982. "Workers' Cooperatives: Remedy for Plant Closings?" In *Workplace Democracy and Social Change,* eds. Frank Lindenfeld and Joyce Rothschild-Whitt, 177–97. Boston: Porter Sargent.

Lloyd, E. A. 1926. *The Cooperative Movement in Italy.* New York: International Publishers.

Lynch, Helena. N.D. *Co-op Options: A Study of Worker Co-ops in Ireland.* Dublin: Workers Unity Trust.

Mancomunidad del Alto Deba. 1982. *Datos y series estadísticas de la comarca del Alto Deba.*

Mandel, Ernest. 1975. *Late Capitalism.* New York: Verso.

————. 1978. *The Second Slump: A Marxist Analysis of Recession in the Seventies.* London: New Left Books.

Marsh, J. S. and Pamela J. Swanney. 1980. *Agriculture and the European Community.* London: Allen & Unwin.

Marshall, Ray. 1987. *Unheard Voices: Labor and Economic Policy in a Competitive World.* New York: Basic Books.

Martínez-Alier, Juan. 1971. *Laborers and Landowners in Southern Spain.* Totowa, NJ: Rowman and Littlefield.

Maynard, David. 1991. "French Socialism and Breton Ethnic Politics, 1980–1988." *Socialism and Democracy* 13: 87–101.

Mendizabal, José Antonio. 1989. "Las sociedades anónimas laborales en el contexto de la economía social." Tesis doctoral, Universidad del País Vasco.

Menzies, Charles. 1992. "On Permanent Strike: Class and Ideology in a Producers' Co-operative." *Studies in Political Economy* 38: 85–108.

Midwest Center for Labor Research. 1989. *Participation in Managment: Union Organizing on a New Terrain.* Chicago: Midwest Center for Labor Research.

Milbrath, Robert Stephen. 1986. "Institutional Development and Capital Accumulation in a Complex of Basque Worker Cooperatives." Doctoral dissertation, University of Michigan.

Mishel, Lawrence and Paula B. Voos, eds. 1992. *Unions and Economic Competitiveness.* Armonk, N.Y. and London: M.E. Sharpe.

Monreal, Gregorio. 1980. "Anotaciones sobre el pensamiento político tradicional vasco en el siglo XVI." Madrid: Instituto Nacional de Estudios Jurídicos, Anuario de Historia del Derecho español.

Morrison, Roy. 1991. *We Build the Road as We Travel.* Philadelphia: New Society Publishers.

Moulinier, Jacques. 1949. "The Rh Factor in Southwestern France. An Examination of the Basque and Bearnais Populations." *American Journal of Physical Anthropology* 7: 545–49.

Moreno, Amparo. 1977. *Mujeres en lucha. El movimiento feminista en España.* Barcelona: Editorial Anagrama.

Moye, A. Melissa. 1993. "Mondragón: Adapting Co-operative Structures to Meet the Demands of a Changing Environment." *Economic and Industrial Democracy* 14: 251–76.

Nadal, Jordi. 1976. "The Failure of the Industrial Revolution in Spain 1830–1914." In *The Emergence of Industrial Societies. The Fontana Economic History of Europe,* ed. Carlo M. Cipolla, 532–627. New York: Harvester Press.

Nash, June. 1985. "Segementation of the Work Process in the International Division of Labor." in *The Americas in the New International Division of Labor,* ed. Steven Sanderson, 253–72. New York: Holmes and Meier.

———. 1989. *From Tank Town to High Tech: The Clash of Community and Industrial Cycles.* Albany: State University of New York Press.

Nash, June, Jorge Dandler, and Nicholas S. Hopkins, eds. 1976. *Popular Participation in Social Change: Cooperatives, Collectives, and Nationalized Industry.* The Hague: Mouton.

Newman, Katherine S. 1989. *Falling from Grace: The Experience of Downward Mobility in the American Middle Class.* New York: Vintage Books.

Núñez, Luis C. 1977. *Clases sociales en Euskadi.* San Sebastián: Txertoa. [p. 127–28]

Oakeshott, Robert. 1975 [1973]. "Mondragón, Spain's Oasis of Democracy." In *Self-Management: Economic Liberation of Man,* ed. Jaraslov Vanek, 290–296. Baltimore: Penguin Books.

———. 1978a. *The Case for Workers' Co-ops.* London: Routledge Kegan and Paul.

———. 1978b. "Industrial Co-operatives: The Middle Way." *Lloyds Bank Review,* January (187): 44–58.

Oktubre Taldea. 1987. *Arrasate 1936: Una generación cortada.* Mondragón: Oktubre Taldea.

Ormaechea, José María. 1991. *La experiencia cooperativa de Mondragón.* Mondragón: Grupo Cooperativo Mondragón.

———. N.d. *El Grupo Cooperativo Mondragón:* Textos básicos de Otalora. Mondragón: Caja Laboral Popular.

Ornelas, Carlos. 1980. "Producer Cooperatives and Schooling: The Case of Mondragón, Spain." Doctoral dissertation, Stanford University School of Education.

Ortzi. 1978. *Los Vascos. Síntesis de su historia.* Donostia: Hordago.

Otazu y Llana, Alfonso de. 1986. *El "Igualitarismo" Vasco: mito y realidad.* San Sebastián: Editorial Txertoa.

Parker, Mike. 1985. *Inside the Circle: A Union Guide to QWL.* Detroit: Labor Notes.

Parker, Mike, and Jane Slaughter. 1988. *Choosing Sides: Unions and the Team Concept.* Detroit: Labor Notes.

Payne, Stanley G. 1961. *Falange. A History of Spanish Fascism.* Stanford: Standford University Press.

Peiss, Kathy Lee. 1986. *Cheap Amusements: Working Women and Leisure in New York City, 1880–1920.* Philadelphia: Temple University Press.

Pimentel, Felipe Zerbi. 1987. "Democratization, Modernization, and De-Radicalization: Spanish Socialism during the Consolidation of a New Political Regime 1976–1982." *Political Culture* 3: 67–97.

Piore, Michael J., and Charles F. Sabel. 1984. *The Second Industrial Divide.* New York: Basic Books.

Poggi, Gianfranco. 1967. *Catholic Action in Italy: The Sociology of a Sponsored Organization.* Stanford: Standford University Press.

———. 1978. *The Development of the Modern State: A Sociological Introduction.* Stanford: Standford University Press.

Quigley, Martin, Jr., and Monsignor Edward M. Connors. 1963. *Catholic Action in Practice: Family Life, Education, International Life.* New York: Random House.

Rodríguez de Coro, Francisco. 1980. *Guipúzcoa en la democracia revolucionaria (1868–1876). Génesis de nacionalismo vasco.* San Sebastián: Caja de Ahorros Provincial de Guipúzcoa.

Rosen, Corey. 1981. *Employee Ownership: Issues, Resources, and Legislation.* Arlington, VA: National Center for Employee Ownership.

Rothstein, Frances A., and Michael Blim, eds. 1991. *Anthropology and the Global Factory: Studies of the New Industrialism in the Late Twentieth Century.* New York: Praeger.

Royal Arsenal Co-operative Society, Ltd. N.d. "Mondragón. The Basque Co-operatives." Royal Arsenal Co-operative Society.

Russell, Raymond. 1984. "Using Ownership to Control: Making Workers Owners in the Contemporary United States." *Politics and Society* 13(3): 253–94.

———. 1985. *Sharing Ownership in the Workplace.* Albany: State University of New York Press.

Sarti, Roland. 1971. *Fascism and the Industrial Leadership in Italy, 1919–1940; A Study in the Expansion of Private Power under Fascism.* Berkeley: University of California Press.

Sartre, Jean-Paul. 1975. "The Burgos Trial." In *Life/Situations: Essays Written and Spoken by Jean-Paul Sarte,* trans. Paul Austen and Lydia Davis, 135–61. New York: Random House.

Schiller, Nina Glick. 1987. "Management by Participation: The Division of Labor, Ideology and Contradiction in a U.S. Firm." In *Perspectives in U.S. Marxist Anthropology,* eds. David Hakken and Hannah Lessinger, 211–31. CO: Westview.

Schneider, P., J. Schneider, and E. Hansen. 1972. "Modernization and Development: the Role of Regional Elites and Noncorporate Groups in the European Mediterranean." *Comparative Studies in Society and History* 14: 328–350.

Schweickart, David. 1984. "Plant Relocations: A Philosophical Reflection." *Review of Radical Political Economics* 16(4): 32–51.

Searjeant, Graham. 1978. *Sunday Times* (London), 19 November.

Secretariado Social Diocesano. 1974. "Conflictos en el Movimiento Cooperativo." Mimeographed.

Shapiro, Jack H., and Teresa Cosenza. 1987. *Reviving Industry in America: Japanese Influences on Manufacturing and the Service Sector.* Cambridge, MA: Ballinger.

Simmons, John, and William Mares. 1985. *Working Together: Employee Participation in Action.* New York: New York University Press.

Skoggard, Ian. 1993. "Dependency and Rural Industrialism in Taiwan." Doctoral dissertation, City University of New York.

Sociedad de Investigación Aplicada para el Desarrollo Económico. SIADECO. 1970. *Datos del estudio socio-económico sobre Mondragón.* San Sebastián: SIADECO.

———. 1972. *Mondragón y su futuro.* San Sebastián: SIADECO.

Taylor, Peter. 1988. "The Gas Tap Work Groups of Copreci, S. Coop." unpublished paper.

———. 1994. "The Rhetorical Construction of Efficiency: Restructuring and Industrial Democracy in Mondragón, Spain." *Sociological Forum* 9(3): 459–87.

Thomas, Henk, and Chris Logan. 1982. *Mondragón: An Economic Analysis.* London: Allen & Unwin.

Thompson, E. P. 1966. *The Making of the English Working Class.* New York: Vintage Books.

Touraine, Alain. 1985. "An Introduction to the Study of Social Movements." *Social Research* 54(4): 749–87.

Turner, Victor. 1967. *The Forest of Symbols: Aspects of Ndembu Ritual.* Ithaca: Cornell University Press.

Unión Cerrajera. N.d. *Unión Cerrajera: 75 años de historia.* Unpublished manuscript.

Unzueta, Patxo. 1988. *Los nietos de la ira. Nacionalismo y violencia en el País Vasco.* Madrid: El País, Aguilar.

Uribe-Echebarria, Agustín. 1981. *¿Burocracia o participación? Un ensayo sobre organización y las cooperativas de Mondragón.* Bilbao.

Urla, Jacqueline. 1987. "Being Basque, Speaking Basque: The Politics of Language and Identity in the Basque Country." Doctoral dissertation, University of California, Berkeley.

————. 1989. "Reinventing Basque Society." In *Essays in Basque Social Anthropology and History*, ed. William A. Douglass, 149–79. Reno: Basque Studies Program.

Urtiaga. 1962. "El problema de la propiedad en la futura euzkadi." Reprinted in ETA (1981) 2: 364–66, 372–74, 382–84.

Valle, Teresa del. 1988. *Korrika. Rituales de la lengua en el espacio.* Barcelona: Anthropos.

Valle, Teresa del, et al. 1985. *La mujer vasca. Imagen y realidad.* Barcelona: Anthropos Editorial del Hombre.

Vanek, Jaroslav. 1977. *The Labor-Managed Economy.* Ithaca: Cornell University Press.

Weiner, Hans, and Robert Oakeshott. 1987. *Worker-Owners: Mondragón Revisited. A New Report on the Group of Co-operatives in the Basque Provinces of Spain.* London: Algo-German Foundation for the Study of Industrial Society.

Wells, Donald M. 1987. *Empty Promises: Quality of Working Life Programs and the Labor Movement.* New York: Monthly Review Press.

Wells, Miriam J. 1984. "What Is a Worker? The Role of Sharecroppers in Contemporary Class Structure." *Politics and Society* 13(3): 295–320.

Whyte, William F. 1982. "Social Inventions for Solving Human Problems." *American Sociological Review* 47: 1–13.

Whyte, William F., and Kathleen King Whyte. 1988. *Making Mondragón: The Growth and Dynamics of the Worker Cooperative Complex.* Ithaca, NY: ILR Press.

————. 1991. *Making Mondragón: The Growth and Dynamics of the Worker Cooperative Complex.* Second Edition. Ithaca, NY: ILR Press.

Williams, Brackette F. 1989. "A Class Act: Anthropology and the Race to Nation across Ethnic Terrain." *Annual Reviews in Anthropology* 18: 401–44.

Withers, Charles W. J. 1988. *Gaelic Scotland. The Transformation of a Cultural Region.* London: Routledge.

Witte, John F. 1980. *Democracy, Authority and Alienation in Work: Workers' Participation in an American Corporation.* Chicago: University of Chicago Press.

Wolf, Eric. 1982. *Europe and a People without History.* Berkeley: University of California Press.

Wright, Erik Olin. 1976. "Class Boundaries in Advanced Capitalist Societies." *New Left Review* 98: 3–41.

Zapirain Karrika, David and Juan Carlos Mora Afán. 1993. "La gestión de la vida familiar y municipal de Arrasate en el siglo XVI." Mondragón: Ayuntamiento de Mondragón.

Zulaika, Joseba. 1988. *Basque Violence: Sacrament and Metaphor.* Reno: University of Nevada Press.

Index

Note: As in the text, place names are generally in Basque in the index.

Index